Grade 5

To Our Valued Customers:

We would like to welcome you to join our Popular Parents' Club Rewards Program. By scanning the QR code above and signing up to become a member of "**Popular Canada Parents' Club**", you will enjoy the following benefits:

- free educational videos of learning tips by Canadian teachers
- our newsletter informing you of our most recent product releases
- promotional codes for exclusive discounts which can be used during your next purchase
- free educational printables
- eligibility to win a quarter end prize for an iPad
- eligibility to win a quarter end prize worth $100 in workbooks
- eligibility to win other gifts

Your Partner in Education,
Popular Book Company (Canada) Limited

ISBN: 978-1-77149-203-4

ISBN: 978-1-77149-203-4

A Message to Parents

Advanced Complete MathSmart is an extension of our bestselling *Complete MathSmart* series. This series focuses on challenging word problems that require the application of the math concepts and skills that children have learned in the *Complete MathSmart* series.

The two sections in this book are designed to gradually develop your child's problem-solving and critical-thinking skills. In Section 1, each unit covers one core topic and begins with basic skills questions, followed by problem-solving questions that increase in difficulty as the unit progresses. It reinforces your child's math concepts and skills in the topic in focus. Working through this section, your child should be able to proficiently explain and illustrate the solutions to the word problems.

Section 2 provides abundant critical-thinking questions, each combining multiple topics from Section 1. The topics are integrated in different ways to provide a wide range of complex and challenging questions that help stimulate your child's mathematical reasoning and develop his or her critical-thinking skills.

An answer key with step-by-step solutions is also provided at the end of this comprehensive book. All the solutions are presented in a clear and organized way to allow your child to have a thorough understanding of the math concepts.

Advanced Complete MathSmart will not only improve your child's core math understanding and skills, but also develop his or her critical-thinking skills which are essential in solving daily life challenges.

Your Partner in Education,
Popular Book Co. (Canada) Ltd.

Advanced Complete MathSmart®

Section 1:
Basic Problem-solving Questions

ISBN: 978-1-77149-203-4

Contents

Section 2:
Critical-thinking Questions

Level 1 – with hints

Level 2 – without hints

ISBN: 978-1-77149-203-4

ISBN: 978-1-77149-203-4

Section 1:
Basic Problem-solving Questions

ISBN: 978-1-77149-203-4

Whole Numbers

solving a variety of word problems that involve addition, subtraction, multiplication, and division of whole numbers

Math Skills

①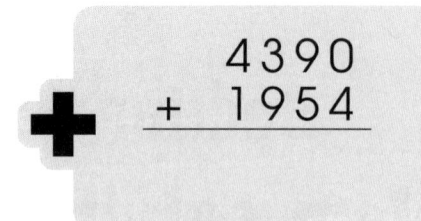

$$\begin{array}{r} 4390 \\ + 1954 \\ \hline \end{array}$$

a. 5217 + 891 = _____

b. 3147 + 4603 = _____

c. 4389 + 2687 = _____

d. 2980 + 6477 = _____

e. 7816 + 1989 = _____

②

$$\begin{array}{r} 5881 \\ - 967 \\ \hline \end{array}$$

a. 9000 – 7246 = _____

b. 4838 – 1739 = _____

c. 7109 – 2644 = _____

d. 5806 – 4437 = _____

e. 7915 – 2069 = _____

③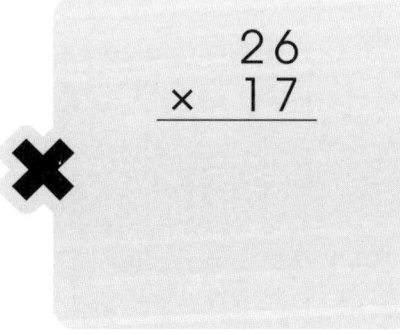

$$\begin{array}{r} 26 \\ \times 17 \\ \hline \end{array}$$

a. 35 × 28 = _____

b. 19 × 43 = _____

c. 73 × 24 = _____

d. 39 × 74 = _____

e. 28 × 50 = _____

④

$$3\overline{)468}$$

a. 798 ÷ 7 = _____

b. 1260 ÷ 9 = _____

c. 2013 ÷ 6 = _____

d. 4296 ÷ 5 = _____

e. 5011 ÷ 7 = _____

ISBN: 978-1-77149-203-4

Problem Solving

Try This!

How many crayons are there in a box of 52 packages?

Solution:

Step 1: **Write a number sentence.**

Think:

1 package = 24 crayons

52 packages = ? crayons

$24 \times 52 =$ ☐

One package has 24 crayons.

Step 2: **Do the multiplication.**

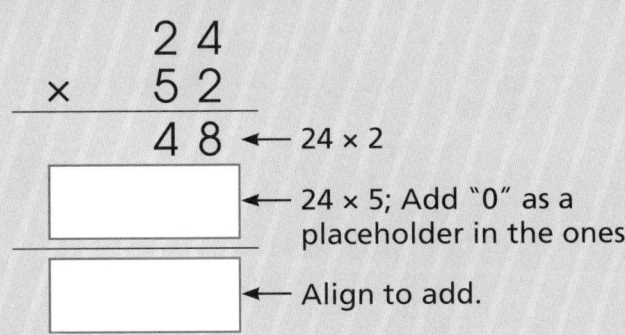

$$
\begin{array}{r}
2\,4 \\
\times \quad 5\,2 \\
\hline
4\,8 \quad \leftarrow 24 \times 2 \\
\hline
\end{array}
$$

☐ ← 24 × 5; Add "0" as a placeholder in the ones.

☐ ← Align to add.

Step 3: **Write a concluding sentence.**

There are ☐ crayons in the box.

① Ms. McNeal's class is doing an art project with Popsicle sticks. Each student needs 46 Popsicle sticks. How many Popsicle sticks are needed for 28 students?

_____ Popsicle sticks are needed.

② My recipe requires 23 g of flour for each cupcake and 45 g of flour for each bun.

Billy

a. How much flour does Billy need if he makes 36 cupcakes?

Billy needs _____ g of flour.

b. Does Billy need more or less flour if he makes 16 buns instead?

Billy needs _____ flour.
                 more / less

c. Billy takes 15 bananas and cuts each banana into 15 slices to decorate a cake. How many banana slices are there?

There are _____ banana slices.

ISBN: 978-1-77149-203-4

③

This novel has 344 pages. I will read 8 pages each day.

How many days will it take Jill to finish the novel?

Jill

It will take Jill _____ days.

④ Stewart took 455 photos during his trip. He puts them equally into 7 photo albums. How many photos are there in each album?

There are _____ photos in each album.

⑤ Bella has 1632 mL of fruit punch. She pours it equally into 8 cups. How much fruit punch does each cup have?

Each cup has _____ mL of fruit punch.

ISBN: 978-1-77149-203-4

⑥ Davis has 475 beads and he will use them to make 9 identical necklaces.

    a. How many beads will be left over?

_____

    b. If Davis makes 7 necklaces instead, will there be any beads left over? If so, how many?

_____

⑦ A school wants to order 450 slices of pizza for the school dance. Each pizza is divided into 8 slices.

    a. How many pizzas does the school need to order?

**Hints**

Individual slices cannot be ordered.

_____

    b.

Our budget for this order is $500. Each pizza costs $9.

How many pizzas can be ordered at most?

_____

ISBN: 978-1-77149-203-4

⑧ A candy store mixed 1502 red candies and 748 yellow candies together. The candies were then equally packaged into 9 bags. How many candies were there in each bag?

> **Tips**
>
> Use brackets to show the part that needs to be done first.
> e.g. (12 + 3) ÷ 5
>   ↑
> Do this part first.

⑨ A box has 12 cans of soup. Amy's grocery store had 25 boxes and 126 cans have been sold. How many cans of soup are left?

⑩ A toy factory has produced 5346 wheels but 342 of them are broken. How many toy cars can be produced if each car needs 4 wheels?

⑪ Jimmy types 45 words per minute. If he can type 5 more words per minute, how many words can he type in 35 minutes?

ISBN: 978-1-77149-203-4

⑫ A building block starter kit contains 1248 toy blocks. Each expansion kit contains 368 toy blocks.

a. David has 1 starter kit and 6 expansion kits.
How many blocks does he have?

_____

b.

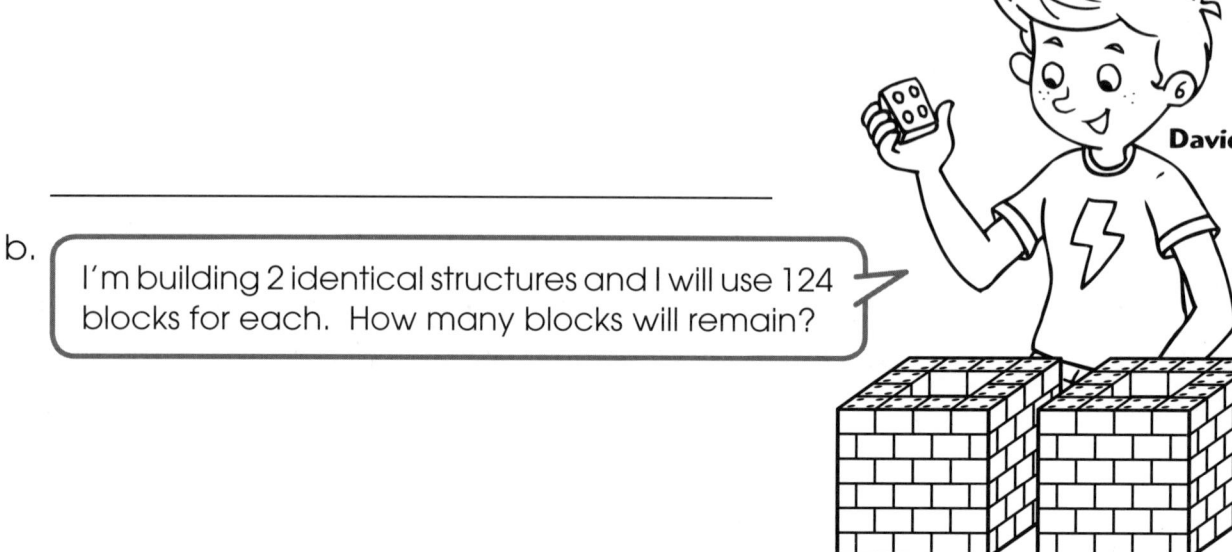

I'm building 2 identical structures and I will use 124 blocks for each. How many blocks will remain?

_____

c. If David shares the rest of his blocks equally with his 3 siblings, how many blocks will each child get?

_____

⑬ 2000 newspapers were printed but 147 of them were torn. The remaining newspapers are packaged into bundles of 8.

a. How many bundles of newspapers are there?

_____

b. How many more newspapers are needed so that there are no newspapers left?

_____

ISBN: 978-1-77149-203-4

⑭ Shuttle Bus A carries 35 passengers on 1 trip and it makes 24 trips in a day. Shuttle Bus B carries 52 passengers on 1 trip and it makes 18 trips in a day.

a. How many passengers does Shuttle Bus A carry in a week?

_____

b. How many more passengers can Shuttle Bus B carry in a week?

_____

⑮ 2456 plastic straws are packaged into 50 boxes with some left over. How many plastic straws are there in 27 boxes?

_____

⑯ An arcade is 2153 m from a bookstore and Mrs. Wynn's house is 1207 m from the bookstore. Mrs. Wynn walks 60 m in 1 min. How long will it take her to walk from her house to the arcade if she passes by the bookstore?

_____

⑰ The cost of coffee beans is determined by its weight. 490 g of coffee beans costs $10. Dan bought some coffee beans and shared them with his sister. If they each paid $6, how many grams of coffee beans did they get together?

_____

Fractions

solving a variety of word problems that involve addition and subtraction of fractions with like denominators

 **Math Skills**

① Put the fractions in order from least to greatest.

a. $\dfrac{7}{5}$ $\dfrac{2}{5}$ $1\dfrac{1}{5}$ $\dfrac{3}{5}$

b. $\dfrac{3}{4}$ $\dfrac{3}{7}$ $1\dfrac{1}{2}$ $\dfrac{1}{2}$

_____

_____

c. $1\dfrac{3}{6}$ $\dfrac{11}{6}$ $\dfrac{4}{3}$ $1\dfrac{2}{3}$

d. $\dfrac{10}{4}$ $\dfrac{16}{6}$ $\dfrac{11}{4}$ $1\dfrac{5}{6}$

_____

_____

② Do the addition.

a.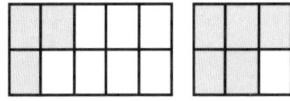

$\dfrac{3}{10} + \dfrac{7}{10} =$ _____

b. $\dfrac{2}{3} + \dfrac{1}{3} =$ _____

c. $\dfrac{3}{4} + \dfrac{3}{4} =$ _____

d. $1\dfrac{2}{5} + \dfrac{2}{5} =$ _____

e. $\dfrac{4}{7} + \dfrac{6}{7} =$ _____

f. $\dfrac{9}{4} + 1\dfrac{3}{4} =$ _____

g. $\dfrac{12}{5} + \dfrac{7}{5} =$ _____

h. $2\dfrac{1}{3} + 1\dfrac{1}{3} =$ _____

③ Do the subtraction.

a.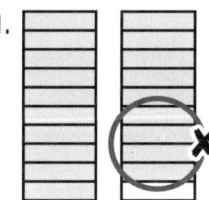

$1\dfrac{9}{10} - \dfrac{4}{10} =$ _____

b. $\dfrac{3}{5} - \dfrac{2}{5} =$ _____

c. $1 - \dfrac{1}{4} =$ _____

d. $1\dfrac{5}{6} - \dfrac{4}{6} =$ _____

e. $2\dfrac{1}{3} - \dfrac{5}{3} =$ _____

f. $\dfrac{11}{4} - 1\dfrac{1}{4} =$ _____

g. $\dfrac{10}{7} - \dfrac{3}{7} =$ _____

h. $2\dfrac{4}{6} - 1\dfrac{1}{6} =$ _____

ISBN: 978-1-77149-203-4

 **Problem Solving**

Try This!

Aaron biked for $\frac{8}{3}$ hours and Lewis biked for $2\frac{1}{3}$ hours. How much longer did Aaron bike for than Lewis?

Solution:

Step 1: Write a number sentence.

$$\frac{8}{3} - 2\frac{1}{3} = \boxed{}$$

Step 2: Convert the mixed number into an improper fraction and then solve it.

$$\frac{8}{3} - 2\frac{1}{3}$$

$$= \frac{8}{3} - \boxed{} \leftarrow 2\frac{1}{3} = \frac{2 \times 3 + 1}{3}$$

$$= \boxed{}$$

You can also convert the improper fraction into a mixed number, so that both fractions are mixed numbers.

Step 3: Write a concluding sentence.

Aaron biked for $\boxed{}$ hour longer than Lewis.

① Roger has $1\frac{1}{4}$ chocolate bars and Donna has $\frac{7}{4}$ chocolate bars. How many chocolate bars do they have altogether?

Roger and Donna have _____ chocolate bars altogether.

ISBN: 978-1-77149-203-4

② The boys ate $3\frac{3}{5}$ pizzas and the girls ate $\frac{20}{5}$ pizzas. Who ate more pizzas? By how much more?

The _____ ate _____ more pizzas.
   boys / girls

③ Samuel's house is $\frac{16}{5}$ km away from school and Mark's house is $2\frac{4}{5}$ km away from school.

a. How much farther away from school does Samuel live than Mark?

Samuel lives _____ km farther than Mark.

b.

Teresa

I live $\frac{14}{5}$ km farther from school than Mark.

How far does Teresa live from school?

Remember to give the final answer as a mixed number whenever possible.

Teresa lives _____ km from school.

ISBN: 978-1-77149-203-4

④ A recipe for jelly requires $2\frac{1}{4}$ cups of fruit juice and $1\frac{3}{4}$ cups of water. How many cups of liquid are needed in total?

_____ cups of liquid are needed in total.

⑤ Armin's bakery sold $1\frac{3}{7}$ chocolate cakes and $\frac{9}{7}$ vanilla cakes.

a. How many chocolate and vanilla cakes did he sell in all?

Armin sold _____ chocolate and vanilla cakes in all.

b.

I sold $1\frac{2}{7}$ more strawberry cakes than the total of chocolate and vanilla cakes.

How many strawberry cakes did he sell?

Armin

Armin sold _____ strawberry cakes.

ISBN: 978-1-77149-203-4

⑥ Rosie drank $3\frac{4}{5}$ bottles of water in the morning and $2\frac{3}{5}$ bottles in the afternoon. How many bottles of water did she drink?

_____

⑦ Aunt Vivian baked 5 lemon pies and she gave away $3\frac{1}{2}$ pies. How many pies does she have left?

_____

⑧

I'm 12 years old. I have a cat and a rabbit.

Amy

a. How much older is the cat than the rabbit?

$4\frac{7}{12}$ years old

$6\frac{1}{12}$ years old

_____

b. How much older is Amy than her cat?

_____

ISBN: 978-1-77149-203-4

⑨ Josh weighs the fruits in a grocery store.

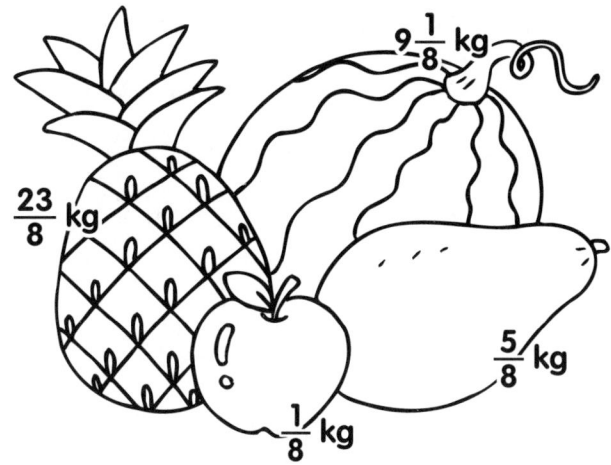

a. How much do the apple and the papaya weigh altogether?

_____

b. How much do the watermelon and the pineapple weigh altogether?

c. How much heavier is the watermelon than the papaya?

_____

_____

d. How much heavier is the papaya than the apple?

e. Which 2 fruits weigh exactly 3 kg altogether?

_____

_____

f. Which fruit is 9 kg lighter than the watermelon?

g. What is the total weight of all 4 fruits?

_____

_____

⑩ Tina ordered 10 boxes of toy cars for her store. $4\frac{1}{6}$ boxes were sold, $3\frac{5}{6}$ boxes are on the shelves, and the rest are in storage. How many boxes are in storage?

_____

⑪ Chef Nigel mixed $6\frac{4}{5}$ cups of vegetables with $3\frac{3}{5}$ cups of rice to make fried rice. He saved $2\frac{2}{5}$ cups of fried rice and served the rest. How many cups of fried rice were served?

_____

⑫ Michael owns a total of 20 baseball cards. He has put $\frac{3}{4}$ of his baseball card collection up for sale.

a. How many baseball cards are for sale?

Hints

Draw the number of baseball cards. Then divide them into 4 groups.

_____

b. If 5 baseball cards have been sold, what fraction of the collection remains?

_____

⑬ Scott has $2\frac{1}{4}$ boxes of crayons. Each box has 8 crayons. How many crayons does Scott have?

_____

ISBN: 978-1-77149-203-4

⑭ Johnson has $6\frac{7}{12}$ cartons of eggs. He needs $2\frac{5}{12}$ cartons to make 30 omelettes.

a. How many cartons of eggs will be left if he makes 30 omelettes?

_____

b. Johnson makes 90 omelettes. How many cartons are needed?

_____

c. How many more cartons does Johnson need to make 90 omelettes?

_____

⑮

I want to put these books on a shelf.

a. What is the total weight of the books?

_____

b. The shelf can hold up to 10 kg. How many more kilograms can it hold?

_____

ISBN: 978-1-77149-203-4

Decimals

solving a variety of word problems that involve addition, subtraction, multiplication, and division of decimals to 2 decimal places

Math Skills

①
```
    3.42          4.16
  + 1.78        + 5.70
```

a. 6.82 + 2.27 = _____

b. 10.36 + 7.5 = _____

c. 7 + 2.19   = _____

d. 9.26 + 2.9 = _____

e. 8.06 + 15.1 = _____

②
```
    5.68          9.40
  - 3.21        - 4.13
```

a. 7.15 – 2.49 = _____

b. 10 – 6.77   = _____

c. 17.32 – 9.87 = _____

d. 15.9 – 6.51 = _____

e. 12.61 – 0.9 = _____

③
```
    4.96          2.63
  ×    6        ×    9
```

a. 8.2 × 8   = _____

b. 0.16 × 5   = _____

c. 6.34 × 4   = _____

d. 7.06 × 20 = _____

e. 1.9 × 300 = _____

④
```
  3 ) 16.2       4 ) 2.2
```

a. 17.64 ÷ 7 = _____

b. 5.4 ÷ 6   = _____

c. 24.8 ÷ 8   = _____

d. 5 ÷ 2   = _____

e. 12.4 ÷ 10 = _____

ISBN: 978-1-77149-203-4

 **Problem Solving**

Try This!

A plant was 8.6 cm tall and it has grown 1.94 cm. How tall is the plant now?

Solution:

Step 1: **Write a number sentence.**

Starting height: 8.6 cm
Height grown: 1.94 cm

8.6 + 1.94 = ⬜

> Remember that to add and subtract decimals, the digits are aligned by the decimal points, not to the right like whole numbers.

Step 2: **Do the addition.**

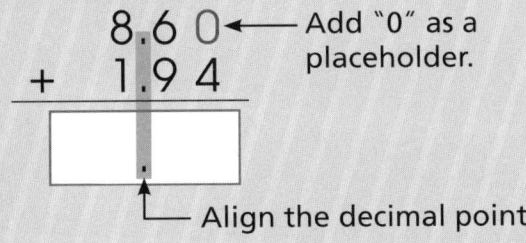

8.6 0 ← Add "0" as a placeholder.
+ 1.9 4
⬜

└── Align the decimal points.

Step 3: **Write a concluding sentence.**

The plant is ⬜ cm tall.

① Judy bought 3.79 kg of almonds and used 1.28 kg. How many kilograms of almonds does Judy have left?

Judy has _____ kg of almonds left.

ISBN: 978-1-77149-203-4

② Brenda has a piece of red yarn that was 2.14 m long and a piece of blue yarn that was 1.96 m long.

a. What was the total length of yarn that Brenda had?

Brenda had _____ m of yarn.

b. Brenda used 1.08 m of the yarn to make a braided bracelet. How many metres of yarn is left?

_____ m of yarn is left.

③ The school bus's route from Travis's home to school is shown. How long is the route?

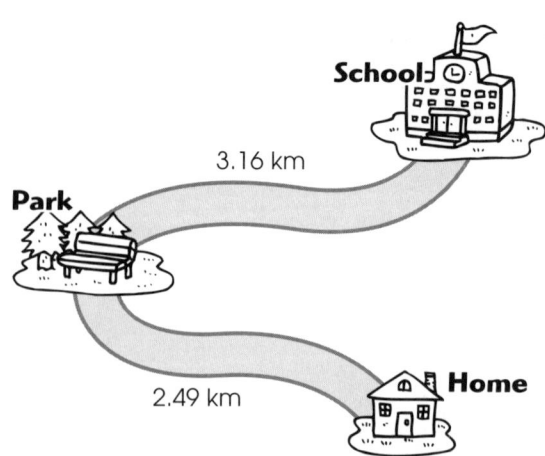

3.16 km

Park

2.49 km

School

Home

The route is _____ km long.

ISBN: 978-1-77149-203-4

④ A small bridge has a maximum weight limit of 10 tonnes. A truck carries 3 containers with weights of 0.78 tonnes, 1.05 tonnes, and 1.2 tonnes.

a. What is the total weight of the containers?

The total weight of the containers is _____ tonnes.

b. The weight of the truck is 2.7 tonnes. How many more tonnes can the bridge support?

The bridge can support _____ more tonnes.

⑤ A bag has 1.33 L of milk. A glass holds 0.24 L. How much milk is left in the bag after pouring 3 glasses of milk?

Hints

You will need to subtract 3 times.

_____ L of milk is left.

ISBN: 978-1-77149-203-4

⑥ Shawn has three 5.65-m rolls of ribbon. How many metres of ribbon does he have in total?

_____

⑦ A bag of 9 oranges weighs 3.24 kg. What is the average weight of an orange?

_____

⑧ Chef Leo made 7.36 L of soup for 20 customers. How much soup was each customer served?

_____

⑨

> A table is 1.78 m long. I put 5 tables together to form a rectangle for food trays at the party.

What is the total length of the tables?

_____

ISBN: 978-1-77149-203-4

⑩ Kenzie has a 4-L tub of ice cream.

a. If she serves 8 guests equal amounts of ice cream, how much ice cream will each guest get?

_____

b. If 2 more guests decide to come, how much ice cream will each guest get instead?

_____

⑪ The weight of a robot is 3.08 kg. What is the total weight of 6 robots?

_____

⑫

My goal is to practise the violin 5 h a week.

If Anita practises 0.8 h each day, will she reach her goal?

Anita

_____

ISBN: 978-1-77149-203-4

⑬

My car can travel 9 km for each litre of gas.

Ms. Lee's car had 60 L of gas and 24.16 L has been used. How much farther can she drive?

⑭ A bag with 100 chocolate eggs weighs 362 g. What is the weight of 60 chocolate eggs?

⑮ Penelope has opened a tea shop. She uses 0.453 kg of tea leaves to make 100 cups of tea. How many kilograms of tea leaves are needed for 2000 cups?

⑯ Gordon's home and his school are 1.21 km apart. He bikes to and from school every day.

a. How far does Gordon bike in 4 days?

b. One Friday, Gordon biked to school in the morning and he biked 2.45 km to his grandma's house after school to stay over for the weekend. How far did he bike that week?

ISBN: 978-1-77149-203-4

⑰ Felix and Ricky were competing to solve 5 Rubik's cubes. Felix's average time for each cube was 15.24 s and Ricky's total time was 78.8 s.

   a. What was the difference between their total times in seconds?

   _____

   b. Felix's best time was 14.57 s. If he completed all 5 cubes at his best time, how much sooner would he have completed all of the cubes?

   _____

   c. Ricky's best time was 13.09 s. What was the difference between his best time and his average time?

   _____

⑱ Shawn swam an average of 16.5 laps each day over 6 days.

   a. How many laps did Shawn swim in 6 days?

   _____

   b.
   > On the 7th day, I swam 3.5 laps more than my average. What is my new average number of laps each day?

   _____

ISBN: 978-1-77149-203-4

Money

solving a variety of word problems that involve basic operations with money

 **Math Skills**

① Find the total amounts.

a.     $_____

b.     $_____

c. 6 $50 bills, 5 $20 bills, 3 quarters, 7 dimes $_____

d. 5 $20 bills, 4 $10 bills, 3 toonies, 14 quarters $_____

e. 3 $100 bills, 7 $10 bills, 5 dimes, 9 nickels $_____

② Find the change.

a.  **$7.55**

Paid: $10

Change:

_____

b.  **$29.40**

Paid: $30.40

Change:

_____

③ Check the exact bills and coins needed to pay for each toy.

a. **$33.60**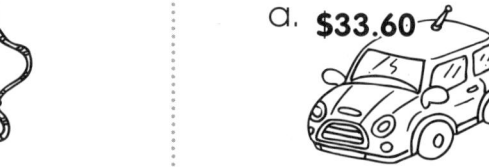

b. **$71.15**

ISBN: 978-1-77149-203-4

 **Problem Solving**

Try This!

> I paid 3 $20 bills for a $50.35 helmet. What was my change?

Solution:

Step 1: Write a number sentence.

Think: Amount paid – Cost of item = Change

Amount paid: $20 x 3 = $60 ← 3 $20 bills

Cost of helmet: $50.35

$60 – $50.35 = $ ☐

Ethan

Step 2: Do the subtraction.

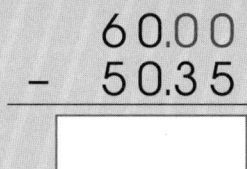

```
  60.00
– 50.35
 _____
|_____|
```

Step 3: Write a concluding sentence.

Ethan's change was $ ☐ .

① Laurie wants to buy a chair for $80.95. If she has 1 $50 bill and 1 $20 bill, how much more money does she need?

Laurie needs $_____ more.

ISBN: 978-1-77149-203-4

② Mr. Davidson is at an electronics store. He has 5 $50 bills.

Electronics Sales Event

$159.95

$78.45

$107.80

a. What will his change be if he uses all of his bills to buy a camera and a pair of headphones?

His change will be $_____ .

b. How much more money does he need if he buys a camera and a cell phone?

He needs $_____ more.

c.

> I want to buy 2 pairs of headphones as gifts.

Mr. Davidson

How many $50 bills will Mr. Davidson use? What will his change be?

Mr. Davidson will use _____ $50 bills. His change will be $_____ .

ISBN: 978-1-77149-203-4

③ Bonnie got $1.65 in change after paying 3 $100 bills, 3 $5 bills, and 2 toonies. What was the cost of the purchase?

The cost of the purchase was $_____ .

④ Morgan's car is in the auto shop for maintenance.

a. What is the total cost of the maintenance service?

Auto Shop Service

Customer: Mr. Morgan Young
Vehicle: APLX 127

Service Item	Amount
Tire Alignment	$79.95
Oil Change	$60.85
Filter Replacement	$145.50

The total cost is $_____ .

b. If Morgan pays with 2 $100 bills and 2 $50 bills, how much change will he get back?

Morgan will get $_____ back.

ISBN: 978-1-77149-203-4

⑤ Hugh is shopping at a grocery store.

   a. If he pays for 3 watermelons and 4 pineapples with 2 $20 bills, what is his change?

$4.80

$5.95

_____

   b. If he wants to buy 2 watermelons and 3 pineapples, will 5 $5 bills be enough? If not, how much more does he need?

_____

⑥ Conrad and his 4 friends have rented a car for a road trip for $202.60. The cost is split evenly among Conrad and his friends.

   a. How much more money does Conrad need if he pays with 2 $10 bills and 4 $5 bills?

**Hints**

Do not forget to include Conrad when splitting the cost.

_____

   b. If he pays with a $50 bill instead, what will his change be?

_____

ISBN: 978-1-77149-203-4

⑦ Joyce and Ellen went to a restaurant for lunch.

a. Joyce ordered all 3 items. Would 3 $5 bills be enough to pay? If so, what would her change be?

Menu

Soup of the day $4.95

Sandwich $7.50

Tea $2.75

Order all 3 items and save $2!

_____

b. Ellen paid for a sandwich and a cup of tea. She got 1 $5 bill, 2 toonies, and 3 quarters back in change. How much did she pay?

_____

⑧ Leo and Lenna plan to buy their mom a dress for $150.70. They are splitting the cost evenly.

a. Leo has saved 2 $20 bills, 3 $5 bills, and 1 quarter. How much more does he need to save?

_____

b. Lenna has saved 1 $50, 2 $5 bills, and 9 toonies. How much will she have left after paying for the dress?

_____

⑨ Ms. Jones needs to park her car for 8 hours. Parking Lot A charges $9.75 for the first hour and $0.50 for each additional hour. Parking Lot B charges $1.75 for each hour.

a. Which parking lot has a better deal? What is the difference in cost?

_____

b. Ms. Jones pays to park at Parking Lot A with 2 $5 bills and 2 toonies. What is her change?

_____

⑩ A store has a promotion of "buy 5 get 1 free". A T-shirt costs $23.40 and a sweater costs $36.10.

a. If Sara buys 6 T-shirts, how much will each T-shirt cost on average?

_____

b. If Sara buys 3 sweaters and 3 T-shirts, how much will each item cost on average? (The free item is the cheapest item.)

_____

c.

> I bought 3 sweaters and 3 T-shirts and got 2 $20 bills, 2 toonies, and 9 dimes in change.

Sara

How much did Sara pay?

_____

ISBN: 978-1-77149-203-4

⑪ Jackson has 4 $20 bills, 2 $10 bills, and 3 $5 bills and he wants to buy some CDs and DVDs. A CD costs $19.99 and a DVD costs $25.99.

    a. How much will he have left if he buys 3 CDs and 2 DVDs?

_____

    b. How much more money does Jackson need for 6 DVDs?

_____

⑫ A shoe store is having a clearance sale. Each pair of shoes gets an additional discount of $2 for every $25 spent.

    a. How much will a pair of shoes that costs $34.76 be with the discount?

> **Hints**
>
> Spending $34.76 will only give a $2 discount.

_____

    b. Which item will be cheaper: a pair of boots that costs $168.26 or a pair of heels that costs $175.29?

_____

    c. Will 10 $5 bills be enough to pay for 2 pairs of running shoes if each pair costs $27.23? If not, how much more money is needed?

_____

ISBN: 978-1-77149-203-4

Time and Temperature

solving a variety of word problems that involve finding elapsed time and changes in temperature

 **Math Skills**

① Write the times and find the elapsed times.

a.
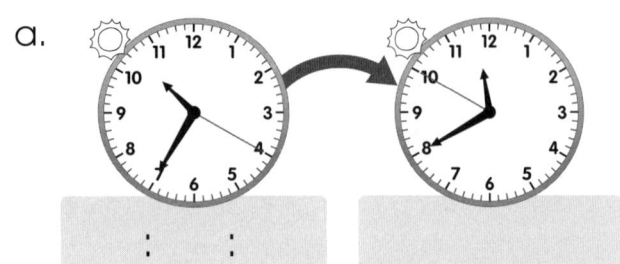

Elapsed time: _____ h _____ min _____ s

b.
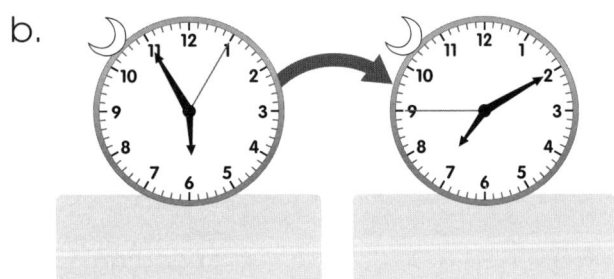

Elapsed time: _____

c. 10:35:10 a.m. → 11:42:25 a.m.

_____

d. 3:45:05 p.m. → 5:28:40 p.m.

_____

e. 4:46:20 p.m. → 8:09:15 p.m.

_____

f. 11:26:30 a.m. → 1:50:40 p.m.

_____

g. 9:08:27 a.m. → 3:54:30 p.m.

_____

② Write the temperatures and describe the changes.

a.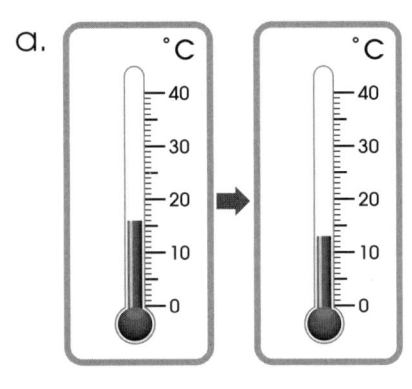

b.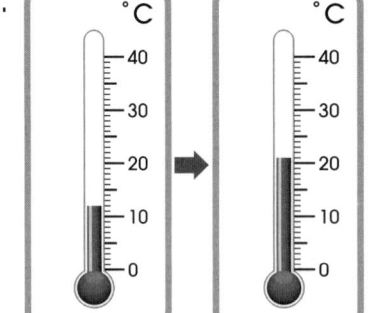

c.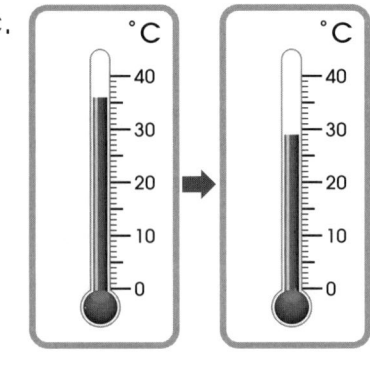

_____ °C _____

_____ by _____ °C
rose/dropped

_____ _____

_____ _____

ISBN: 978-1-77149-203-4

 **Problem Solving**

Try This!

Penny began driving at 10:15:25 a.m. and arrived at her destination at 1:10:55 p.m. How long was her drive?

Solution:

Step 1: **Write the times in 24-h notation.**

10:15:25 a.m. → 10:15:25
1:10:55 p.m. → 13:10:55

Step 2: **Subtract to find the elapsed time.**

$$\begin{array}{r} \overset{12}{\cancel{13}}:\overset{70}{\cancel{10}}:55 \\ -\ 10:15:25 \\ \hline 2:55:30 \end{array}$$

> Always add or subtract hours, minutes, and seconds separately. When needed, trade 1 h for 60 min or 1 min for 60 s.

Step 3: **Write a concluding sentence.**

Penny's drive was ⬚ long.

① Charles went to school at 7:45:15 a.m. and returned home at 3:10:26 p.m. How long did he stay at school?

Tips

Keep in mind that "a.m." refers to before noon and "p.m." refers to after noon.

Charles stayed at school for _____ .

ISBN: 978-1-77149-203-4

② Margo started working at 2:42:10 p.m. and worked for 4 h 37 min. What time did Margo get off work?

Margo got off work at _____ .

③ Ben completed his puzzle at 8:56:31 p.m. It took him 3 h 28 min 10 s to complete the puzzle. What time did he start the puzzle?

Ben started the puzzle at _____ .

④

I painted the first coat at 2:48:51 p.m. and the second coat at 10:31:05 a.m. the next day.

How long did Lisa wait between the two coats?

Lisa

Lisa waited _____ between the two coats.

ISBN: 978-1-77149-203-4

⑤ It takes Miranda 1 h 24 min 8 s to bake 1 batch of cookies. What is the latest time Miranda has to start baking if she needs to have 2 batches baked by 1:16:20 p.m.?

The latest time Miranda has to start baking is _____ .

⑥ At a movie theatre, Movie A begins at 7:46:12 p.m. and is 1 h 35 min 47 s long. Movie B begins at 7:21:02 p.m. and is 2 h 5 min 37 s long.

a. Which movie will end first?

Movie _____ will end first.

b. How much earlier will the first movie end?

The first movie will end _____ earlier.

⑦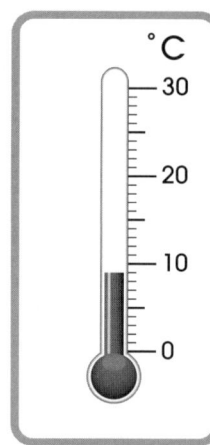

The thermometer shows the outdoor temperature in the morning.

  a. The temperature has risen by 7°C. What is the current temperature?

  _____

  b. The thermometer on the right shows the indoor temperature. How much warmer is it indoors than outdoors?

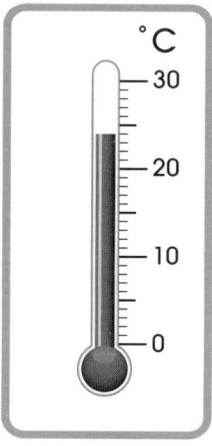

  _____

⑧ A frozen turkey was 12°C below 0°C. After it thawed, its temperature has risen by 16°C.

  a. What is the temperature of the turkey now?

Tips

Visualize the change on a thermometer if needed.

  _____

  b. How much hotter is the turkey after cooking compared to its temperature when it was frozen?

  _____

ISBN: 978-1-77149-203-4

⑨ A frozen microwave dinner was 4°C below 0°C before cooking and 52°C after cooking. How much hotter was the microwave dinner after cooking?

_____

⑩ The temperature in the morning was 2°C below 0°C. It rose by 5°C in the afternoon and dropped by 10°C at night. What was the temperature at night?

_____

⑪ In an experiment, the temperature of a liquid was 13°C below 0°C at 9:03:15 a.m. After 4 min 32 s, its temperature rose to 3°C.

a. What time was it when the liquid reached 3°C?

_____

b. By how much had the temperature risen?

_____

ISBN: 978-1-77149-203-4

⑫ A soccer game began at 4:57:22 p.m. and ended at 6:45:09 p.m. If a soccer game is 90 minutes long with a 15-minute intermission, how much extra time did the soccer game have?

_____

⑬ Damien sent an e-mail at 11:34:24 a.m. and received a reply at 3:45:21 p.m. How long did it take for Damien to get the reply?

Tips

Converting the times into 24-h notation can help you figure out the answer easily.

_____

⑭ A boat left the dock on September 24 at 11:47:03 a.m. and arrived at its destination on September 29 at 5:03:17 p.m. How long was the voyage?

_____

⑮ The opening hours of a swimming pool are shown.

a. How long is the pool open on Fridays?

Opening Hours

Monday to Thursday
8:00 a.m. – 9:30 p.m.

Friday to Sunday
10:00 a.m. – 11:45 p.m.

_____

b.

How much longer is the pool open on Saturdays than Tuesdays?

_____

ISBN: 978-1-77149-203-4

⑯ A flight that is 5 hours and 19 minutes long takes off from the airport at 10:36 p.m. on June 15 from Toronto.

a. When will the flight arrive at its destination which is in the same time zone?

Hints

Remember to convert 24 hours into 1 day.

_____

b. What time will the flight arrive if the destination is Vancouver, which is 3 hours behind Toronto?

_____

c. If there is a delay of 1 hour and 57 minutes, what time will the flight arrive in Vancouver?

_____

⑰ An air conditioner cools a room by 2°C every 16 minutes.

a. What time will a room cool from 30°C to 22°C if the air conditioner is turned on at 5:53 p.m.?

_____

b. If the air conditioner is turned on from 9:43 a.m. to 11:19 a.m., how much cooler will the room be?

_____

ISBN: 978-1-77149-203-4

Perimeter and Area

solving a variety of word problems that involve finding the perimeters and areas of shapes

Math Skills

① Find the perimeters and areas.

1 cm

1 cm

A

B

C

D

E

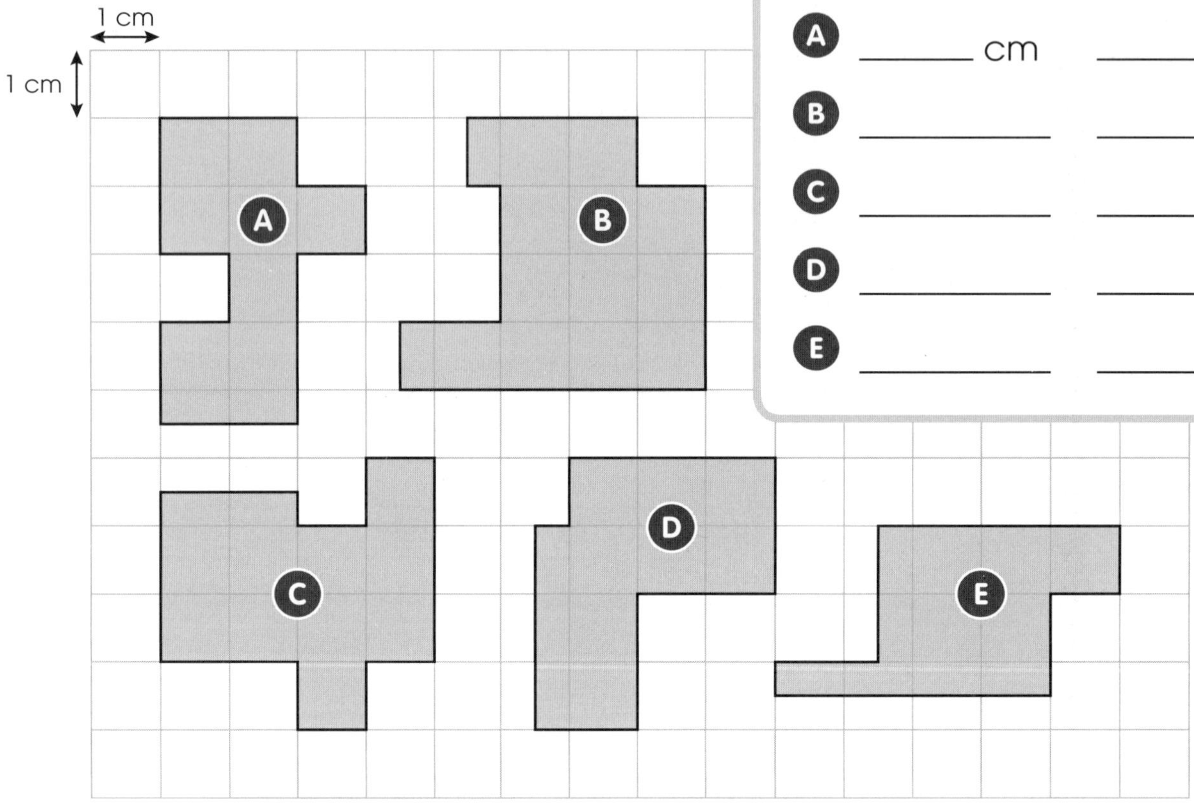

Perimeter and Area

A _____ cm   _____ cm²

B _____   _____

C _____   _____

D _____   _____

E _____   _____

②

5 cm

Perimeter:

_____

= _____ (cm)

Area:

_____

= _____ (cm²)

③

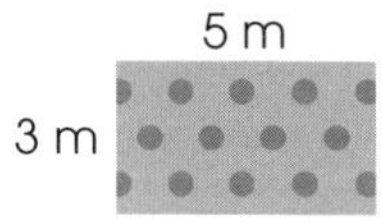

5 m

3 m

Perimeter:

_____

= _____

Area:

_____

= _____

④

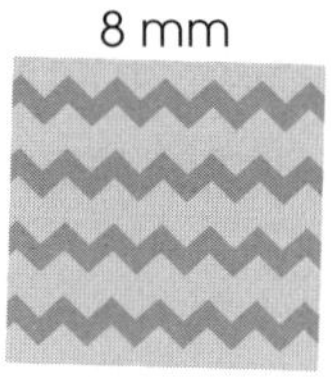

8 mm

Perimeter:

_____

= _____

Area:

_____

= _____

ISBN: 978-1-77149-203-4

 **Problem Solving**

Leo has a square mirror that has a side length of 15 cm. What is the perimeter of the mirror?

Solution:

> Use these formulas to find the perimeters and areas of squares and rectangles.

Step 1: Make a sketch of the mirror.

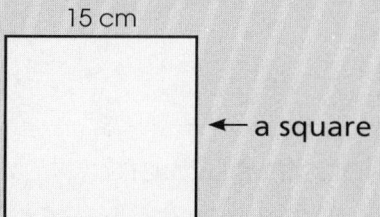

15 cm

← a square

Step 2: Find the perimeter.

15 × 4 = ⬚

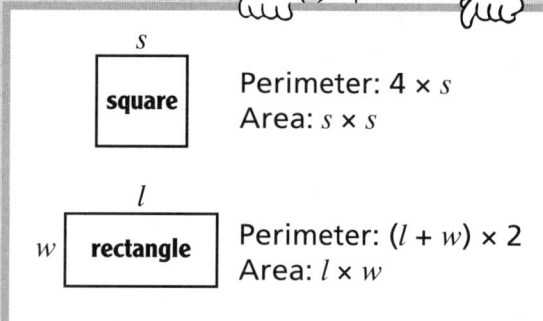

s

| square | Perimeter: 4 × s
 Area: s × s |

l

w | rectangle | Perimeter: (l + w) × 2
 Area: l × w |

Step 3: Write a concluding sentence.

The perimeter of the mirror is ⬚ cm.

① George wants to add trimmings to a rug that measures 80 cm by 60 cm. How many centimetres of trimmings does he need?

George needs _____ cm of trimmings.

ISBN: 978-1-77149-203-4

② Peter has drawn a rectangle on his driveway with chalk. It measures 0.8 m by 1.2 m. What is the perimeter of the rectangle?

The perimeter of the rectangle is _____ m.

③ Anne's square handkerchief has a side length of 23 cm.

a. What is the perimeter of her handkerchief?

The perimeter of her handkerchief is _____ cm.

b. The side length of Tessa's square handkerchief is 1.5 cm greater than Anne's. What is the perimeter of Tessa's handkerchief?

The perimeter of her handkerchief is _____ cm.

ISBN: 978-1-77149-203-4

④ Zoe has the 2 pieces of cardboard on the right.

    a. She glued a piece of 26.9-cm yarn along the edges of one of them. Which one was it?

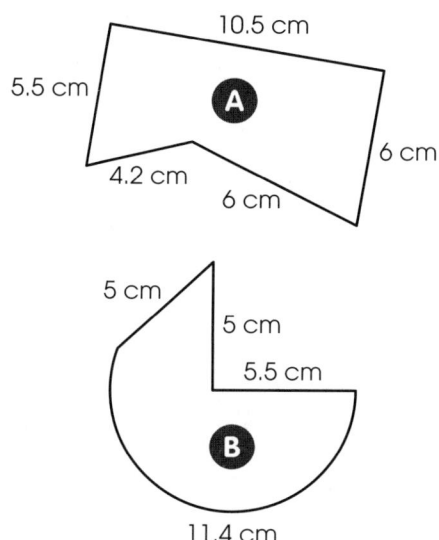

Zoe glued yarn on Shape _____ .

b.

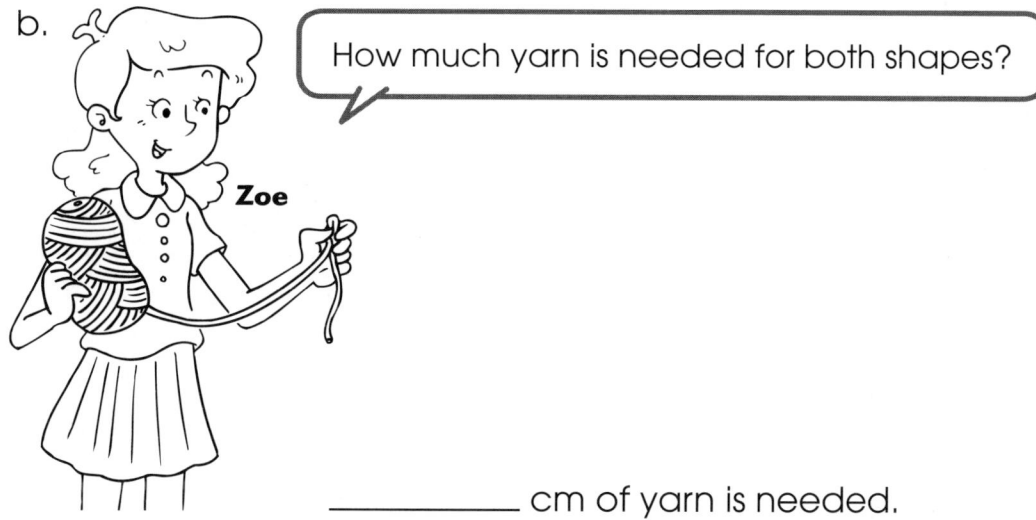

How much yarn is needed for both shapes?

Zoe

_____ cm of yarn is needed.

⑤ Measure each shape in the diagram. Which shape has the greatest perimeter?

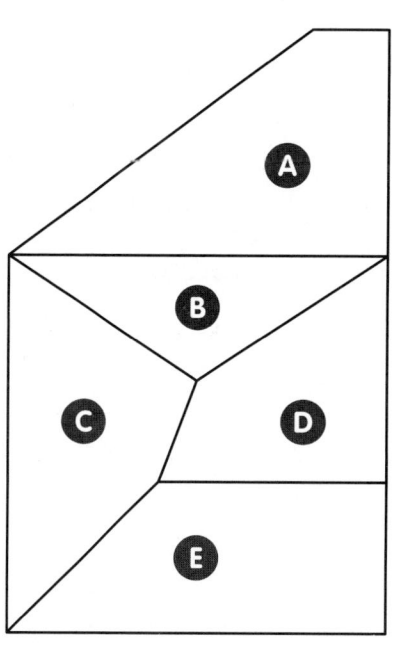

Shape _____ has the greatest perimeter.

ISBN: 978-1-77149-203-4

⑥ A square table has a side length of 72 cm. What is the area of the table?

_____

⑦ A rectangular board has a length of 16 cm and an area of 200 cm². What is the width of the board?

_____

⑧ The dimensions of a rectangular tile are 15 cm by 8 cm.

a. What is the area of the tile?

_____

b.
> Will 200 tiles be enough to cover a panel that measures 290 cm by 85 cm?

_____

  ISBN: 978-1-77149-203-4

⑨ Janice has placed a photo into her new picture frame. The frame is 2 cm thick on all four sides.

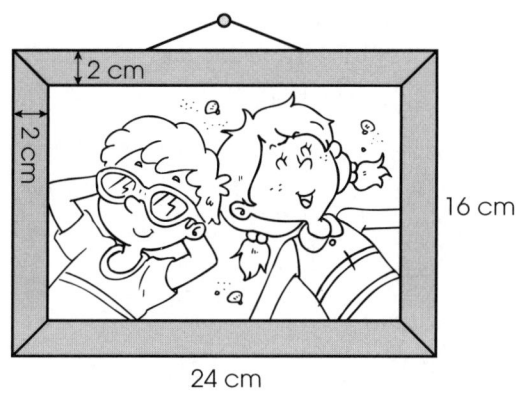

24 cm

a. What is the area of the photo?

_____

b. What is the area of the frame alone?

Hints

You can find the area of the frame by finding the difference of the areas of the two shapes.

_____

⑩ Troy has a rectangular parking space that is 3 m long and 2.6 m wide.

a. What is the area of the parking space in m²?

_____

b. What is the area of the parking space in cm²?

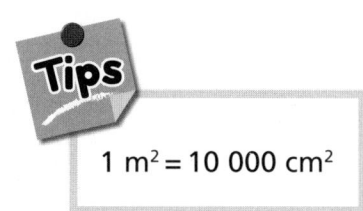

Tips

1 m² = 10 000 cm²

_____

ISBN: 978-1-77149-203-4

⑪ Farmer Sarah measured a rectangular section of her farm to plant tomatoes.

Sarah

I measured a length of 0.24 km and a width of 4000 cm.

a. What is the area in m²?

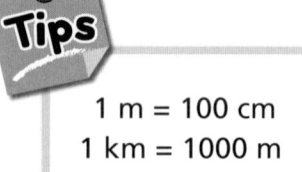

Tips

1 m = 100 cm
1 km = 1000 m

_____

b. What is the perimeter in km?

_____

⑫ Cyrus uses a piece of string to make a rectangle that is 32 cm by 16 cm.

a. How long is the piece of string? What is the area of the rectangle?

_____

b. If Cyrus changes the rectangle to a square instead, what will the area of the square be?

_____

⑬ A picture frame has a width of 16 cm and its length is 8 cm longer than the width. What is the perimeter and the area of the picture frame?

Hints

Find the length first.

_____

ISBN: 978-1-77149-203-4

⑭ Renée has a wooden door that is 2 m by 50 cm. She wants to make a square cut-out that has a side length of 30 cm into the door for a window. What is the area of the door in cm² after the cut-out?

---

⑮ The floor plan of James's and his sisters' bedrooms is shown.

a. What is the area of the biggest room?

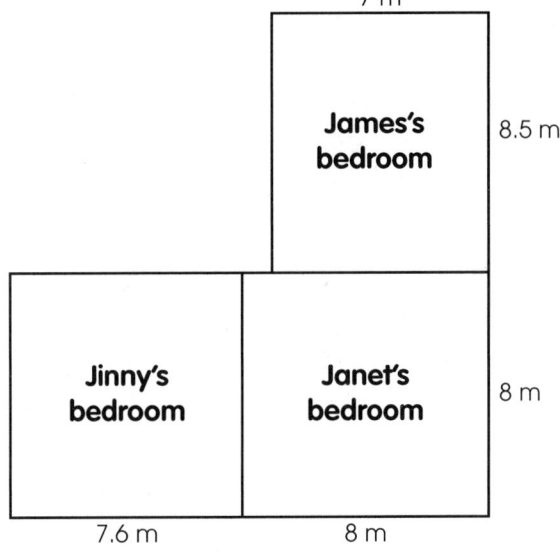

---

b. The sisters' bedrooms are connected. What is the total area?

---

⑯ Two rectangular paintings have the same area. Painting A has a length of 16 cm and a width of 15 cm. The width of Painting B is 3 cm shorter than the width of Painting A.

a. What is the length of Painting B?

---

b. Which painting has a greater perimeter?

ISBN: 978-1-77149-203-4

Volume, Capacity, and Mass

solving a variety of word problems that involve finding volume, capacity, and mass

Math Skills

① Find the volume, capacity, and mass.

Volume

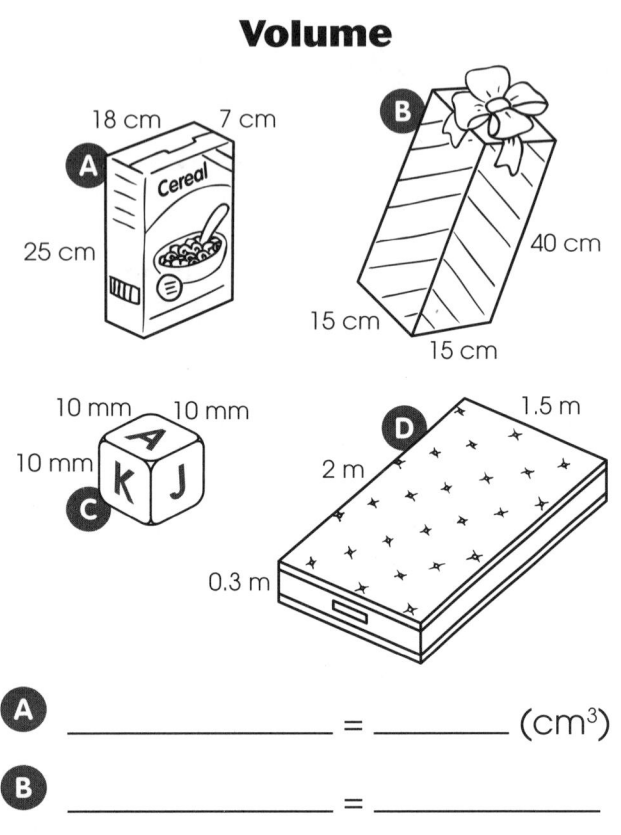

A _____ = _____ (cm³)

B _____ = _____

C _____ = _____

D _____ = _____

Capacity

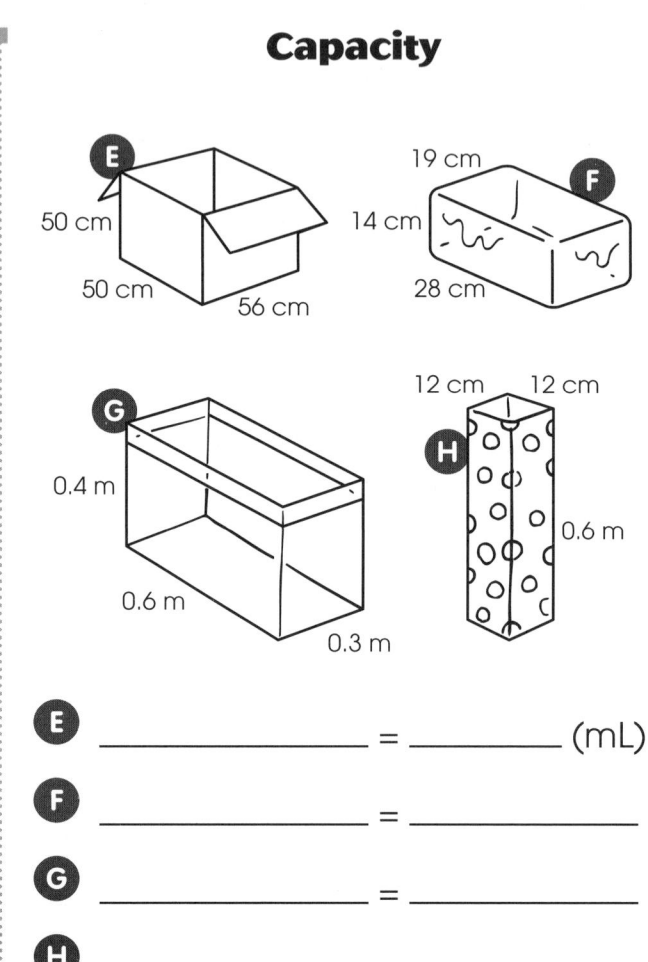

E _____ = _____ (mL)

F _____ = _____

G _____ = _____

H _____ = _____

Mass

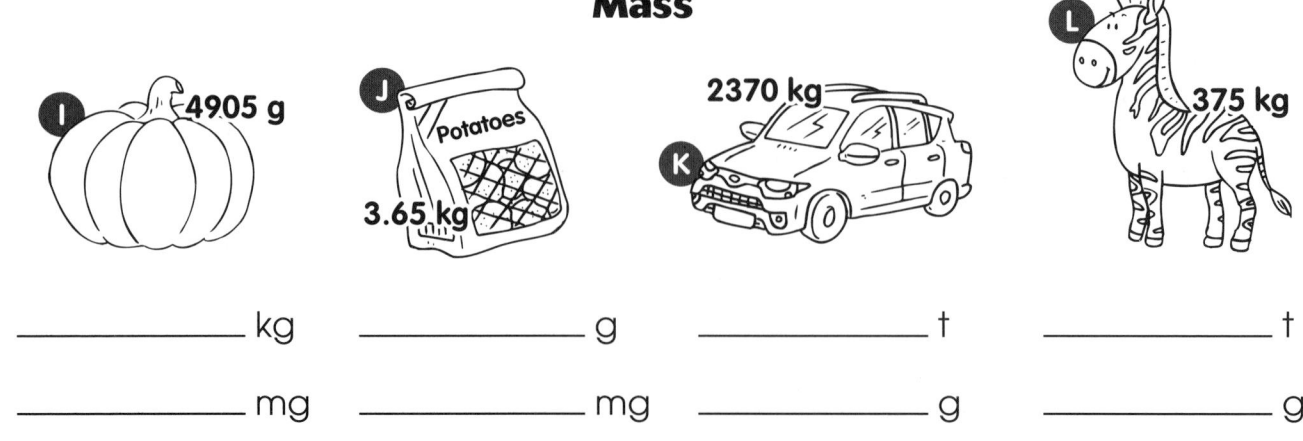

_____ kg   _____ g   _____ t   _____ t

_____ mg   _____ mg   _____ g   _____ g

ISBN: 978-1-77149-203-4

 **Problem Solving**

Try This!

Elliot has a rectangular prism that has a length of 8 cm, a width of 8 cm, and a height of 6 cm. What is the volume?

Solution:

Step 1: Make a sketch of the rectangular prism.

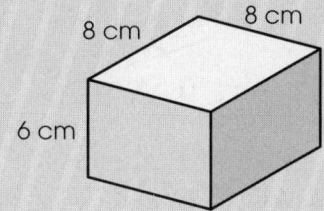

The volume of a rectangular prism is the product of its length, width, and height.

Step 2: Find the volume.

8 × 8 × 6 = ⬚

Step 3: Write a concluding sentence.

The volume of the rectangular prism

is ⬚ cm³.

① A juice box has a length of 5 cm, a width of 3 cm, and a height of 12 cm. What is the volume of the juice box?

The volume of the juice box is _____ cm³.

ISBN: 978-1-77149-203-4

② I cut this rectangular wooden block out of a tree trunk. What is its volume?

0.42 m

0.54 m **30 cm**

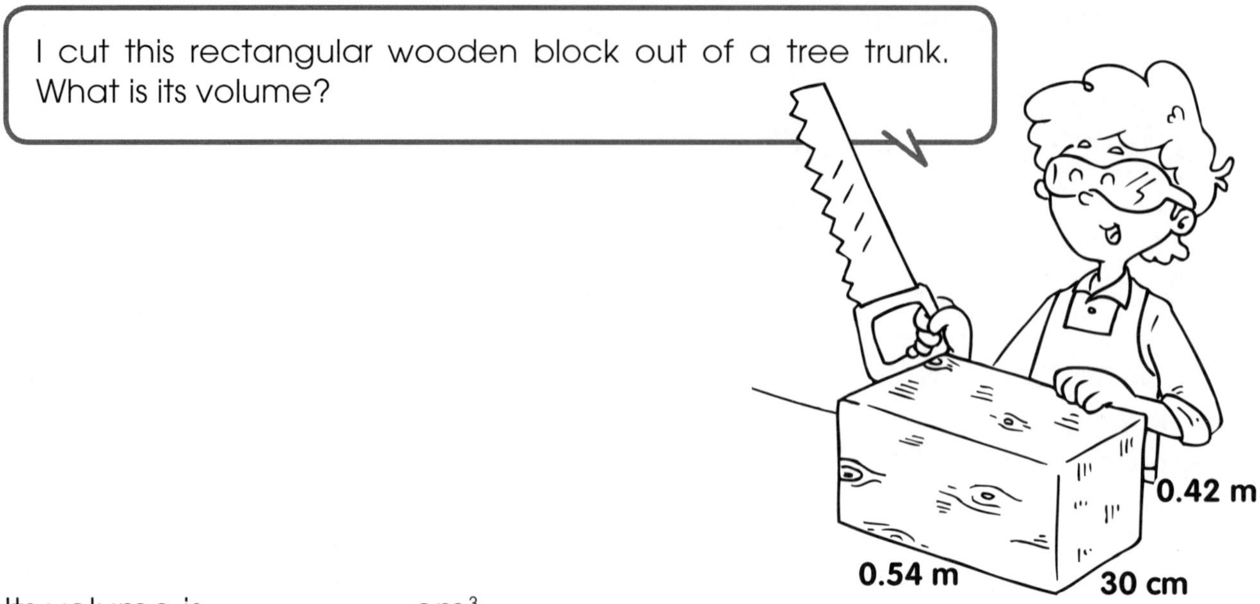

Its volume is _____ cm³.

③ A cookie container has a length of 12 cm, a width of 12 cm, and a height of 7.5 cm. What is its volume?

Its volume is _____ cm³.

④ A cardboard box has a volume of 2000 cm³. It has a width of 10 cm and its height is twice the width. What is the length of the cardboard box?

The length of the cardboard box is _____ cm.

ISBN: 978-1-77149-203-4

⑤ A garbage bin has a length of 35 cm, a width of 28 cm, and a height of 45 cm. What is its capacity?

Its capacity is _____ mL.

⑥ Abby has made a gift box out of construction paper. Its dimensions are 13 cm by 13 cm by 20 cm. What is the capacity of the gift box?

The capacity of the gift box is _____ mL.

⑦ An aquarium has a length of 600 cm, a width of 240 cm, and a height of 280 cm. What is the capacity of the aquarium in litres?

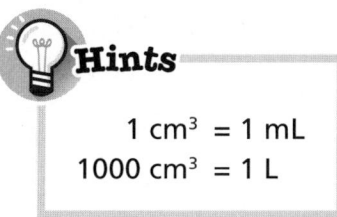

Hints

$1 \text{ cm}^3 = 1 \text{ mL}$
$1000 \text{ cm}^3 = 1 \text{ L}$

The capacity of the aquarium is _____ L.

⑧ A glass cube has a side length of 9 cm. Can it hold 1 L of water?

_____

⑨ A sandbox measures 152 cm by 75 cm by 18 cm. What is its capacity in L?

_____

⑩ Emily has a cooler in the shape of a rectangular prism. The cooler is 65 cm in length and 48 cm in width.

a. The capacity of the cooler is 78 L. What is its height?

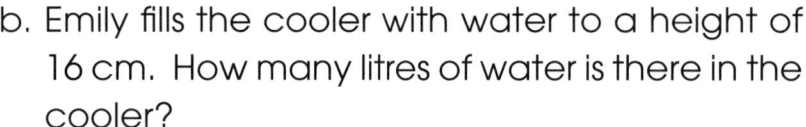

Emily

_____

b. Emily fills the cooler with water to a height of 16 cm. How many litres of water is there in the cooler?

_____

ISBN: 978-1-77149-203-4

⑪ A mailman has 3 parcels to deliver. He wants to put the heaviest parcel at the bottom and the lightest parcel at the top.

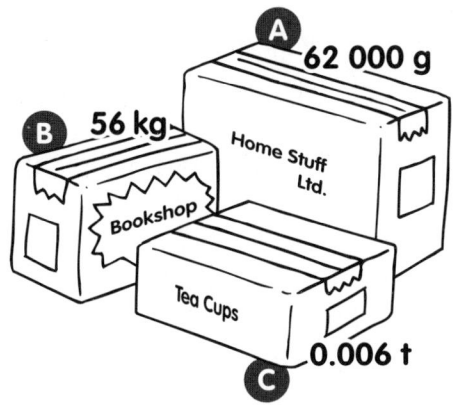

a. How should the mailman stack the parcels?

_____

b. The mailman uses a trolley to deliver the parcels. If the trolley has a maximum mass limit of 180 kg, can the trolley be used to move all 3 parcels at once?

_____

⑫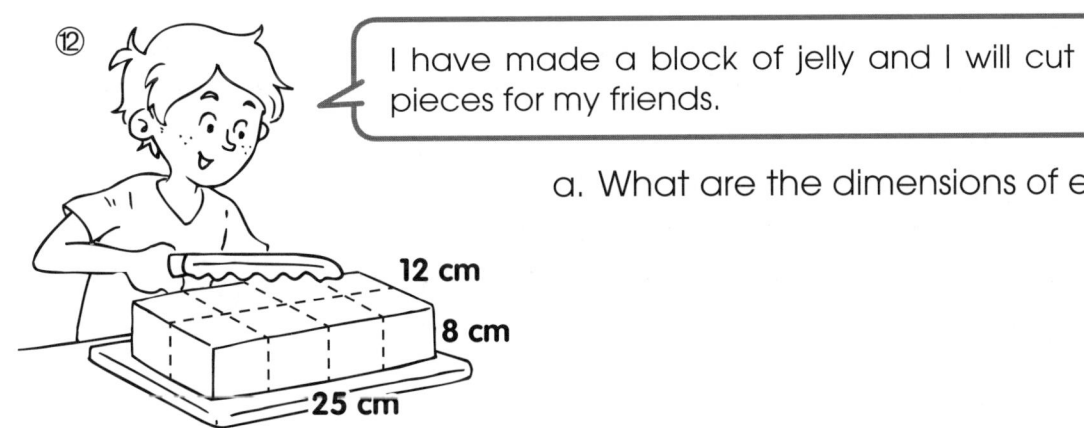

I have made a block of jelly and I will cut it into 8 equal pieces for my friends.

a. What are the dimensions of each piece?

_____

b. The total mass of the jelly is 1.648 kg. What is the mass of each piece?

_____

ISBN: 978-1-77149-203-4

⑬ An inflated swimming pool has a length of 3.5 m, a width of 2 m, and a depth of 0.9 m.

a. What is the capacity of the swimming pool in m³?

_____

b. If the water level in the swimming pool is at 0.6 m, how much water is there in mL?

_____

c. Alex fully submerges himself into the swimming pool and the water level rises by 20 cm. What is his volume?

_____

⑭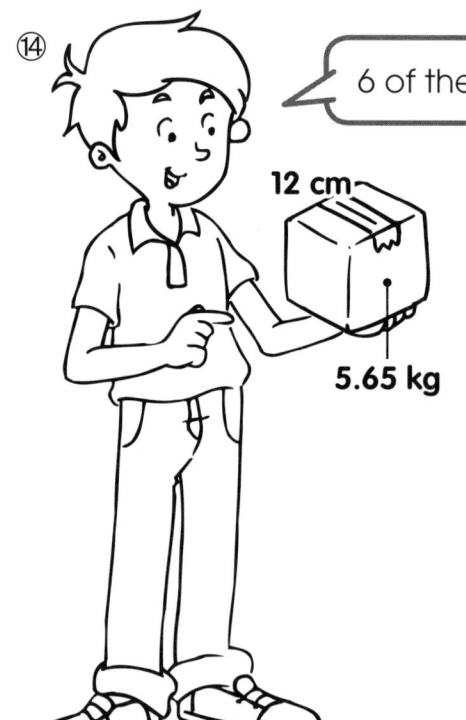

6 of these cube boxes fit perfectly into one bin.

a. What is the volume of the bin?

12 cm

5.65 kg

_____

b. What is the mass of the bin when it is fully packed with the cube boxes?

_____

ISBN: 978-1-77149-203-4

⑮ Peter's aquarium has a capacity of 9 L. He filled his aquarium with 7.2 L of water and the water level was at 16 cm.

a. The width of the aquarium is 15 cm. What is its length?

_____

b. Peter puts 5 identical decorations into the aquarium and the water level rises to 18 cm. What is the volume of 1 decoration?

_____

c. How many more of the identical decorations can the aquarium hold without overflowing?

_____

⑯ At a water purification facility, a cube tank that has a side length of 6 m is first filled with lake water, which is then filtered into a smaller tank.

a. The smaller tank has a base of 12 m². How tall is it if it has a capacity of 72 000 L?

Tips

$1 \text{ m}^3 = 1000 \text{ L}$

_____

b. By how many metres will the water level in the cube tank decrease after 72 000 L of water is filtered out?

_____

ISBN: 978-1-77149-203-4

Shapes and Solids

solving a variety of word problems that involve the geometric properties of shapes and solids

 **Math Skills**

① Name the shapes.

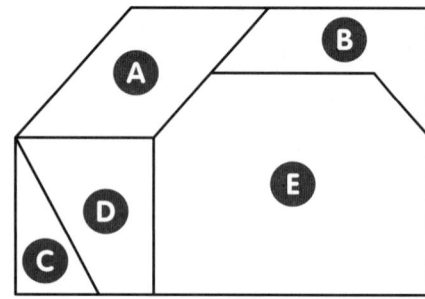

A _____

B _____

C _____

D _____

E _____

② Name each triangle by sides and by angles.

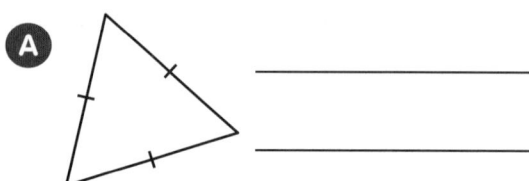

_____

_____

_____

_____

_____

_____

③ Complete the skeletons of the 3-D figures and the chart.

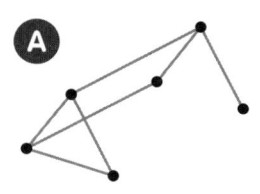   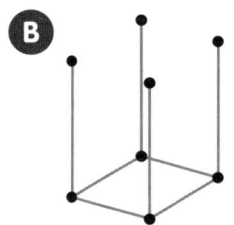   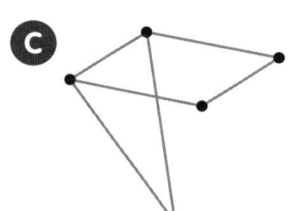   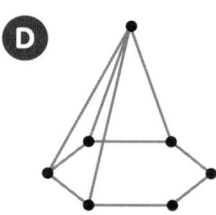

	Name	Number of Faces	Number of Vertices	Number of Edges
A				
B				
C				
D				

ISBN: 978-1-77149-203-4

Problem Solving

Stacy has drawn a parallelogram. How many acute angles and obtuse angles are there?

Solution:

Step 1: **Draw a parallelogram.**

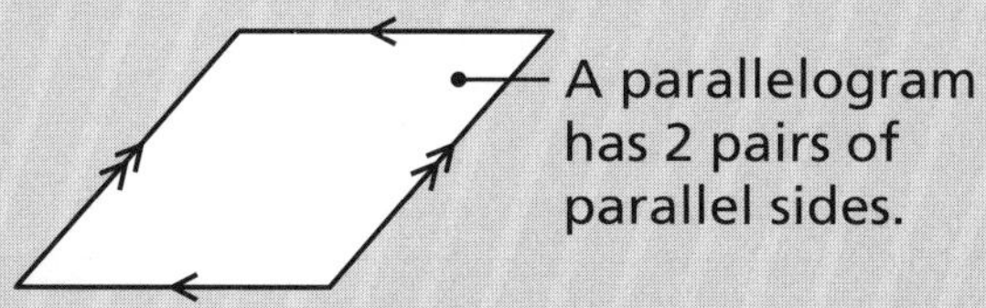

A parallelogram has 2 pairs of parallel sides.

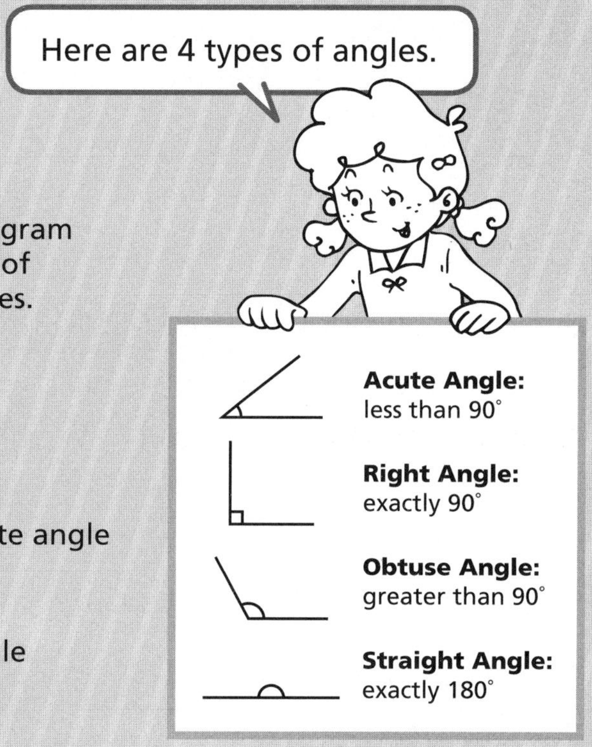

Here are 4 types of angles.

Step 2: **Identify the angles.**

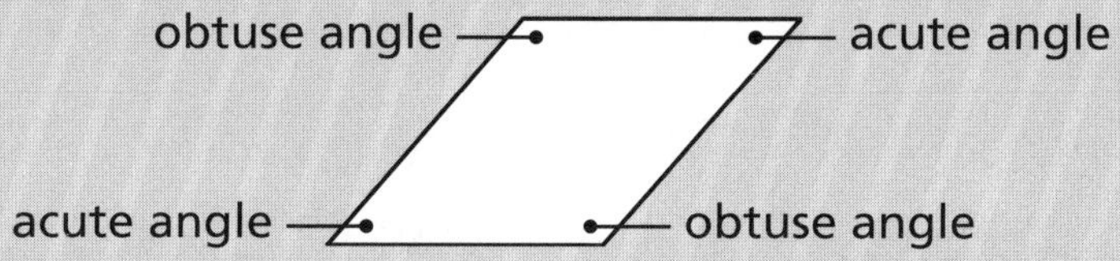

obtuse angle — • — • — acute angle

acute angle — • — • — obtuse angle

Acute Angle:
less than 90°

Right Angle:
exactly 90°

Obtuse Angle:
greater than 90°

Straight Angle:
exactly 180°

Step 3: **Write a concluding sentence.**

There are ☐ acute angle(s) and ☐ obtuse angle(s).

① Andrew drew a trapezoid that has no right angles. Name the types of angles and record the number of each type.

There are _____ .

②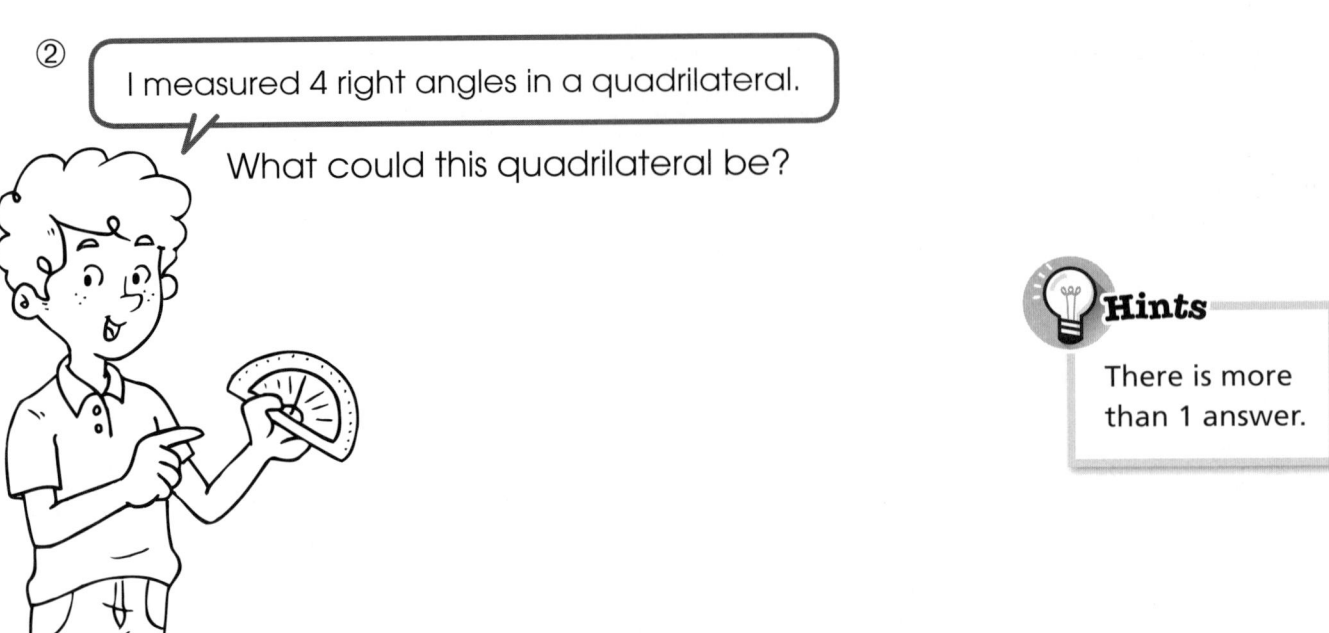

I measured 4 right angles in a quadrilateral.

What could this quadrilateral be?

Hints

There is more than 1 answer.

This quadrilateral could be _____ .

③ Ginny took a picture of a road sign. It is in the shape of a regular polygon that has 8 lines of symmetry. What is this shape?

Hints

A regular polygon has all sides equal and all angles equal.

This shape is a(n) _____ .

④ Aaron folded a square handkerchief diagonally to form a triangle. Name this triangle in 2 ways.

This triangle is a(n) _____ and a(n) _____ .

ISBN: 978-1-77149-203-4

⑤ Ms. White cut a regular pentagon into 5 equal triangles. Name the triangles in 2 ways.

The names of these triangles are _____ and _____ .

⑥ Sandra has 8 identical equilateral triangles.

   a. She composed 2 of them to make a quadrilateral. Name the quadrilateral.

The quadrilateral is a _____ .

  b.

> I will compose the rest of the triangles to make a regular polygon.

Name the regular polygon.

Sandra

The regular polygon is a(n) _____ .

ISBN: 978-1-77149-203-4

⑦ I'm cutting this regular octagon along all of its lines of symmetry.

How many pieces will there be? Name the shape of each piece.

_____

⑧ Christina has drawn a trapezoid that has 1 line of symmetry. She wants to divide it into 1 square and 2 right triangles. Is it possible?

_____

⑨ Jack says, "A triangle that is made by combining 2 identical right triangles is always an isosceles triangle." Is he correct?

_____

⑩ Derek folds a square piece of paper as shown to make a smaller square. Then he cuts off a corner of the square and unfolds it. Name the shape.

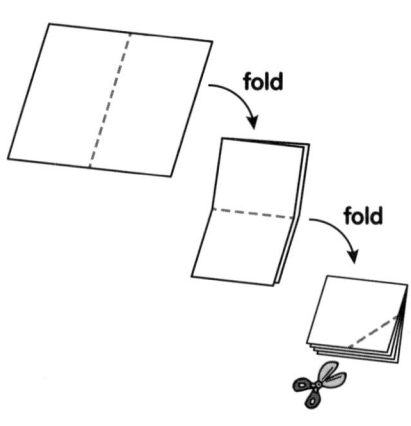

_____

   ISBN: 978-1-77149-203-4

⑪ Teresa is making models of buildings. Find the number of faces, edges, and vertices each model has.

a. A hotel is a square-based pyramid.

_____

b. A hospital is a rectangular prism.

_____

⑫ Draw and name the solid

a. with 4 faces, 6 edges, and 4 vertices.

b. with 6 faces, 10 edges, 6 vertices, and is not a prism.

_____   _____

c. without flat faces.

d. with 8 faces, 18 edges, 12 vertices, and is not a pyramid.

_____   _____

ISBN: 978-1-77149-203-4

⑬ Stephan made 3 solids using the nets below.

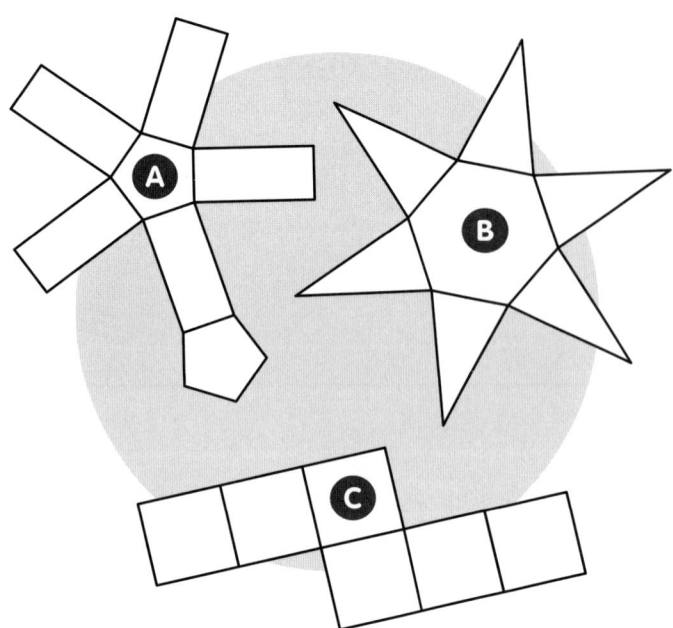

a. Draw and name the solid that each net forms.

b. Which net makes the solid that

• has the fewest faces?

_____

• has the most edges?

_____

• has the fewest vertices?

_____

ISBN: 978-1-77149-203-4

⑭

I want to build the skeleton of a heptagonal pyramid. I have 8 balls of clay and 12 sticks.

a. Does Lucy have enough materials? If not, which material does she need more of?

**Hints**

A heptagon has 7 sides.

b. A heptagonal pyramid has 7 identical triangular faces. Name the triangles in 2 ways.

⑮ Avery built a solid that has exactly 1 hexagonal face. How many triangular faces does it have?

⑯ An aquarium is a hexagonal prism. Its rectangular faces are identical. Is the base a regular hexagon?

⑰ The bases of a prism are trapezoids. How many rectangular faces does it have?

ISBN: 978-1-77149-203-4

Cartesian Coordinate Plane

solving a variety of word problems that involve locations and movements on a Cartesian coordinate plane

 **Math Skills**

① Write the coordinates of each fruit.

a. _____

b. _____

c. _____

d. _____

e. _____

f. _____

g. _____

h. _____

② Name the fruits that have the given coordinates.

a. (1,4) _____   b. (5,4) _____

c. (4,10) _____   d. (4,2) _____

③

I just picked up the apple. How should I get to the...

a. banana? _____

b. strawberry? _____

ISBN: 978-1-77149-203-4

 **Problem Solving**

Try This!

Emily wants to get the book and the pencil. Describe the shorter route to get both of them.

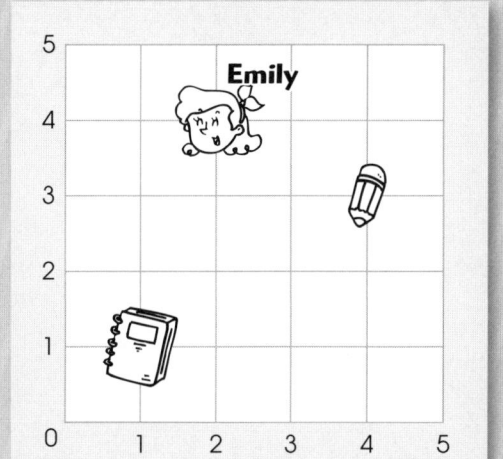

Solution:

Step 1: Identify the possible routes.

Route 1: Emily → pencil → book
Route 2: Emily → book → pencil

Step 2: Find the length of each route.

Route 1: 8 units ← shorter
Route 2: 9 units

You can go up/down first, or left/right first.

Step 3: Write a concluding sentence.

Emily should go [unit(s)] and

[unit(s)], and then [unit(s)]

and [unit(s)] .

① Emily's sister, Emma, is at (4,0). Describe the shorter route for Emma to get both items.

Emma should go _____

_____ .

ISBN: 978-1-77149-203-4

② Look at the map.

Map of Greensvilla

a. Write the coordinates of the places.

- forests

- houses

_____   _____

- mountains

- ponds

_____   _____

b. Rena is at (2,2) and Samuel is at (6,5). Locate and label them on the map.

c. Rena is hiking. How should she go to

- the closest forest?

She should go _____ .

- the farthest forest?

She should go _____ .

ISBN: 978-1-77149-203-4

d. Samuel wants to visit a pond. How should he go if he wants to go to

  • the closest pond?

   He should go _____ .

  • the farthest pond?

   He should go _____ .

e. Each unit on the map is 2 km. How many kilometres does Samuel travel to visit the closest pond?

   Samuel travels _____ km.

f. Samuel's house is the one that is farthest from the mountains. Label his house.

g. Rena's house is the one that is farthest from where she is. Label her house.

h.
> To get to the mountains from my house, how far do I have to travel?

Rena

   Rena has to travel _____ km.

i.
> How far is the closest pond from my house in km?

Samuel

   It is _____ km.

j. Rena and Samuel want to meet up. If they each travel 4 km from their houses, at which coordinates will they meet?

   They will meet at _____ or _____ .

ISBN: 978-1-77149-203-4

③ Look at the map of Jeannie's neighbourhood.

a. Locate and draw.

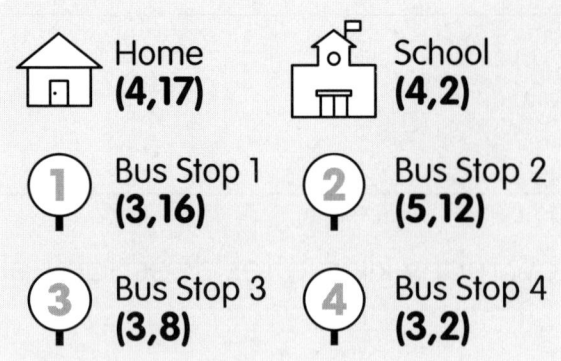

Home **(4,17)**   School **(4,2)**

① Bus Stop 1 **(3,16)**   ② Bus Stop 2 **(5,12)**

③ Bus Stop 3 **(3,8)**   ④ Bus Stop 4 **(3,2)**

b. Jeannie goes to school by bus. How many units does she travel on the bus?

_____

c. Jeannie returns home by train. How many units does she travel on the train?

_____

d. How many metres will Jeannie travel on the train if each unit is 100 m?

_____

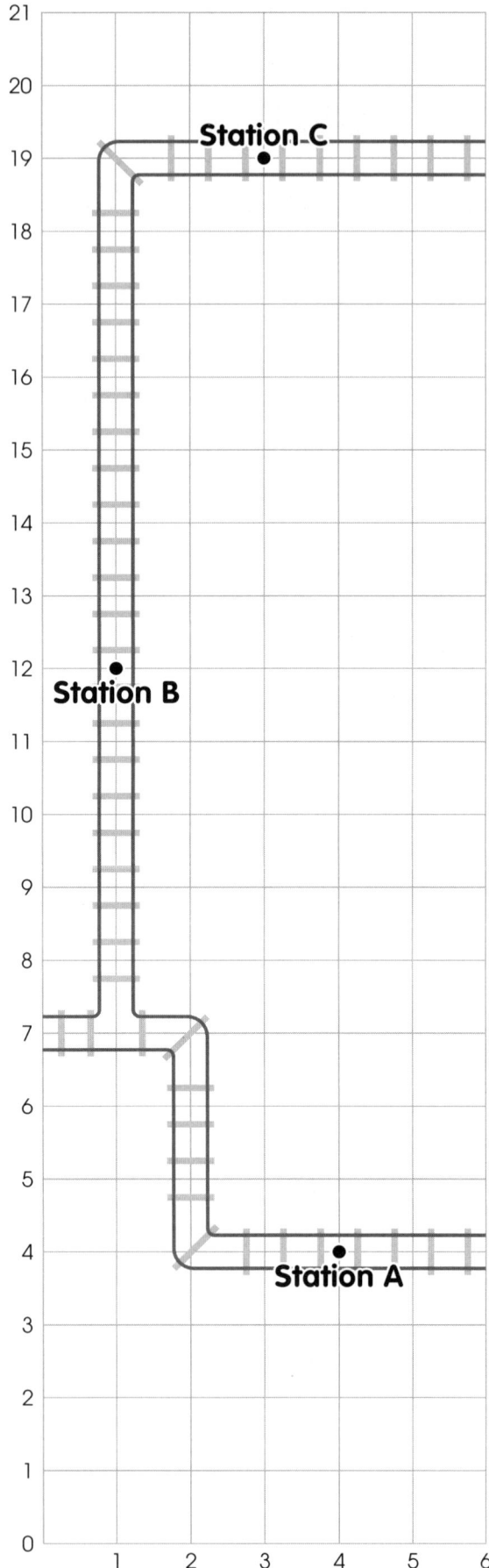

ISBN: 978-1-77149-203-4

④ Oscar drew the shapes on the Cartesian coordinate plane.

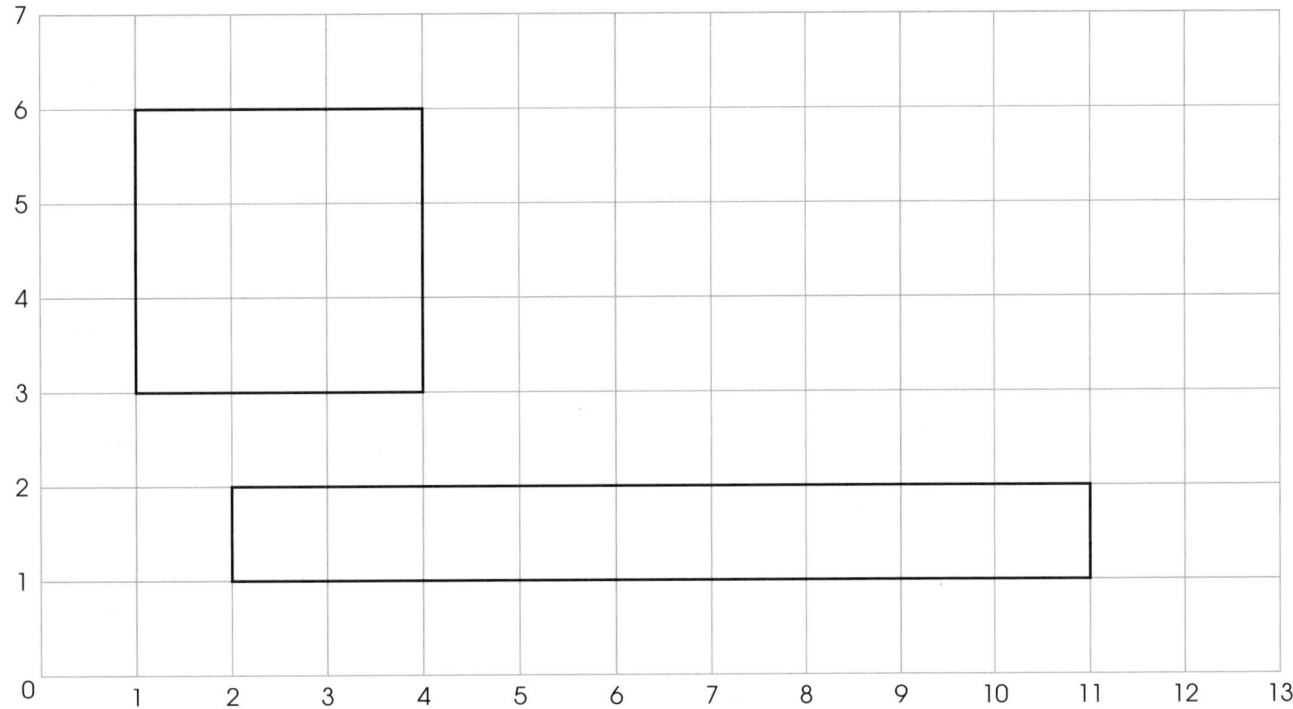

a. What are the coordinates of the shapes' vertices?

_____

_____

b.

> The next shape that I'll draw has these coordinates as its vertices.

Draw the shape and name it.

Oscar

| (6,6) | (9,6) |
| (5,3) | (9,3) |

_____

c. Finally, Oscar wants to draw the largest possible right triangle without touching the other shapes or the borders of the Cartesian coordinate plane. Draw the shape and write the coordinates of its vertices.

_____

ISBN: 978-1-77149-203-4

⑤ Below are Farmer Frank's animal pens.

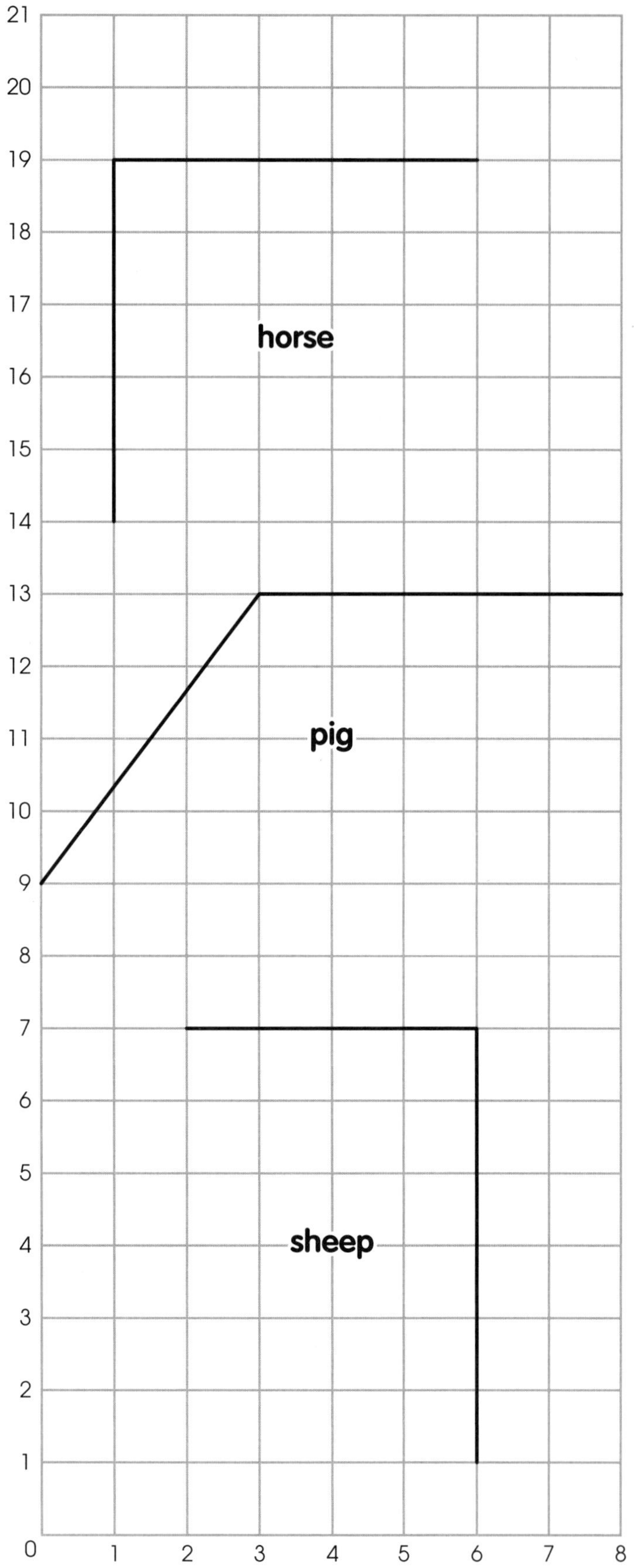

a. These are the shapes of the pens.

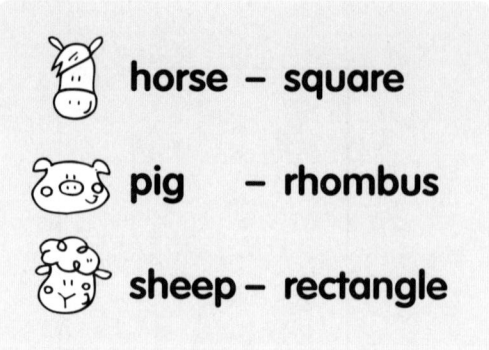

horse – square

pig – rhombus

sheep – rectangle

Draw 2 lines to complete each pen.

b. Write the coordinates of the missing vertices.

_____

_____

c. Count to find the pen that has the greatest area.

_____

d. The pig pen is a rhombus. What is its perimeter in units?

_____

e. Each unit represents a length of 10 m. What is the total length of fencing of all 3 pens?

_____

ISBN: 978-1-77149-203-4

⑥

I dug up 1 dinosaur fossil at an excavation site and I'm looking for 2 more. Each fossil takes up 5 sets of coordinates.

Jack

a. Jack tried the coordinates below but none of them uncovered the fossils. Mark an "✗" for each.

(1,2)   (2,2)   (4,4)

(2,1)   (1,3)   (4,3)   (3,4)

b. On the next three attempts at (3,2), (4,1), and (3,3), Jack uncovered part of one of the fossils. Circle the coordinates.

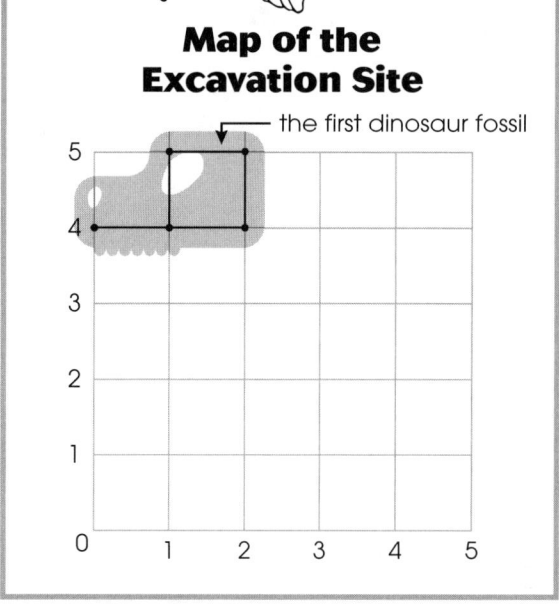

Map of the Excavation Site

the first dinosaur fossil

c. Can Jack uncover the remaining parts of the fossil? If so, write the coordinates of the remaining parts.

_____

d. Where could the other fossil be located? Write all the possible coordinates.

Hints

There are 6 pairs of possible coordinates.

_____

e. Of the possible coordinates, which ones must contain part of a fossil?

_____

ISBN: 978-1-77149-203-4

Transformations

solving a variety of word problems that involve transformations, similar and congruent shapes, and tiling

Math Skills

① Describe the transformations.

a. **A → B**

_____

_____

b. **B → C**

_____

_____

c. **A → D**

_____

_____

d. **W → X**

_____

_____

e. **X → Y**

_____

_____

f. **Y → Z**

_____

_____

g.

Is Figure A congruent to Image B? Explain.

_____

_____

_____

ISBN: 978-1-77149-203-4

 **Problem Solving**

Try This!

Mr. Argent moved a flag from 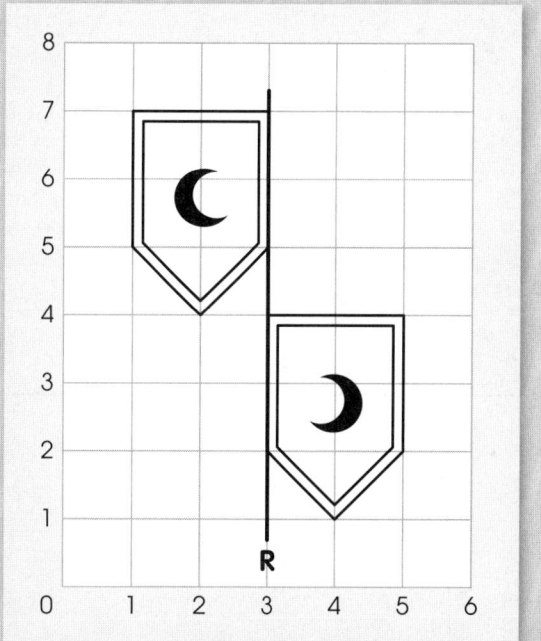 to in 2 transformations.
How was it transformed?

Solution:

Step 1: **Identify the transformations.**

translation ✔
rotation
reflection ✔

Step 2: **Describe the transformations.**

Translate it ☐ units down.

Reflect it in ☐ .

In this case, you can also reflect the flag before translating it.

Step 3: **Write a concluding sentence.**

It was translated ☐ units down.

Then it was reflected in ☐ .

① Refer to the grid above. What are the coordinates of the vertices of the flag now?

Hints

Remember which is the transformed image.

The coordinates of the vertices are _____ .

② Below is the floor plan of Aiden's bedroom.

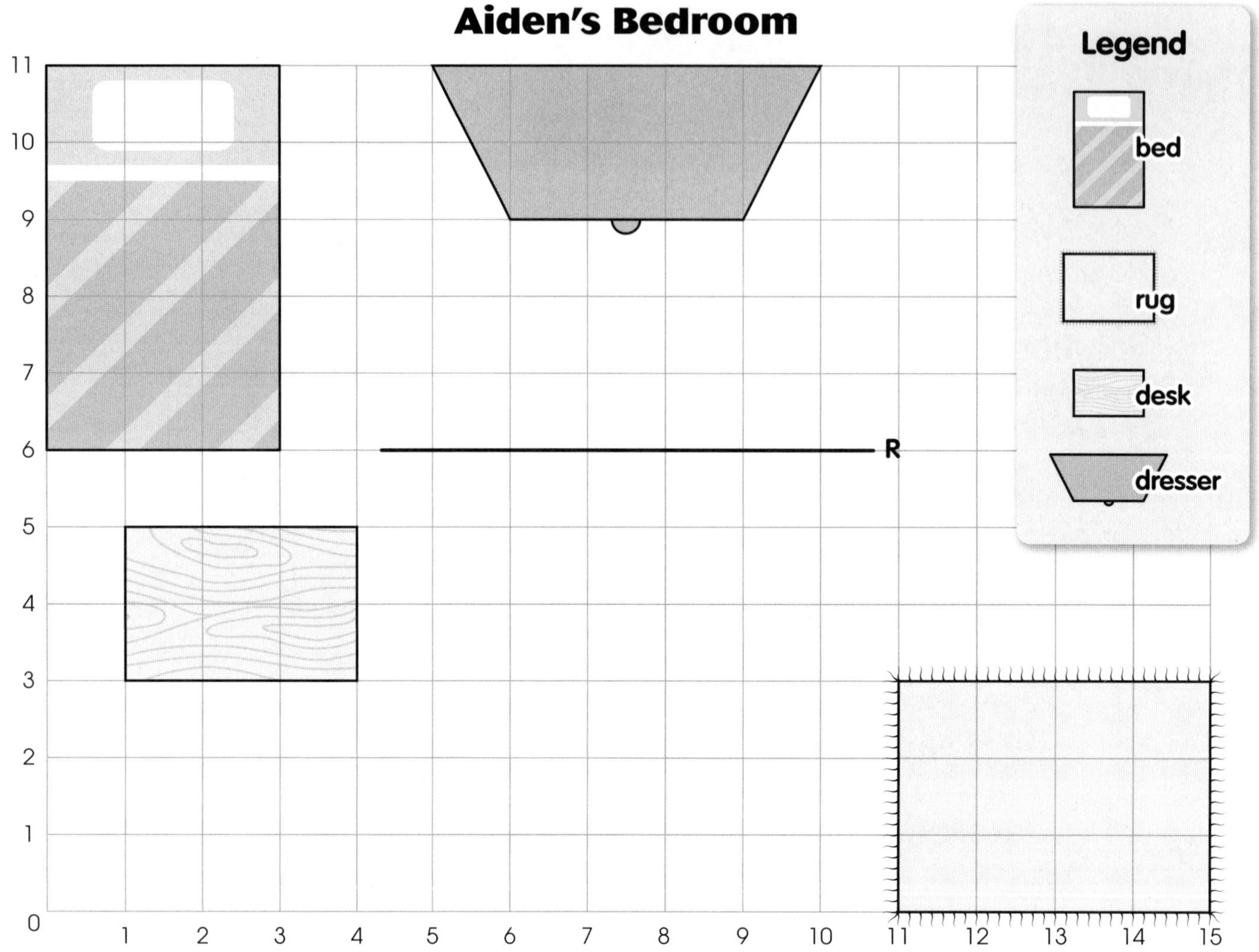
Aiden's Bedroom
Legend
bed
rug
desk
dresser
R
0
1
2
3
4
5
6
7
8
9
10
11
12
13
14
15

a. Aiden rearranges the furniture on the floor plan. Draw to show the new layout with the given transformations.

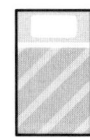

Translate it 3 units down and 2 units to the right. Then rotate it $\frac{1}{4}$ counterclockwise about (5,3).

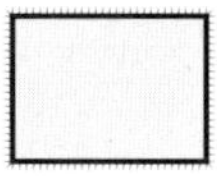

Translate it 1 unit up and 4 units to the left. Then reflect it in Line R.

b. The new coordinates of the desk's corners are shown below.

(7,1) (7,4) (9,1) (9,4)

Draw to show where the desk is.

ISBN: 978-1-77149-203-4

c. Identify and describe the transformations of the desk.

_____

_____

d. The coordinates of the dresser's corners are now (0,11), (2,10), (2,7), and (0,6). Draw to show where the dresser is.

e. Identify and describe the transformations of the dresser.

_____

_____

f.

> Another way of moving the bed to the new position is to first rotate it $\frac{1}{4}$ clockwise about (3,6), and then translate it 6 units down and 3 units to the left.

Aiden

Is Aiden correct? Explain.

_____

_____

g. Identify and describe an alternate set of transformations to move the pieces of furniture to their current positions.

• the bed

_____

_____

• the rug

_____

_____

• the desk

_____

_____

ISBN: 978-1-77149-203-4

③

Nathan

Transforming Figure A to Image B can only be done by translation.

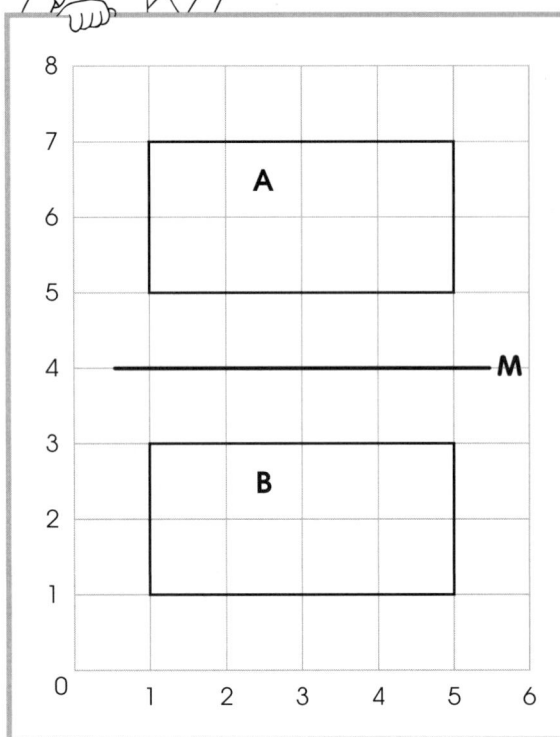

a. Is Nathan correct? If not, which transformation(s) can also be done?

_____

_____

_____

b. Describe the transformation(s).

_____

_____

_____

④

Transforming Figure A to Image B can only be done by reflection.

Nancy

a. Is Nancy correct? If not, which transformation(s) can also be done?

_____

_____

_____

b. Describe the transformation(s).

_____

_____

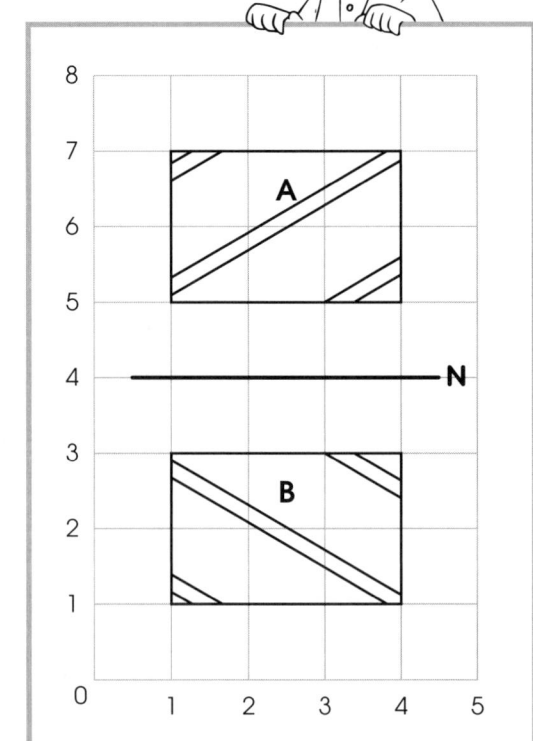

ISBN: 978-1-77149-203-4

⑤ Melody wants to complete a design.

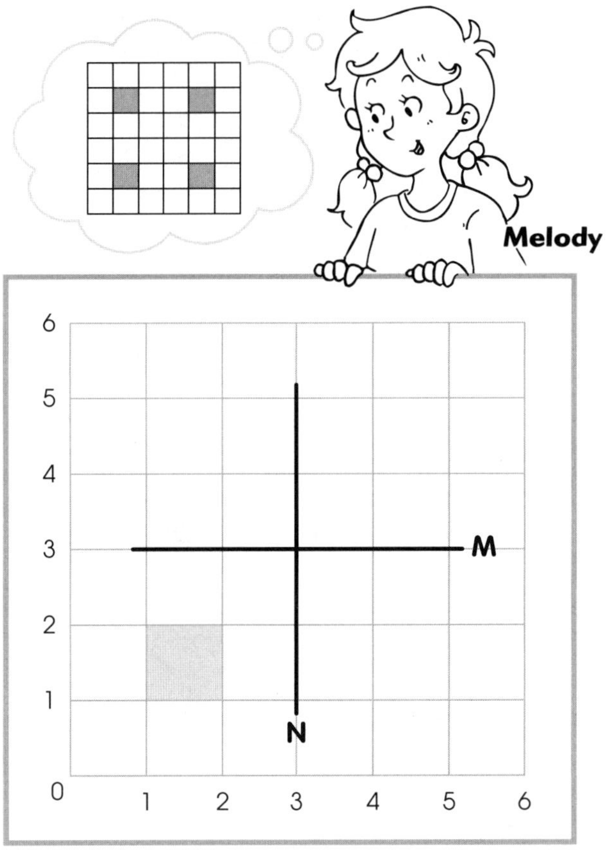

a. How should she transform the square if she uses only

• translations?

_____

_____

_____

• rotations?

_____

_____

_____

b. Can Melody complete the design by rotation using another point as the centre? If yes, write the coordinates.

_____

_____

c. Transform the squares and label them 1 to 4. Then write the coordinates of the corners of each square.

Square 1

_____
_____
_____
_____

Square 2

_____
_____
_____
_____

Square 3

_____
_____
_____
_____

Square 4

_____
_____
_____
_____

ISBN: 978-1-77149-203-4

⑥ Lisa transformed Figure A into Images B to F.

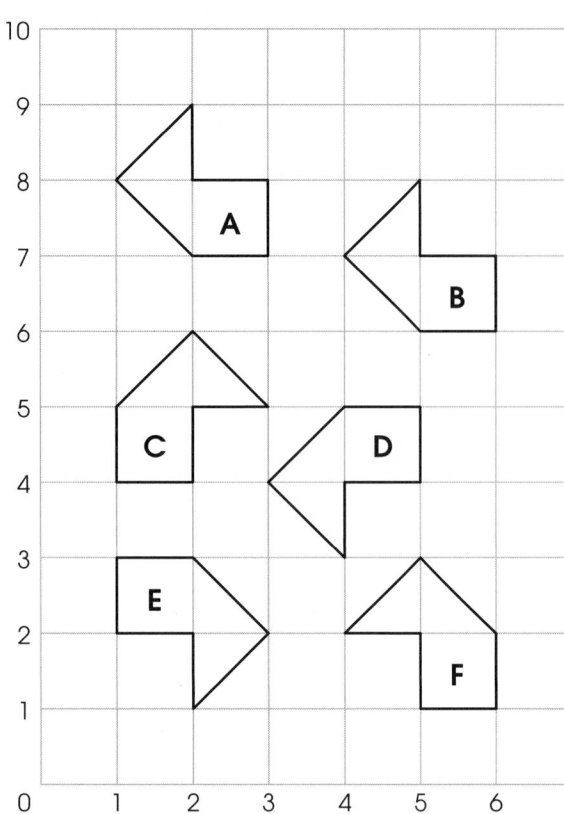

a. Which images are congruent to Figure A?

_____

b. Which transformations will create congruent images?

_____

c. If Image G is created through a rotation and a reflection of Image F, is Image G congruent to Figure A?

_____

I drew some triangles.

d. Identify the similar pairs of triangles. Which one is remaining?

_____

_____

e. Lisa draws a triangle that is similar to Triangle C. Two of its vertices are (0,11) and (6,11). What are the possible coordinates of the last vertex?

_____

_____

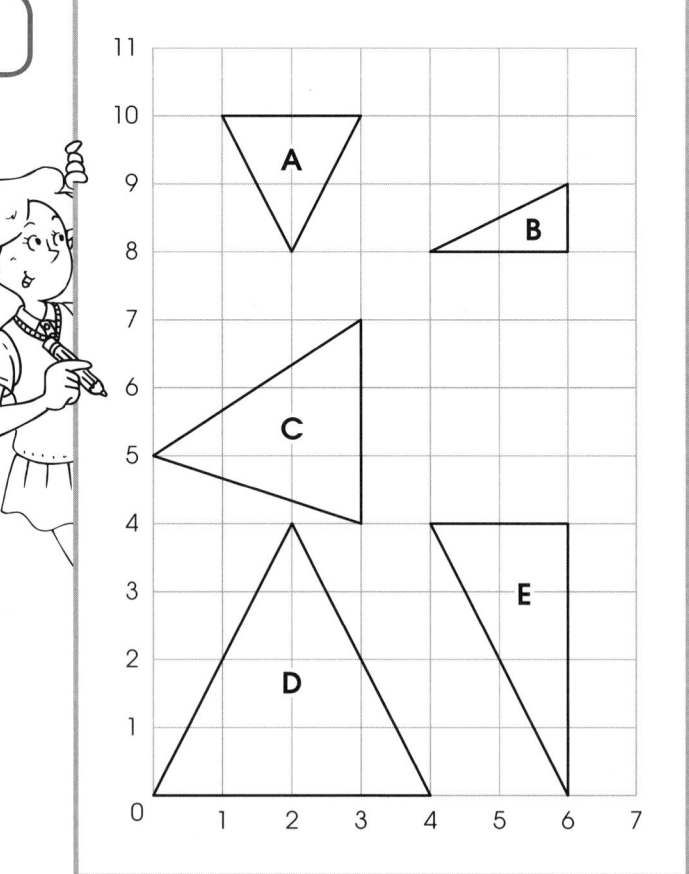

ISBN: 978-1-77149-203-4

⑦ Use the two figures to create a tiling pattern.

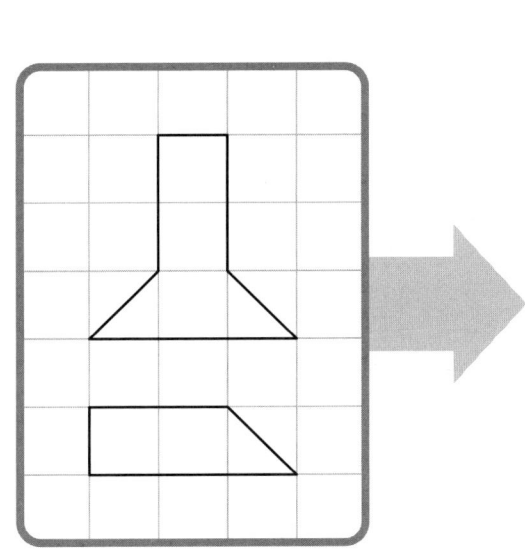

⑧ I want to complete a tiling pattern by transforming Figure X.

Roger

Describe the transformation Roger used to transform Figure X to each image.

a. Image A

_____

_____

b. Image B

_____

_____

c. Image C

_____

_____

d. Complete the pattern.

Patterning

solving a variety of word problems that involve extending patterns and describing pattern rules

 **Math Skills**

① Complete each pattern. Then write the pattern rule.

a. 4   7   10   13   16   _____   _____   _____

Pattern Rule: _____

b. 65   58   51   44   37   _____   _____   _____

Pattern Rule: _____

c. 5   10   20   40   80   _____   _____   _____

Pattern Rule: _____

d. 7   8   10   13   17   _____   _____   _____

Pattern Rule: _____

② Complete the charts. Then answer the questions.

Jane's Savings

No. of Days	Amount ($)
1	4
2	8
3	12
4	16
5	
6	

Chloe's Savings

No. of Days	Amount ($)
2	6
4	12
6	18
8	24
10	
12	

Write the pattern rules that relate the number of days to the amount of savings.

- Jane's Savings

  _____

  _____

- Chloe's Savings

  _____

  _____

ISBN: 978-1-77149-203-4

Problem Solving

Try This!

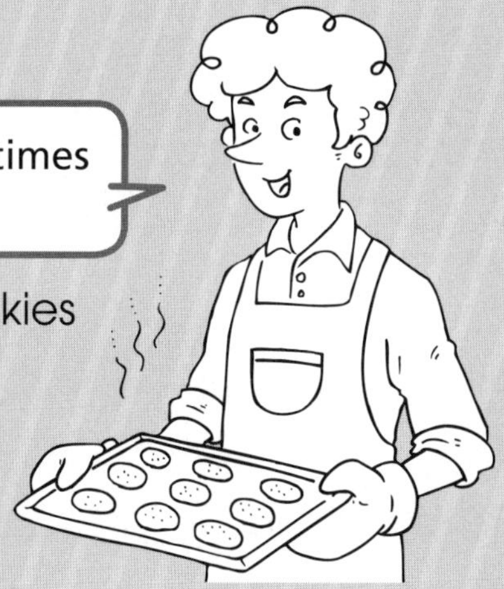

> The total number of cookies baked each hour is 2 times that in the previous hour.

If Finn bakes 9 cookies at 2:00, how many cookies will he bake at 5:00?

Solution:

Step 1: Identify the pattern rule.

Start at ☐ . Multiply the number by ☐ each time.

Step 2: Extend the pattern.

Time	2:00	3:00	4:00	5:00
No. of Cookies	9	☐	☐	☐

×2   ×2   ×2

Step 3: Write a concluding sentence.

Finn will bake ☐ cookies at 5:00.

① Simon starts by doing 5 push-ups on Monday. He increases the number of push-ups by 3 every day. How many push-ups will he do on Saturday?

Simon will do _____ push-ups on Saturday.

② A candle is 28 cm tall. Its height is 27 cm after 1 hour of burning, 25 cm after 2 hours, 22 cm after 3 hours, and so on. How many hours will the candle last?

The candle will last _____ hours.

③

> I cooked 512 kernels of corn to make popcorn. After 1 min, 256 kernels remained unpopped. After 2 min, 128 kernels remained unpopped.

Kermit

a. How many kernels remained unpopped after 4 min?

_____ kernels remained unpopped after 4 min.

b. If Kermit wants to have fewer than 10 kernels unpopped, at least how many minutes should Kermit cook the kernels for?

 **Hints**

He can stop cooking once there are fewer than 10 kernels unpopped.

Kermit should cook the kernels for at least _____ min.

ISBN: 978-1-77149-203-4

④ Billy records the number of paper cranes he folds in the chart.

Billy's Paper Cranes

Day	No. of Cranes
1	1
2	3
3	5
4	7
5	9

a. How many cranes will he fold on Day 8?

Billy will fold _____ cranes.

b. On which day will he fold 19 cranes?

Billy will fold 19 cranes on _____ .

⑤

I filled a vase with water and recorded the amount of water left each week.

How much water was there in Week 6?

Week	Amount of Water (mL)
1	300
2	156
3	84
4	48

There was _____ mL of water.

ISBN: 978-1-77149-203-4

⑥ Molly has 2 plants. She has recorded their heights in the chart.

Heights of Molly's Plants

Height (cm) \ Month	1	2	3	4	5
Plant A	10	14	22	38	___
Plant B	8	13	23	43	___

a. Name the plant that follows the pattern.

- Add 5 each time. _____

- Subtract by 3 and multiply by 2 each time. _____

- Multiply by 2 and subtract by 3 each time. _____

b. Complete the chart. Which plant was taller after 5 months?

_____

> After 5 months, Plant A grew 15 cm each month and Plant B grew 12 cm each month.

Molly

c. How tall were the plants after 7 months? Which plant was taller?

_____

d. How long did it take Plant A to reach 130 cm?

_____

ISBN: 978-1-77149-203-4

⑦ Julia has created the pattern below using sticks.

Julia's Pattern

Frame 1

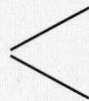

Frame 2

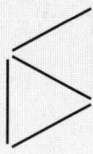

Frame 3

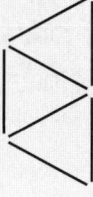

Frame 4

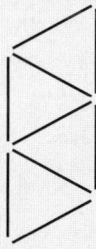

Frame 5

a. Draw to extend the pattern.

b. Complete the chart.

Frame No.	1	2	3	4	5
No. of Sticks	3	5			

c. Write a pattern rule to describe the number of sticks used for the frames.

_____

_____

d. Write a pattern rule to describe how the frame number relates to the number of sticks.

_____

_____

_____

e. How many sticks does Julia need to make

• Frame 7?

_____

• Frame 10?

_____

• Frame 50?

_____

⑧

> The ball is at a height of 108 cm. Its height decreases by 12 cm after each bounce.

a. What will the ball's height be after 6 bounces?

_____

b. How many bounces will it take the ball to stop bouncing?

_____

⑨ Cory has won a contest and he can choose between 2 prizes. Prize A is $50. Prize B is $10 in the first week and then double that amount the next week for 3 weeks. Which is a better prize?

_____

**Hints**

Remember to add the prizes from each week together.

⑩ Sheila invested $200. The amount will double every 5 years.

a. How much money will Sheila have after 30 years?

_____

b. If Sheila withdraws $100 at the end of every 5 years, how much will she have after 30 years instead?

_____

ISBN: 978-1-77149-203-4

⑪ A turtle walks 10 cm every minute. A grasshopper hops 5 cm in the first minute, and doubles its distance every minute. If both start at the same location, how long will it take the grasshopper to catch up with the turtle?

_____

⑫ Michael got a score of 30 on Quiz 1 and 46 on Quiz 2. If he improves his next score by half of the difference between his previous two quizzes each time, what will his score be on Quiz 6?

_____

⑬ Marcus only fills his tank by 8 L when he has used half his gas. If he starts with a full tank of 80 L of gas, how much gas will he have after filling his tank 6 times?

_____

⑭ An Internet cafe charges $7 for the first 2 hours and $3 for every hour after.

a. Julie's bill was $16. How many hours did she spend at the Internet cafe?

_____

b. I get 1 stamp for every $5 spent. At least how many hours do I need to complete the stamp card?

Stamp Card

Julie

_____

ISBN: 978-1-77149-203-4

Data Management

solving a variety of word problems that involve finding the mean, median, and mode, and interpreting information from graphs

 **Math Skills**

① Find the mean, median, and mode of each set of data.

A

3	4	6
5	3	9
8	3	4

B

8	4	1
2	6	9
4	8	3

C

18	17	15
	21	9
16	14	10

D

	12	25
23	18	14
12	10	15
	11	9

E

5.7	7.1
6.2	6.7
4.4	3.2
3.2	5.9

F

6.9	6.3	
7.9	8.9	2.3
6.6	7.3	
2.3	5.8	8.9

	Mean	Median*	Mode**
A			
B			
C			
D			
E			
F			

* If there are 2 middle values, the median is half the sum of the middle values.

** There can be more than 1 mode in a data set.

②

$3.60	$3.90
	$2.90
$3.20	$3.90

mean: $ _____

median: _____

mode: _____

15.4 cm	14.7 cm
10.9 cm	12.5 cm
8.3 cm	13.8 cm

mean: _____ cm

median: _____

mode: _____

6 kg	4.3 kg	5 kg
3 kg	4.6 kg	5 kg
	4.3 kg	

mean: _____ kg

median: _____

mode: _____

ISBN: 978-1-77149-203-4

 **Problem Solving**

> I recorded the amount of money I saved last week.

Sally

What are the mean, median, and mode amounts?

Day	Amount
Mon	$6.30
Tue	$5.80
Wed	$7.15
Thu	$4.70
Fri	$7.15

Solution:

Step 1: **Find the mean.**

$$(6.3 + 5.8 + 7.15 + 4.7 + 7.15) \div 5$$

= [   ]

mean
sum of all values $\div$ no. of values

Step 2: **Put the values in order to find the median and mode.**

4.7   5.8   (6.3)   ‹7.15   7.15› ← from least to greatest

median
the middle value in a set of ordered values

mode
the value that appears most often

Step 3: **Write a concluding sentence.**

The mean is $ [   ] , the median is $ [   ] ,

and the mode is $ [   ] .

① Refer to the data above. If Sally saved $3.80 on Tuesday instead, will the mean, median, or mode change? If so, find the correct answer(s).

ISBN: 978-1-77149-203-4

② A hiking trail is divided into 5 sections. The lengths of the sections are 2.3 km, 1.6 km, 3.7 km, 2.2 km, and 3.2 km. What is the mean length of the sections?

The mean length of the sections is ⎯⎯⎯ km.

③ A small cake weighs 0.8 kg and a large cake weighs 1.3 kg. What is the mean weight of 2 small cakes and 3 large cakes?

The mean weight is ⎯⎯⎯ kg.

④ The mean height of 5 children is 1.2 m. What is Eddie's height if the other children's heights are 1.3 m, 1.1 m, 1.5 m, and 0.8 m?

**Hints**

We can work backward to find the missing value. Find the total height of the children by multiplying the mean by the number of children. Then use subtraction to find the missing value.

Eddie's height is ⎯⎯⎯ m.

ISBN: 978-1-77149-203-4

⑤ Dana bought 3 books. The mean cost of the 3 books was $10.40. Which 3 books did Dana buy?

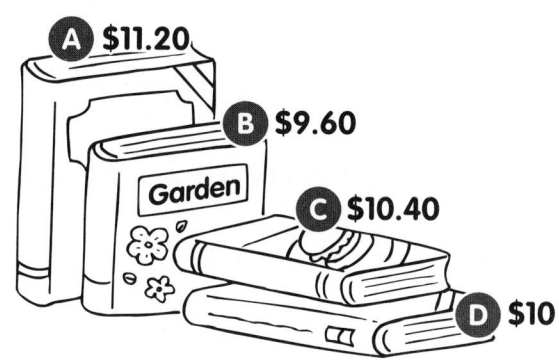

A $11.20

B $9.60

Garden

C $10.40

D $10

Dana bought _____ .

⑥ Romeo recorded the results of his quizzes in the chart.

My Results

Quiz	Result
1	82
2	79
3	81
4	79
5	90
6	?

a. The mean is 82. What was his result on Quiz 6?

Romeo's result on Quiz 6 was _____ .

b. What are the median and mode?

The median is _____ and the mode(s) is/are _____ .

ISBN: 978-1-77149-203-4

⑦ The bar graphs show Jane's and Ashley's test scores.

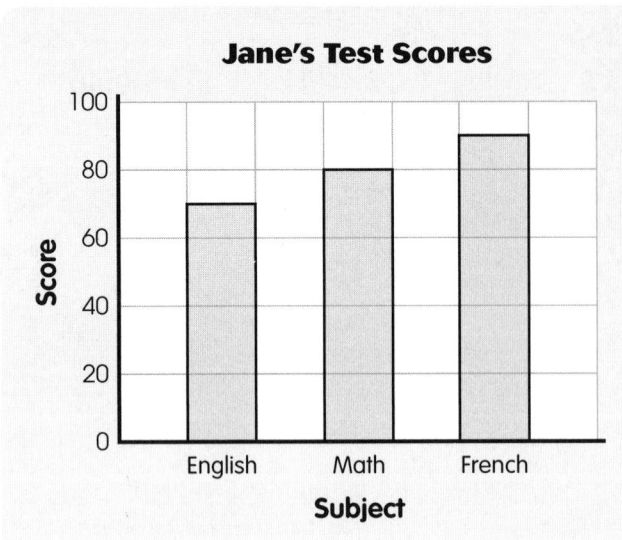

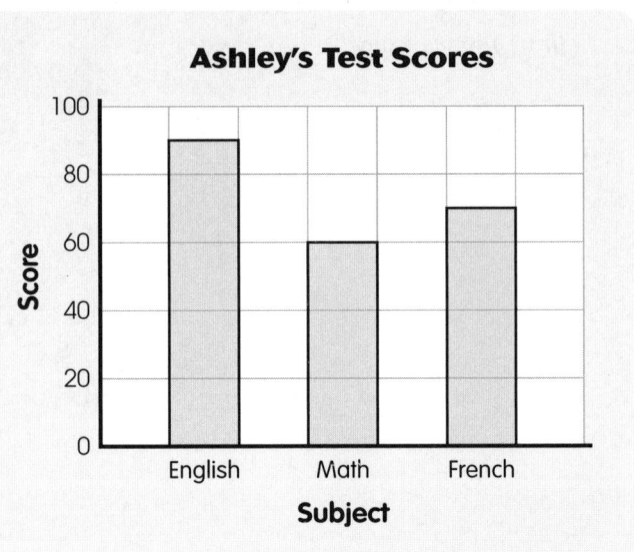

a. Which is Jane's

• best subject?

It is _____ .

• worst subject?

It is _____ .

b. Which is Ashley's

• best subject?

It is _____ .

• worst subject?

It is _____ .

c. Who did better on her Math test? How much higher was her score?

_____ did better. Her score was _____ higher.

d. Who did better on her English test? How much higher was her score?

_____ did better. Her score was _____ higher.

e. The girls just got their Science tests back. Jane's score is 16 higher than her Math test score. Ashley's score is 10 lower than Jane's Science test score.

• What is Jane's Science test score?

Jane's Science test score is _____ .

• What is Ashley's Science test score?

Ashley's Science test score is _____ .

ISBN: 978-1-77149-203-4

⑧ Ryan surveyed Grade 5 students on their favourite colours. Make a bar graph with the results below.

Grade 5 Students' Favourite Colours

Colour	Red	Blue	Green	Yellow	Other
No. of Students	3	10	11	8	3

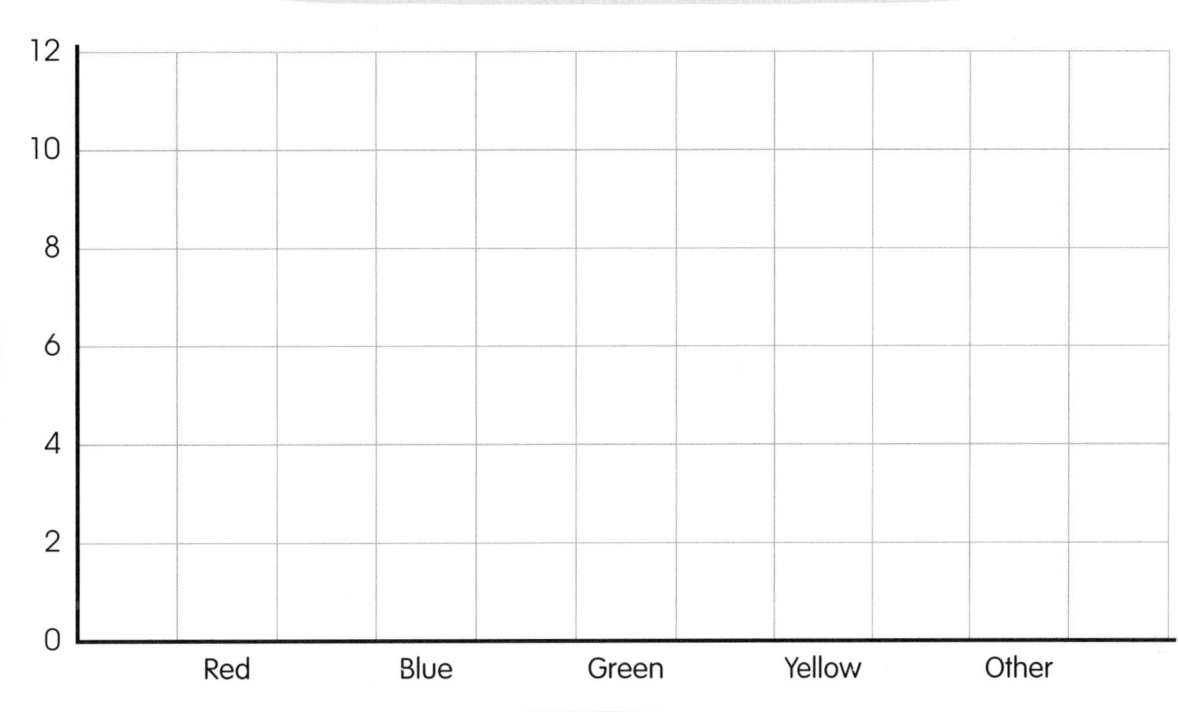

a. How many more students chose

• blue than red?   _____ more students chose blue.

• green than yellow?   _____ more students chose green.

b. What is the mean number of students that chose each colour?

The mean is _____ students.

ISBN: 978-1-77149-203-4

⑨ Mike plotted the temperatures of the past week in a line graph.

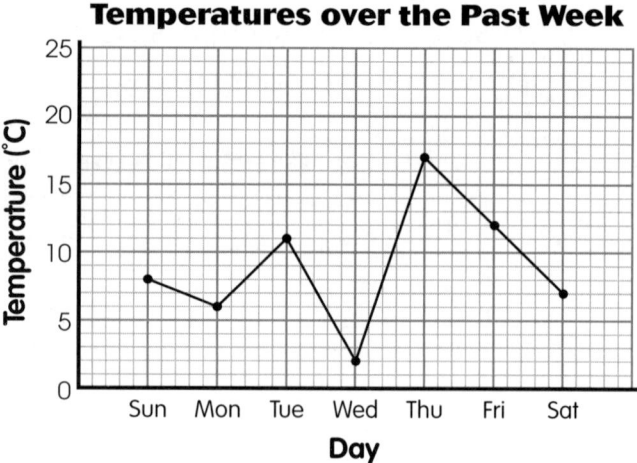

Temperatures over the Past Week

a. On which day was the
   • lowest temperature recorded?

   _____

   • highest temperature recorded?

   _____

b. What was the highest recorded temperature?

   _____

c. What was the mean temperature of the past week?

   _____

d. Between which days did the biggest temperature change occur?

   _____

e. The temperatures of the next 3 days were 5°C, 6°C, and 7°C.

   What were the mean, median, and mode temperatures over the 10 days?

Mike

   _____

ISBN: 978-1-77149-203-4

⑩ Jasper surveyed his friends about their favourite sports. The circle graph shows the results.

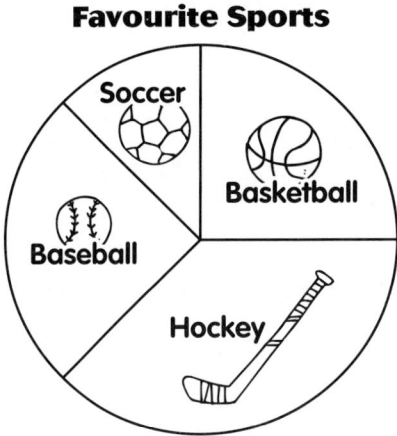

My Friends' Favourite Sports

a. $\frac{3}{8}$ of Jasper's friends picked this sport. Which sport is it?

_____

b. What fraction of Jasper's friends picked the least popular sport? Which sport is it?

_____

c. If 13 people picked soccer, how many people picked basketball?

_____

d. How many people were surveyed in total?

_____

e. How many more people picked baseball or basketball than soccer?

_____

ISBN: 978-1-77149-203-4

Probability

solving a variety of word problems that involve finding the probability

Math Skills

① Write all the possible outcomes. Then find the probabilities.

a.  **Roll the dice.**

Possible outcomes:

_____

Probability of rolling

- 3: _____

- an odd number: _____

- 2 or 6: _____

b. 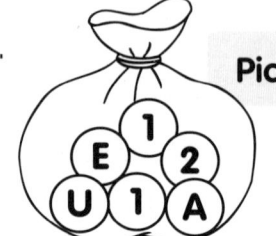 **Pick a ball.**

Possible outcomes:

_____

Probability of picking

- a vowel: _____

- a number: _____

- a consonant: _____

c. 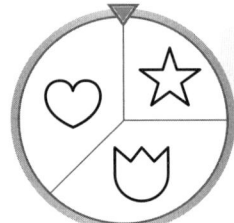 **Spin the wheel.**

Possible outcomes:

_____

Probability of spinning

- ☆ : _____

- ♡ or ♉ or ☆ : _____

- ✸ : _____

d. **Pick a number from 1 to 8.**

Possible outcomes:

_____

Probability of picking

- 5: _____

- 2 or 3: _____

- an odd number: _____

ISBN: 978-1-77149-203-4

Problem Solving

Jenny rolls a dice. What is the probability that she will get a number that is greater than 4?

Solution:

Step 1: **Find all the possible outcomes.**

1   2   3   4   ⑤   ⑥ ← 6 possible outcomes

greater than 4

Step 2: **Find the probability.**

$$\text{Probability} = \frac{\text{no. of favourable outcomes}}{\text{total no. of possible outcomes}}$$

$$= \frac{2}{6}$$

$$= \boxed{}$$

Step 3: **Write a concluding sentence.**

The probability is $\boxed{}$.

Write fractions in simplest form if possible.

① Lynn rolls an 8-sided dice numbered 1 to 8. What is the probability of getting a number smaller than 7?

The probability of getting a number smaller than 7 is _____ .

② Jordan picks a card randomly. What is the probability that he will

a. pick a number?

The probability is _____ .

b. pick a 🖤 ?

c. pick [⭐A] or [🖤2] ?

The probability is _____ .

d. not win?

The probability is _____ .

e. pick a number card with 🌙 ?

The probability is _____ .

The probability is _____ .

ISBN: 978-1-77149-203-4

③ A group of children are divided into different teams.

Number of Children on Each Team

Team \ Number	Boys	Girls
Red	7	11
Blue	6	14
Green	12	10

a. A leader from each team is picked randomly. What is the probability that a girl will be picked for each team?

The probability is _____ for the red team, _____ for the blue team, and

_____ for the green team.

b. There is a running race for boys. If a boy is late to the race, what is the probability that he is from the red or the blue team?

The probability is _____ .

c. One of the children will be the champion of the races. What is the probability that the champion is a boy from the blue team?

The probability is _____ .

ISBN: 978-1-77149-203-4

④ Anna, Cleo, and Daven each created a spinner for a game booth.

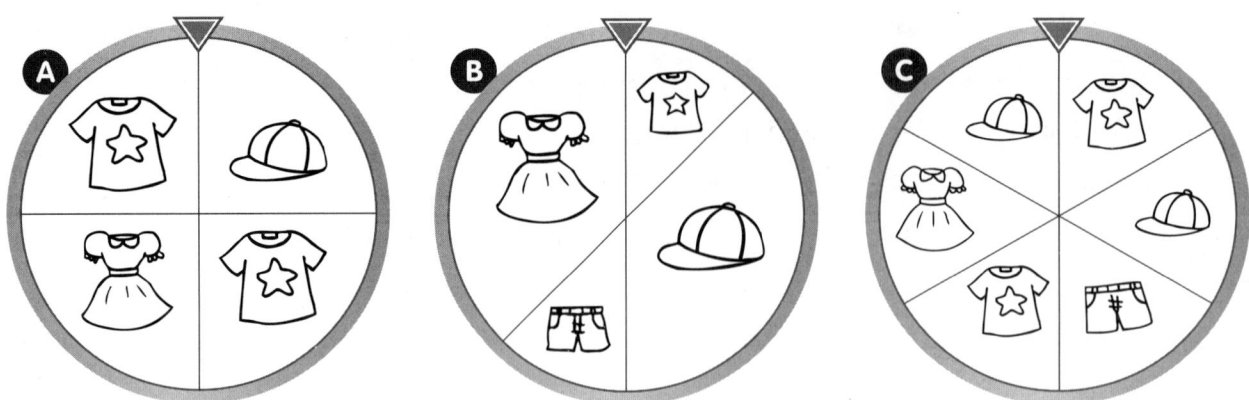

a. Match the correct spinners with each child.

- Anna says, "The probability of getting a shirt or a dress is $\frac{3}{4}$."

  _____

- Cleo says, "The probability of getting a shirt is $\frac{1}{3}$."

  _____

- Daven says, "The probability of getting a shirt or a cap is $\frac{1}{2}$."

  _____

b. If I want to get a shirt, which spinner should I choose?

_____

c. If I don't want to get a cap, which spinner should I choose?

_____

d. If I want a cap or a dress, which spinner should I choose?

Liz

_____

ISBN: 978-1-77149-203-4

⑤ Josie rolls 2 dice and finds their sums.

a. Complete the table to find all the possible outcomes.

b. What is the probability that she

• will get a sum of 3?

Sums of 2 Dice

+	1	2	3	4	5	6
1	2					
2						
3						
4						
5						
6						

_____

• will get a sum greater than 9?

• will roll a 3 on one of the dice?

_____

_____

• will get a sum less than 12?

• will roll a 7 on one of the dice?

_____

_____

c.

If the sum is 6, what is the probability that I will get a 2 and a 4 on the dice?

_____

ISBN: 978-1-77149-203-4

⑥ Make a tree diagram of the game Rock-paper-scissors for 2 players.

Tree Diagram for Rock-Paper-Scissors

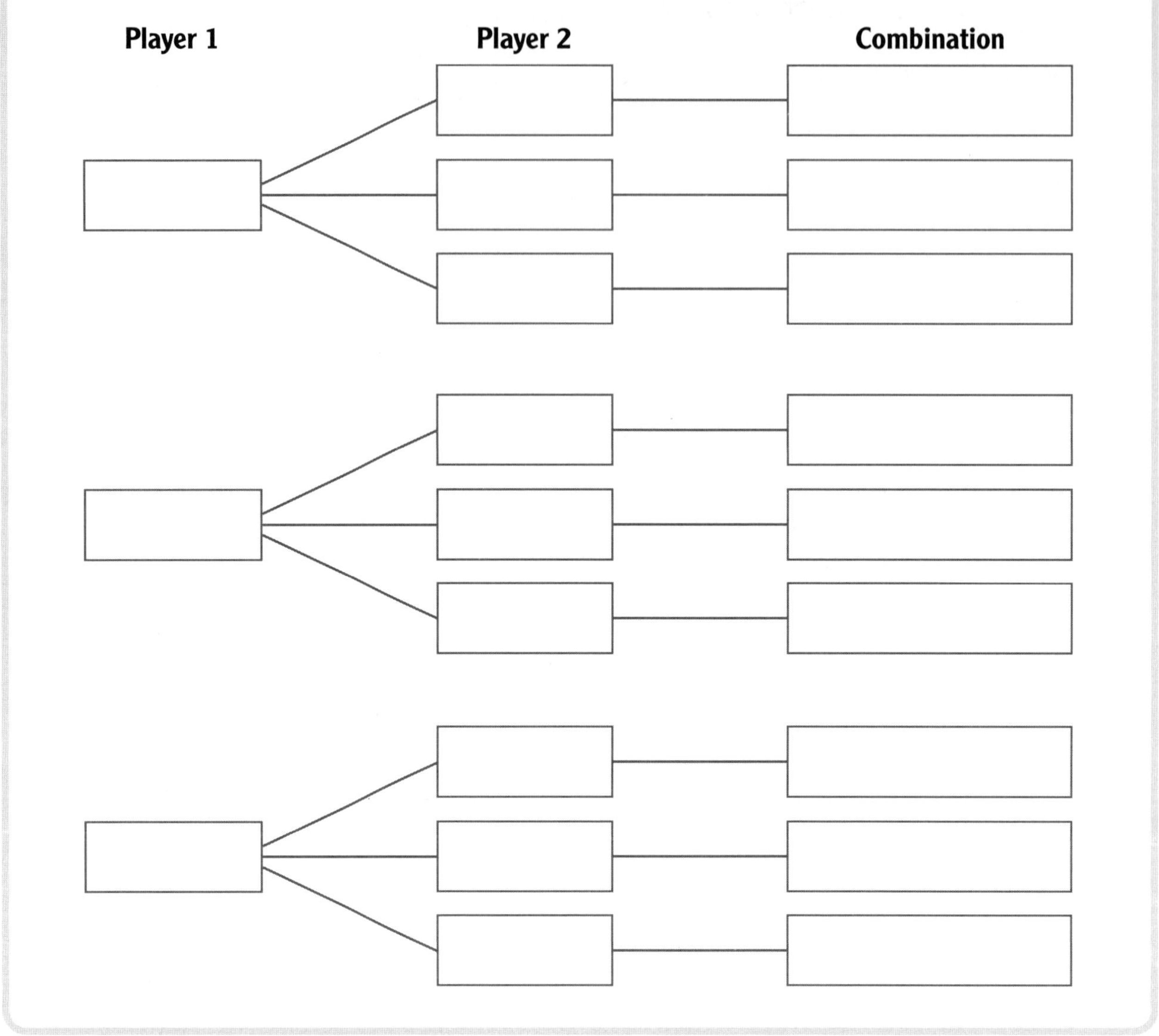

Player 1	Player 2	Combination

a. What is the probability that

- it is a tied game?

- a player plays scissors and loses?

_____   _____

b. If the game is played 100 times, about how many tied games will there be?

**Hints**

Think:
Playing every 3 games will have 1 tied game.
3 games → 1 tied game
100 games → ? tied games

_____

ISBN: 978-1-77149-203-4

⑦ Claire's and Eva's boxes each have 5 balls. There are 2 red, 2 green, and 1 blue balls in Claire's box; there are 4 green and 1 blue balls in Eva's box.

a. What is the probability of picking a green ball from each box?

_____

b. Claire trades a red ball for a green ball with Eva, what is the probability of picking a green ball from each box now?

_____

c. If a ball is picked from Eva's box 50 times, about how many times will a blue ball be picked?

_____

d. Claire then adds 2 red balls to her box, what is the probability of picking a red ball from her box now?

_____

e. If a ball is picked 70 times from Claire's box, about how many times will a red ball be picked?

_____

ISBN: 978-1-77149-203-4

ISBN: 978-1-77149-203-4

Section 2: Critical-thinking Questions

ISBN: 978-1-77149-203-4

Students are required to solve multi-step questions which involve various topics in each.

Topics Covered

	Number Sense and Numeration	Measurement	Geometry and Spatial Sense	Patterning and Algebra	Data Management and Probability	My Record ✔ correct ✗ incorrect
1	decimals money	mass				
2	decimals	time				
3		temperature		patterning		
4	money			patterning		
5			shapes		probability	
6	fractions	volume capacity				
7	decimals				data management	
8		area	shapes / Cartesian coordinate plane			
9	whole numbers				data management	
10	fractions		transformations			
11	decimals	perimeter	shapes			
12	decimals	time				
13	fractions				data management	
14	decimals	time				
15	decimals	volume mass				
16	whole numbers	area	transformations			
17	whole numbers			patterning	data management	
18		volume			data management	
19		perimeter	shapes			
20				patterning	data management	

ISBN: 978-1-77149-203-4

① Jacob paid for 1.536 kg of coffee beans with a $100 bill and got back 1 $20 bill, 3 toonies, and 2 dimes. He divided the beans into 3 jars. How many kilograms of beans are there in each jar? How much does each jar of beans cost?

Amount in 1 jar: _____ ÷ _____ = _____

Total cost: _____ − _____ = _____

Cost of 1 jar: _____ ÷ _____ = _____

There are _____ of beans in each jar. Each jar of beans costs _____ .

② Corey started running at 7:26 a.m. and finished at 8:39 a.m. If he ran 0.22 km each minute, how many kilometres did he run?

③ The weather forecast predicts that the temperature during spring will increase by 2°C every week. If the temperature in Week 1 is 9°C below 0°C, in which week will the temperature be 3°C?

Topics covered:

Question 1	**Question 2**	**Question 3**
• decimals	• decimals	• temperature
• money	• time	• patterning
• mass		

④ Ann gets $8.25 each week for allowance. She spends $3.25 every other week. If she has $10 in Week 1, how many weeks will it take Ann to save $58?

⑤ Sherman cut a trapezoid into 4 triangles as shown. However, he accidentally tore one of the triangles. What is the probability that it was an obtuse triangle?

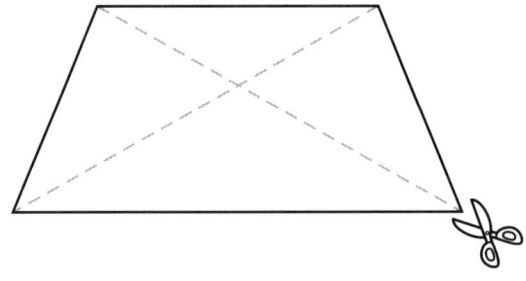

⑥ A glass tank that measures 0.3 m by 0.4 m by 0.6 m is filled with 4.8 L of water. What fraction of the tank is filled?

Topics covered:

Question 4	**Question 5**	**Question 6**
• money	• shapes	• fractions
• patterning	• probability	• volume
		• capacity

ISBN: 978-1-77149-203-4

⑦ April surveyed her classmates about their favourite seasons and created the circle graph below. If 16 people voted for summer, how many people voted for winter?

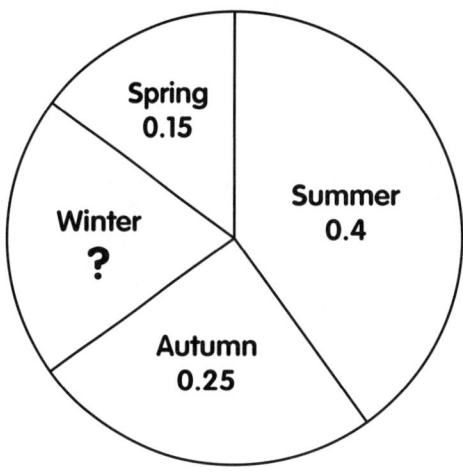

⑧ Britney wants to draw a rectangle that has an area of 135 cm² on the grid. One of its vertices is at (1,4). What are the coordinates of the remaining vertices? What are the length and width of the rectangle?

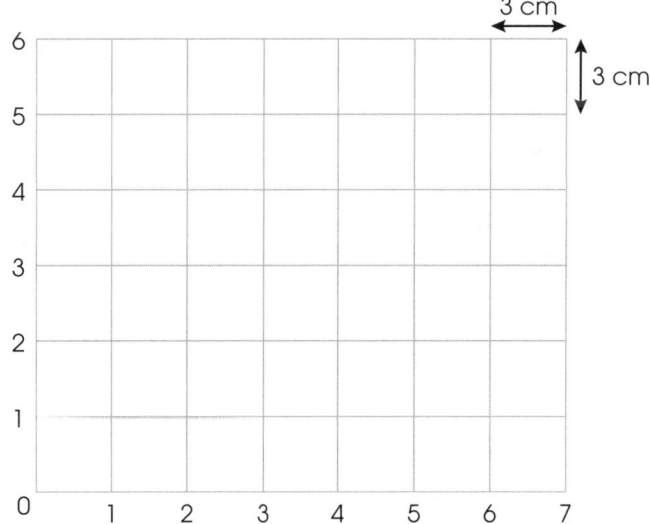

Topics covered:

Question 7
• decimals
• data management

Question 8
• area
• shapes
• Cartesian coordinate plane

ISBN: 978-1-77149-203-4

⑨ William recorded the distance that he ran each day for five days: 2456 m, 2624 m, 1946 m, 1203 m, and 981 m. What is the mean distance that he ran each day?

⑩ Claire and Clement will each rotate identical shapes about (0,0). Claire will rotate her shape $\frac{1}{4}$ clockwise and then $2\frac{1}{2}$ clockwise. Clement will rotate his $\frac{1}{4}$ counterclockwise. Will the rotated shapes be in the same orientation?

⑪ The perimeter of a regular hexagon is 15.3 cm. Jason is cutting out rectangles to make a hexagonal prism using the hexagon as one of the bases. If the height of the prism is 8 cm, what is the area of each rectangle?

⑫ Arnold will record a video from 3:47:17 p.m. to 4:16:02 p.m. If each minute of recording takes up 14 MB of memory, how much memory will Arnold's video use?

 **Hints**

Write the elapsed time in minutes as a decimal.
e.g. 15 s = 0.25 min

Topics covered:

Question 9	Question 10	Question 11	Question 12
• whole numbers	• fractions	• decimals	• decimals
• data management	• transformations	• perimeter	• time
		• shapes	

ISBN: 978-1-77149-203-4

⑬ Damien recorded the amount of time he spent on his supper each day for 5 days. What is the mean, median, and mode elapsed time?

Amount of Time Spent on Supper

Day	Time (h)
Mon	$\frac{7}{6}$
Tue	$\frac{5}{6}$
Wed	$\frac{4}{6}$
Thu	$1\frac{3}{6}$
Fri	$\frac{5}{6}$

⑭ Angela planted a 2.7-cm plant on May 1. It grew 0.02 cm each day. What was its height on August 8?

⑮ A wall that has a volume of 0.5 m³ is being built using bricks. If each brick weighs 2.26 kg, how much will all the bricks for the wall weigh?

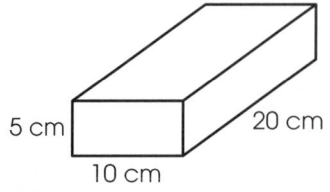

5 cm   10 cm   20 cm

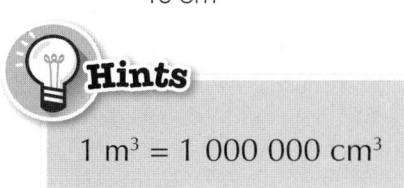

Hints

$1 \text{ m}^3 = 1\ 000\ 000 \text{ cm}^3$

Topics covered:

Question 13
- fractions
- data management

Question 14
- decimals
- time

Question 15
- decimals
- volume
- mass

ISBN: 978-1-77149-203-4

⑯ Janet created a design by transforming a shape. The coordinates of the vertices of the images are as follows:

Image A: (3,3) (3,4) (5,5) (6,3)

Image B: (3,3) (4,3) (5,1) (3,0)

Image C: (0,3) (1,1) (3,3) (3,2)

Describe the transformations. The area of the shape shown is 368 cm². What is the area of each square on the grid?

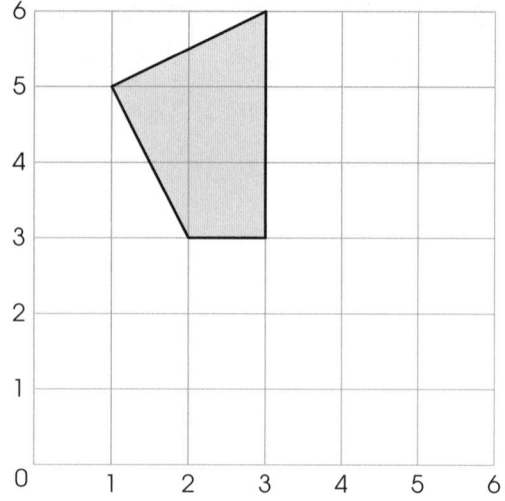

⑰ Jerome created a line graph to show his predictions of the revenue from the heater sales. If the pattern continues, how much revenue could there be from January to July? Complete the line graph.

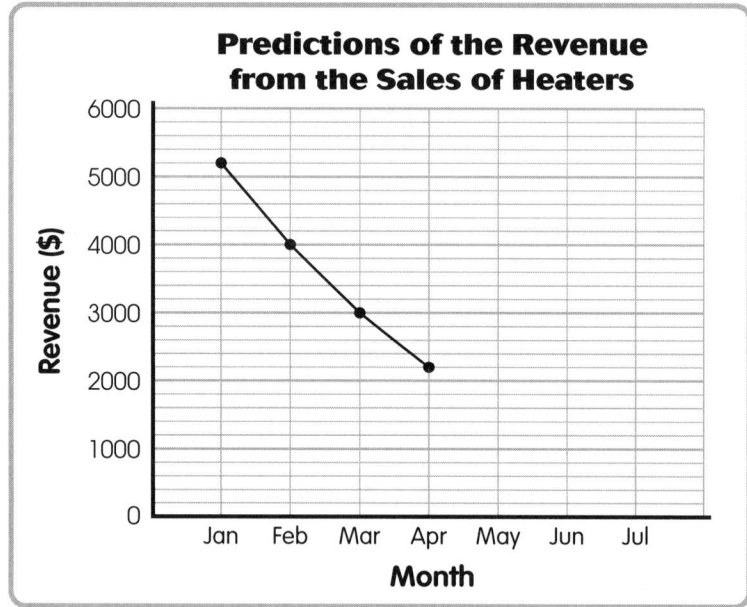

Topics covered:

Question 16
- whole numbers
- area
- transformations

Question 17
- whole numbers
- patterning
- data management

ISBN: 978-1-77149-203-4

⑱ Barbara has 10 containers. Two of them measure 10 cm by 10 cm by 5 cm, four of them are 11 cm by 10 cm by 4 cm, and the rest are 12 cm by 8 cm by 6 cm. What are the mean, median, and mode capacities of the containers?

⑲ A garden in the shape of an isosceles triangle has a perimeter of 24.3 m. One of the sides is 7.1 m long. What are the lengths of the other 2 sides?

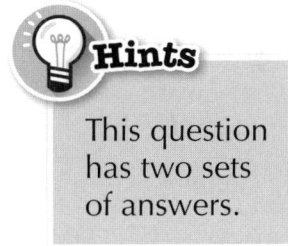

Hints

This question has two sets of answers.

⑳ Dave reads 39 pages on Day 1, 38 pages on Day 2, 36 pages on Day 3, and 33 pages on Day 4. The pattern continues until he finishes the book on the day he reads 18 pages. What is the mean number of pages he reads each day?

Topics covered:

Question 18	**Question 19**	**Question 20**
• volume	• perimeter	• patterning
• data management	• shapes	• data management

ISBN: 978-1-77149-203-4

Students are required to solve multi-step questions which involve various topics in each.

Topics Covered

	Number Sense and Numeration	Measurement	Geometry and Spatial Sense	Patterning and Algebra	Data Management and Probability	My Record ✔ correct ✘ incorrect
1	whole numbers	area				☐
2	whole numbers	time				☐
3	whole numbers	volume				☐
4	whole numbers money			patterning		☐
5	fractions				probability	☐
6	whole numbers decimals	capacity				☐
7	money	perimeter				☐
8	whole numbers	mass		patterning		☐
9	fractions decimals					☐
10			solids		data management	☐
11		perimeter	shapes / Cartesian coordinate plane			☐
12		time			probability	☐
13	money			patterning		☐
14		area		patterning		☐
15			solids transformations			☐
16	fractions decimals					☐
17		time temperature		patterning		☐
18	decimals	area	shapes			☐
19	whole numbers	mass		patterning		☐
20	whole numbers fractions				data management	☐

ISBN: 978-1-77149-203-4

① A patio has 25 rows of wooden planks. Each row has 12 planks. If each plank has an area of 540 cm², what is the area of the patio?

No. of planks = _____ × _____

= _____

Area of patio = _____ × _____

= _____

The area of the patio is _____ .

② A hummingbird flaps its wings 54 times per second and a butterfly flaps its wings 1080 times per minute. How many more times does the hummingbird flap its wings than the butterfly in 5 minutes?

③ There are 20 pencils in a box that measures 15 cm by 13 cm by 2 cm. A number of boxes are packed into a carton. If the carton can hold 1800 pencils, what is its volume?

Topics covered:

Question 1
- whole numbers
- area

Question 2
- whole numbers
- time

Question 3
- whole numbers
- volume

ISBN: 978-1-77149-203-4

④ Simon's Sports sells skateboards. Last week, the amount of money earned each day was twice that of the previous day. If $8816 was earned on Friday, how much was earned last Monday?

⑤ A building has 50 apartments. $\frac{3}{5}$ of them have 2 rooms and the rest have 3 rooms. If rooms are assigned at random, what is the probability of getting a room in a 2-room apartment?

⑥ A cow requires 78 L of water each day. Amy has 77 cows and a water tank that measures 2 m by 2 m by 0.75 m. At least how many times does she need to refill the water tank each day?

Hints

1 m³ = 1000 L

Topics covered:

Question 4	**Question 5**	**Question 6**
• whole numbers	• fractions	• whole numbers
• money	• probability	• decimals
• patterning		• capacity

ISBN: 978-1-77149-203-4

⑦ Ruben buys a piece of wire that can form a rectangle with a length of 2 m and a width of 180 cm. It costs $0.05 for every 8 cm. If Ruben pays with 3 toonies, what will his change be?

⑧ Carl wants to reduce his consumption of chocolate milk. In Week 1, he uses 60 g of chocolate milk powder, 55 g in Week 2, 48 g in Week 3, 39 g in Week 4, and so on. In which week will he use only 15 g?

⑨ A taxi fare is $3.90 for the first 2 km and $1.25 for each additional $\frac{1}{2}$ km. How much will it cost if a route is $4\frac{1}{2}$ km?

⑩ Sharon wants to make 5 triangular prisms, 2 square-based pyramids, and 1 heptagonal pyramid. She will use modelling clay for the vertices. What is the mean number of balls of modelling clay needed?

A heptagon has 7 sides.

Topics covered:

Question 7	**Question 8**	**Question 9**	**Question 10**
• money	• whole numbers	• fractions	• solids
• perimeter	• mass	• decimals	• data management
	• patterning		

⑪ Jessica drew a triangle with its vertices at (1,3), (4,4), and (3,1). Name the triangle in 2 ways. Then measure to find the perimeter.

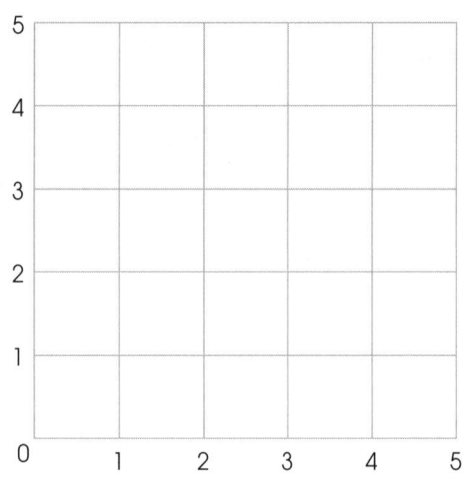

⑫ A package will be delivered anytime within 1:30 p.m. and 5:30 p.m. What is the probability that it will arrive some time within 2:15 p.m. and 3:00 p.m.?

⑬ One sweater costs $17.50. Anita had $5, $10, and $20 bills. She bought sweaters and paid the exact amount with 4 bills. How many sweaters could she have bought?

Topics covered:

Question 11	**Question 12**	**Question 13**
• perimeter	• time	• money
• shapes	• probability	• patterning
• Cartesian coordinate plane		

ISBN: 978-1-77149-203-4

Korra uses squares to form a series of designs. If each square has a side length of 3 cm, what is the area of the 6th design?

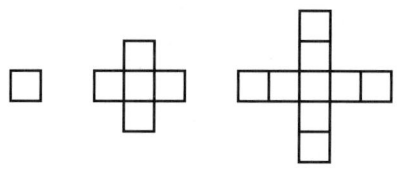

⑮ John has drawn half of a cube's net (the shaded figure as shown on the right). He wants to complete the net by transformations. Which transformed image, A, B, or C, will complete the net? Describe two transformations that are involved.

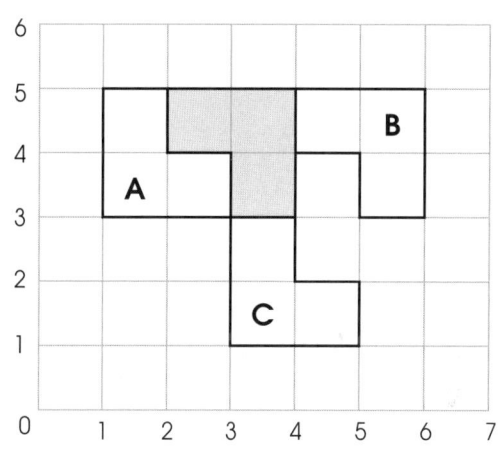

Topics covered:

Question 14
- area
- patterning

Question 15
- solids
- transformations

ISBN: 978-1-77149-203-4

⑯ The results of a survey on students' favourite musicians are recorded. Were there more people who picked male musicians than female musicians?

Musicians	Part of a Whole
Katy	0.37
Drake	$\frac{6}{20}$
Rihanna	0.18
Justin	$\frac{3}{20}$

⑰ The temperature decreased steadily from 8°C at 3:00 p.m. to 4°C below 0°C at 7:00 p.m. Between which hours did the temperature fall below 0°C?

Hints

Use a table to find the temperature at each hour.

⑱ Jordan drew a parallelogram and a triangle. If the area of the triangle is 2.75 cm², what is the area of the parallelogram?

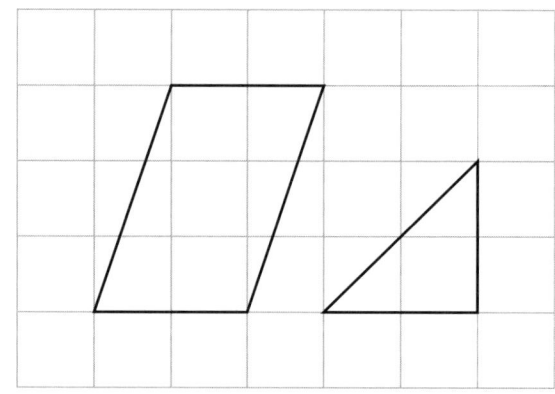

Topics covered:

Question 16
- fractions
- decimals

Question 17
- time
- temperature
- patterning

Question 18
- decimals
- area
- shapes

ISBN: 978-1-77149-203-4

⑲ Marsha built a structure that has 5 layers. There are 4 blocks in Layer 1, 9 blocks in Layer 2, 16 blocks in Layer 3, and so on. If each block weighs 15 g, what is the weight of the structure?

⑳ Jenna created a circle graph to show the sources of raised funds. $4382 was raised from the school dance and $642 was raised from the car wash. How much money was raised from selling raffle tickets?

Sources of Raised Funds

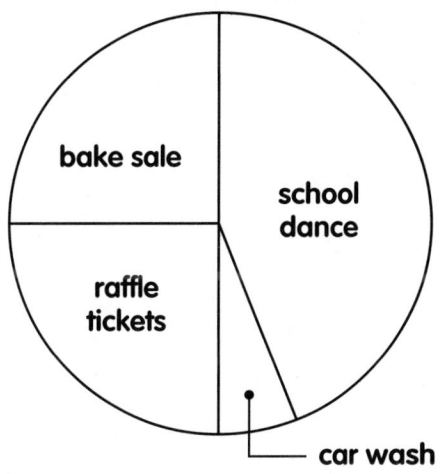

Topics covered:

Question 19
- whole numbers
- mass
- patterning

Question 20
- whole numbers
- fractions
- data management

ISBN: 978-1-77149-203-4

Students are required to solve multi-step questions which involve various topics in each.

Topics Covered

	Number Sense and Numeration	Measurement	Geometry and Spatial Sense	Patterning and Algebra	Data Management and Probability	My Record
1	whole numbers money					
2		area	shapes solids			
3	whole numbers decimals			patterning		
4	fractions	time				
5	money				data management	
6	decimals	perimeter	transformations			
7	decimals fractions			patterning		
8	fractions		shapes			
9	fractions	time	transformations			
10	decimals	perimeter	shapes			
11		volume		patterning	data management	
12		area	Cartesian coordinate plane			
13	whole numbers	time				
14	fractions	volume mass				
15	money				probability	
16	decimals			patterning	data management	
17	fractions money					
18	decimals	perimeter	shapes			
19	whole numbers	capacity			data management	
20	whole numbers	volume			data management	

My Record
✔ correct
✗ incorrect

ISBN: 978-1-77149-203-4

① 500 copies of a school newspaper need to be printed. The newspaper contains 16 pages. A roll of print paper costs $75.20 and it can print 1600 pages. What is the total cost of print paper?

Number of pages: _____ × _____ = _____

Number of rolls needed: _____ ÷ _____ = _____

Total cost: _____ × _____ = _____

The total cost of print paper is _____ .

② Tyler made nets for a triangular prism and a square-based pyramid using squares and triangles that all have a side length of 2 cm. The area of each triangle is 1.7 cm². Which net has a bigger area? By how much?

③ The value of a machine decreases by half each year. If the machine is worth $6504, how much will it be worth after 4 years?

Topics covered:

Question 1	**Question 2**	**Question 3**
• whole numbers	• area	• whole numbers
• money	• shapes	• decimals
	• solids	• patterning

ISBN: 978-1-77149-203-4

④ Tanya finished watching a $2\frac{1}{6}$ -hour-long movie at 1:46 p.m. If she started watching the movie $3\frac{1}{4}$ hours ago, what is the current time?

⑤ Fred has 6 coins that have a mean value of $0.10. The coins are a combination of nickels, dimes, and quarters. How many of each coin does he have?

⑥ Kimmy creates a windmill design by rotating the trapezoid 3 times about Point P: $\frac{1}{4}$ clockwise, $\frac{1}{2}$, and $\frac{1}{4}$ counterclockwise. What is the perimeter of the design?

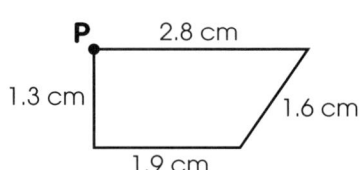

Topics covered:

Question 4	Question 5	Question 6
• fractions	• money	• decimals
• time	• data management	• perimeter
		• transformations

ISBN: 978-1-77149-203-4

⑦ A smoothie shop offers drinks in 5 sizes. The first 3 sizes have capacities of 110 mL, 0.23 L, and $\frac{7}{20}$ L. If the pattern continues, what is the capacity of the biggest cup size?

⑧ Kayla has a right isosceles triangle, an equilateral triangle, and an obtuse triangle. What fraction of the angles are acute?

⑨ Zoe made a paper clock that showed 3:00. She rotated the hour hand $2\frac{1}{4}$ clockwise, and then $1\frac{3}{4}$ counterclockwise, and then $\frac{5}{4}$ clockwise. What time does the clock show now?

⑩ A parallelogram has a perimeter of 14.7 cm. If one of its sides is 5.9 cm, what are the lengths of the other sides?

Topics covered:

Question 7	Question 8	Question 9	Question 10
• decimals	• fractions	• fractions	• decimals
• fractions	• shapes	• time	• perimeter
• patterning		• transformations	• shapes

ISBN: 978-1-77149-203-4

⑪ Wayne is building 6 rectangular prisms that follow a pattern. The first prism has a length of 10 cm, a width of 1 cm, and a height of 16 cm. For each new prism built, the length is 1 cm less, the width is doubled, and the height is 3 cm less than the previous one. What is the mean volume of the prisms?

⑫ A rectangular pool has an area of 1152 m² with the points (1,5) and (3,1) as vertices. Draw the layout of the pool on the grid. What are the dimensions of the pool?

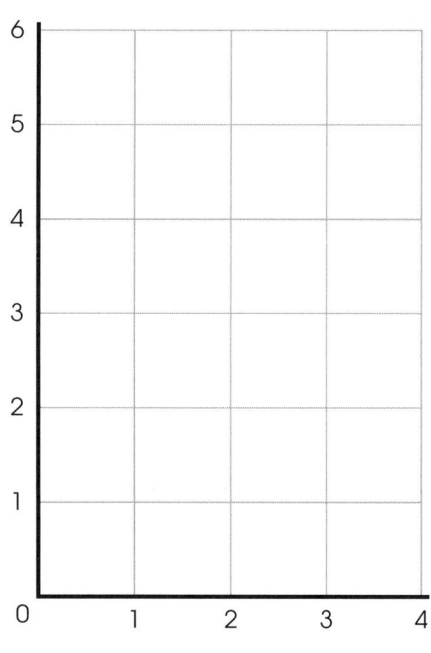

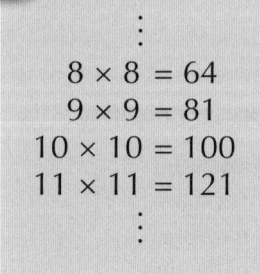
Hints

$$8 \times 8 = 64$$
$$9 \times 9 = 81$$
$$10 \times 10 = 100$$
$$11 \times 11 = 121$$

Topics covered:

Question 11
- volume
- patterning
- data management

Question 12
- area
- Cartesian coordinate plane

ISBN: 978-1-77149-203-4

⑬ Mac lives between 2 bus stops. He is 420 m from Stop A and 0.54 km from Stop B. The bus arrives at Stop A at 2:20 p.m. and Stop B at 2:25 p.m. Mac walks 60 m per minute. Which bus stop should he go to if he leaves home at 2:15 p.m. to catch the bus?

⑭ A 6-kg cake had a length of 36 cm, a width of 25 cm, and a height of 8 cm. Ryan cut off $\frac{1}{6}$ of the cake and another $\frac{2}{5}$ of the remaining cake. What are the volume and mass of the cake that is left?

Hints

Use this diagram to help you.

⑮ Taylor had 4 coins: 1 toonie, 2 loonies, and 1 quarter. He lost 2 of them. What is the probability that he lost more than $2?

Topics covered:

Question 13
- whole numbers
- time

Question 14
- fractions
- volume
- mass

Question 15
- money
- probability

ISBN: 978-1-77149-203-4

⑯ A box of chocolates costs $29.75. During a promotion, each additional box of chocolates costs $1.35 less. If Julie buys 5 boxes of chocolates, what is the mean cost of the boxes of chocolates?

⑰ $\frac{1}{6}$ of a pepperoni pizza costs $1.50. $\frac{1}{2}$ of a vegetarian pizza costs $3.25. If Jim pays for 1 pepperoni pizza and 2 vegetarian pizzas with 2 $20 bills, what will his change be in the fewest bills and coins?

⑱ Bernie's field is in the shape of a right triangle. He has divided it with a fence into an isosceles triangle and an equilateral triangle. How much longer is the perimeter of the isosceles triangle than that of the equilateral triangle? What is the perimeter of his field?

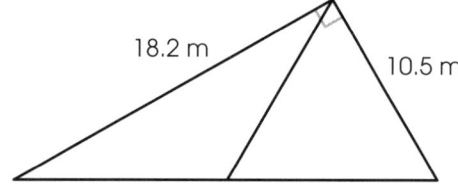

18.2 m   10.5 m

**Hints**

Draw the triangles separately. Then identify the sides that have the same length.

Topics covered:

Question 16	**Question 17**	**Question 18**
• decimals	• fractions	• decimals
• patterning	• money	• perimeter
• data management		• shapes

ISBN: 978-1-77149-203-4

⑲ The capacities of the children's water bottles are shown in the bar graph. Abby filled her bottle 3 times and Danny filled his 2 times. Both children filled their bottles when empty. Who filled more water? By how much more?

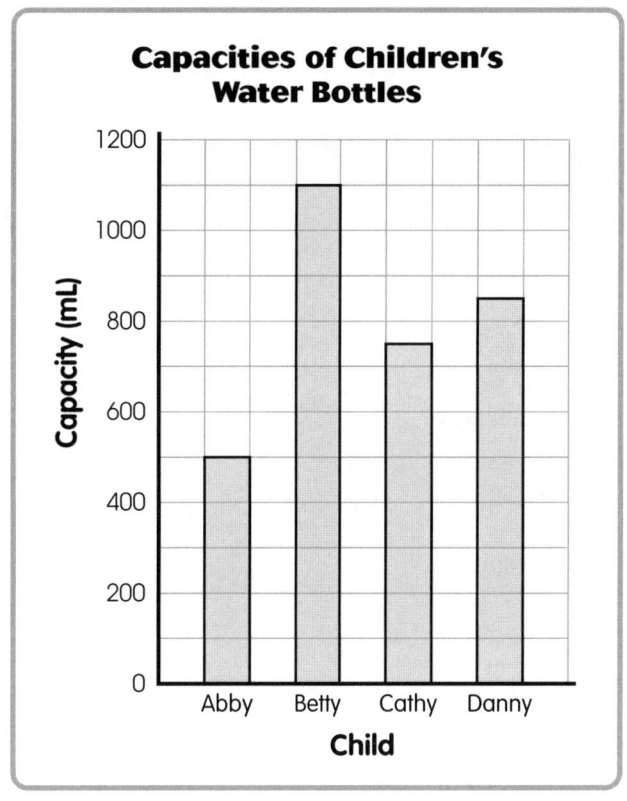

⑳ Refer to Question 19. Two children filled up their water bottles and emptied the water into the fish tank below. Who are the two children?

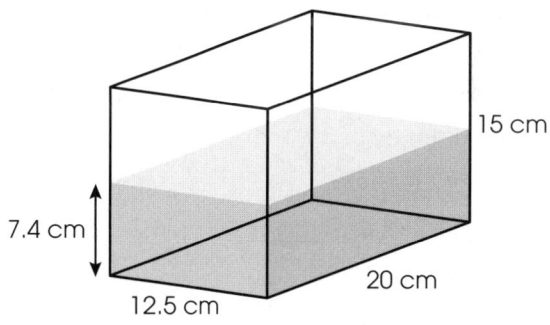

Topics covered:

Question 19
- whole numbers
- capacity
- data management

Question 20
- whole numbers
- volume
- data management

ISBN: 978-1-77149-203-4

Students are required to solve multi-step questions which involve various topics in each.

Topics Covered

	Number Sense and Numeration	Measurement	Geometry and Spatial Sense	Patterning and Algebra	Data Management and Probability	My Record ✔ correct ✘ incorrect
1	decimals				data management	
2	fractions	volume capacity				
3	whole numbers	time				
4	fractions decimals				data management	
5	fractions		transformations	patterning		
6	money		solids			
7		time			probability	
8	whole numbers			patterning		
9	whole numbers money	mass				
10		perimeter area				
11	money	time				
12	whole numbers fractions			patterning		
13	decimals				data management	
14	fractions		shapes / Cartesian coordinate plane			
15	decimals	area				
16		perimeter	shapes transformations			
17	decimals	perimeter				
18	decimals	time capacity				
19	decimals				data management	
20		temperature			data management	

ISBN: 978-1-77149-203-4

① Marty recorded the amount of rainfall in January in 5 cities. How many cities had less rainfall than the mean?

Mean: (_____ + _____ + _____ + _____ + _____) ÷ 5

= _____ ÷ 5

= _____

_____ cities had less rainfall than the mean.

Amount of Rainfall in January in 5 Cities

City	Rainfall (cm)
Portland	3.53
Seattle	5.38
Chicago	1.52
Miami	1.83
New York	2.04

② Juliet drank $\frac{2}{3}$ of a juice box. How many litres of juice did she drink?

9 cm

5 cm

4.2 cm

③ Harry and Sally are 2500 m apart and they walk toward each other. Harry walks 55 m in 1 minute and Sally walks 45 m in 1 minute. If they start walking at 3:15 p.m., what time will they meet each other?

Hints

What is the total distance Harry and Sally cover each minute?

Topics covered:

Question 1
- decimals
- data management

Question 2
- fractions
- volume
- capacity

Question 3
- whole numbers
- time

ISBN: 978-1-77149-203-4

④ The maximum number of points for a game is 60. Carly got $\frac{3}{4}$ of the maximum points, Rae got 12 points more than Jessie, and Jessie got 0.8 of the points that Carly had. Who got the most points? What was the mean number of points?

⑤ Anton has a rectangle that he rotates about a point. If he rotates it $1\frac{3}{4}$ counterclockwise and $1\frac{1}{2}$ clockwise alternately until the 5th rotation, how many of the rectangles would be in the same orientation as the original?

⑥ Nicole wants to buy sticks and balls to build a pentagonal pyramid. Each stick costs 16¢ and each ball costs 75¢. How much will Nicole have left if she pays with 3 toonies and 1 quarter?

Topics covered:

Question 4	**Question 5**	**Question 6**
• fractions	• fractions	• money
• decimals	• transformations	• solids
• data management	• patterning	

ISBN: 978-1-77149-203-4

⑦ There was a blackout at Judy's house from 7:15 a.m. to 8:45 a.m. Her lamp flickered once during the blackout. What is the probability that the lamp flickered at a time that contains the number 6?

⑧ Henry's car has a mileage of 65 000 km and a value of $12 000. The value drops to $11 000 at 75 000 km, and $10 000 at 85 000 km. What is the value at a mileage of 105 000 km?

💡**Hints**

"Mileage" means the total distance a car has travelled.

⑨ 100 g of raisins cost 55 cents. How much change will Jackson get if he pays for 2.6 kg of raisins with a $20 bill?

⑩ A baseball diamond is a rotated square that has a perimeter of 104 m. If 45.8 m² of the diamond is covered with dirt and the rest is covered with grass, what is the area of the diamond that is covered with grass?

Topics covered:

Question 7	**Question 8**	**Question 9**	**Question 10**
• time	• whole numbers	• whole numbers	• perimeter
• probability	• patterning	• money	• area
		• mass	

⑪ A parking lot charges either a flat rate of $3 or $0.75 for the first hour and $0.60 for each additional hour. Michael parks his car from 11:30 a.m. to 5:30 p.m. How much will he pay if he pays the cheaper rate?

⑫ Dan's ball bounces exactly $\frac{1}{2}$ its height when dropped. If its height was 8 cm on the 4th bounce, at what height was it initially dropped?

⑬ There are three Grade 5 classes in a school, with a mean of 25 students and a median of 24 students. The largest class has 0.4 of all the students. How many students are there in each class?

Topics covered:

Question 11	**Question 12**	**Question 13**
• money	• whole numbers	• decimals
• time	• fractions	• data management
	• patterning	

ISBN: 978-1-77149-203-4

⑭ A rectangular path starts at (7,10). Bob walks $\frac{1}{4}$ of the path as shown. If he has 900 m left to complete the path, how long is the path? Find the coordinates of the corners of the path.

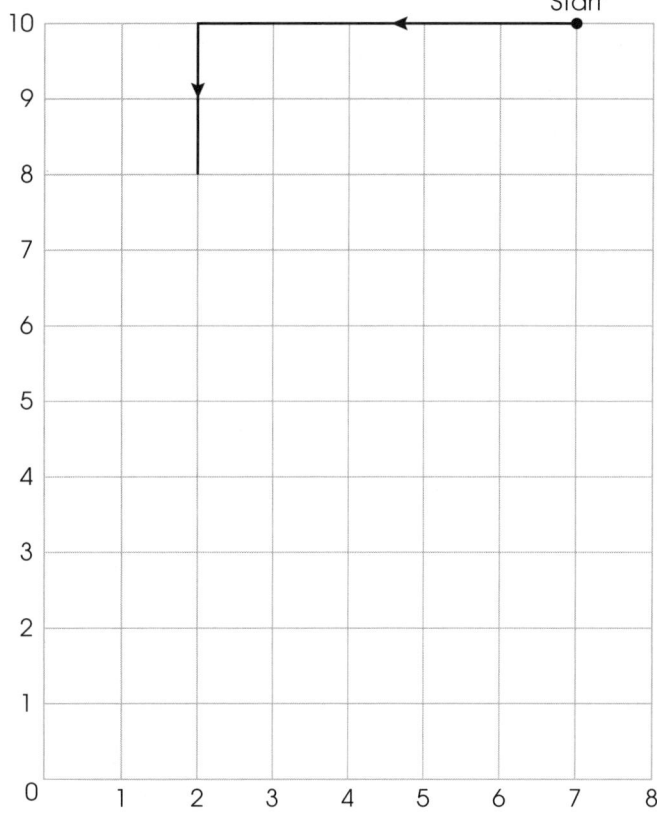

⑮ Nikki is covering her room with tiles, except for her closet. If 3 m² of the tiles cost $65, is $500 enough to cover her room?

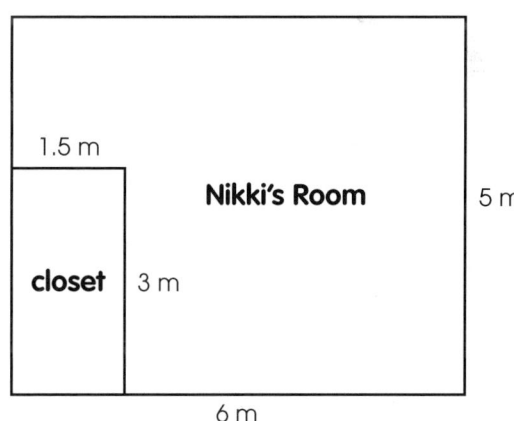

Topics covered:

Question 14
- fractions
- shapes
- Cartesian coordinate plane

Question 15
- decimals
- area

ISBN: 978-1-77149-203-4

⑯ Gordon drew a right triangle that has lengths of 5.4 cm, 3 cm, and 4.5 cm. He reflected the triangle to make a big triangle. Name the big triangle in 2 ways. What is its perimeter?

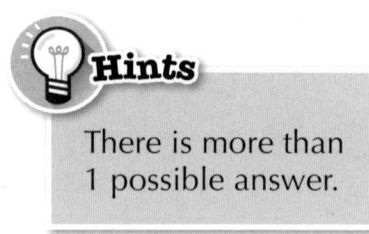

Hints

There is more than 1 possible answer.

⑰ Michael has 10.5 m of fencing. He uses it to fence and divide his backyard into 2 identical square pens as shown. What is the perimeter of each pen?

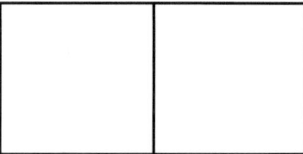

⑱ Katie's doctor told her to use eye drops 3 times a day. She needs to apply 2 drops per eye and each drop is about 0.8 mL. How many 80-mL bottles of eye drops does Katie need in July?

Topics covered:

Question 16	**Question 17**	**Question 18**
• perimeter	• decimals	• decimals
• shapes	• perimeter	• time
• transformations		• capacity

ISBN: 978-1-77149-203-4

⑲ Riley showed the temperatures in the past 6 days in the line graph. What are the mean, median, and mode temperatures?

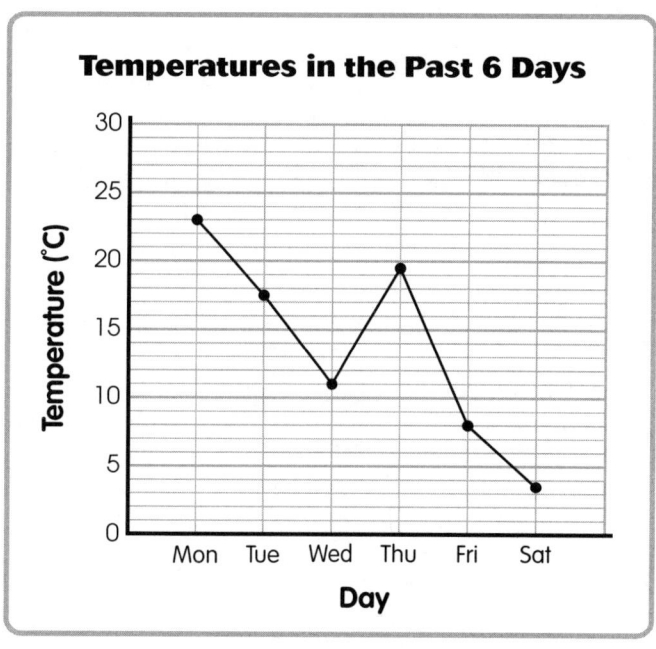

Temperatures in the Past 6 Days

⑳ Refer to Question 19. Today is Sunday and the temperature is 4°C below 0°C. Between which consecutive days did the biggest change in temperature occur?

Topics covered:

Question 19
• decimals
• data management

Question 20
• temperature
• data management

ISBN: 978-1-77149-203-4

Students are required to solve multi-step questions which involve various topics in each.

Topics Covered

	Number Sense and Numeration	Measurement	Geometry and Spatial Sense	Patterning and Algebra	Data Management and Probability	My Record ✔ correct ✘ incorrect
1	whole numbers				data management	
2	fractions	time				
3		area	shapes			
4	fractions	capacity				
5	whole numbers	time				
6		perimeter	solids		probability	
7	fractions	mass				
8		perimeter	shapes		data management	
9	decimals	volume capacity				
10	decimals money			patterning		
11	money			patterning		
12			shapes / Cartesian coordinate plane			
13			shapes transformations			
14	whole numbers decimals				data management	
15	fractions				probability / data management	
16	whole numbers	area volume				
17	money	time				
18			shapes solids			
19	money				probability	
20	decimals	mass		patterning		

ISBN: 978-1-77149-203-4

① A game has 19 rounds. Peter has scored a mean of 32 points in the first 14 rounds. If he wants a mean of 28 points for each round, how many points does he need in the remaining 5 rounds?

Total points in 14 rounds: _____ × _____ = _____

Total points needed in 19 rounds: _____ × _____ = _____

Points needed: _____ – _____ = _____

Peter needs _____ in total in the remaining 5 rounds.

② Anna got home at 5:41 p.m. She studied for $1\frac{1}{2}$ h, had dinner for $\frac{3}{4}$ h, and read until her bedtime. If she went to bed at 9:26 p.m., how long did she read?

③ Tim arranges square tiles into a rectangle that measures 81 cm by 72 cm. What is the area of the smallest tile?

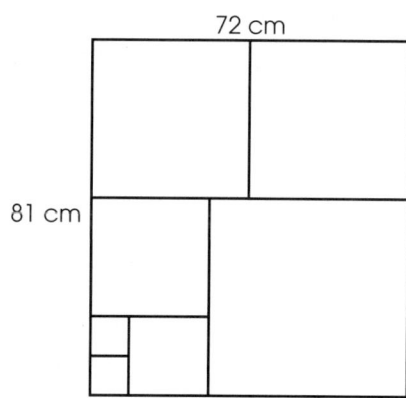

72 cm

81 cm

Topics covered:

Question 1	Question 2	Question 3
• whole numbers	• fractions	• area
• data management	• time	• shapes

ISBN: 978-1-77149-203-4

④ Sally's fish tank is a 20-cm cube. It is $\frac{3}{4}$ full. How many more millilitres of water is needed to fill it so that it is $\frac{7}{8}$ full?

⑤ Dory swam 1250 m. She swam the first 210 m at 3 m in a second and the rest at 2 m in a second. If Dory started swimming at 11:06:48 a.m., what time did she finish swimming?

⑥ George built a pentagonal prism using only 2-cm and 5-cm sticks. The perimeter of the base is 10 cm. If one of the sticks was broken, what is the probability that it is a 5-cm stick?

Topics covered:

Question 4	**Question 5**	**Question 6**
• fractions	• whole numbers	• perimeter
• capacity	• time	• solids
		• probability

ISBN: 978-1-77149-203-4

⑦ Three children each have a bag of candies. Ashley's bag is $\frac{7}{5}$ kg heavier than Brock's, and Cary's is $1\frac{3}{5}$ kg lighter than Ashley's. If Cary's bag weighs 600 g, what is the total mass of the children's candies in kilograms?

⑧ Emily drew the two triangles as shown. They have the same perimeter. The sum of their perimeters is 27 cm. She says that the mean, median, and mode lengths of all the sides of both triangles are the same. Is she correct?

equilateral triangle

isosceles triangle

**Hints**

There is no need to find the measurements of all sides to answer the question.

⑨ A figurine has a volume of 630 cm³. How many millilitres of water can the tank hold after the figurine is placed in the tank?

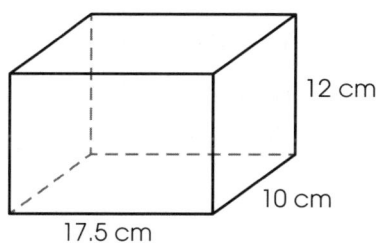
12 cm
10 cm
17.5 cm

Topics covered:

Question 7	**Question 8**	**Question 9**
• fractions	• perimeter	• decimals
• mass	• shapes	• volume
	• data management	• capacity

ISBN: 978-1-77149-203-4

⑩ Damien earns money from his investments. Each year, his earnings double. If his earnings in the first year are $13.75, how many years will it take to earn a total of $220?

⑪ Bill has the same number of dimes and nickels that are worth 90¢ in total. Each dime is 1.22 mm thick and each nickel is 1.76 mm thick. If Bill stacks up all the coins, how tall will the stack be?

⑫ Suzie drew a triangle that has its vertices at A(6,4), B(1,4), and C(6,7). Draw the triangle. Name it in two ways.

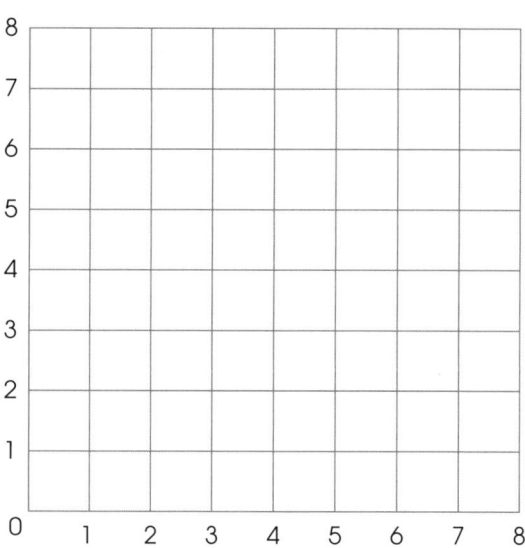

⑬ Refer to Question 12. Point A is translated 5 units to the left and 4 units down. Point B is translated 5 units to the right and 4 units down. What are the coordinates of Point C if the new triangle is congruent to the original? Describe the transformation of Point C.

Topics covered:

Question 10	**Question 11**	**Question 12**	**Question 13**
• decimals	• money	• shapes	• shapes
• money	• patterning	• Cartesian coordinate plane	• transformations
• patterning			

ISBN: 978-1-77149-203-4

⑭ Gloria surveyed 1200 people about the dogs and cats they own and she created the circle graph. How many people own at least one dog?

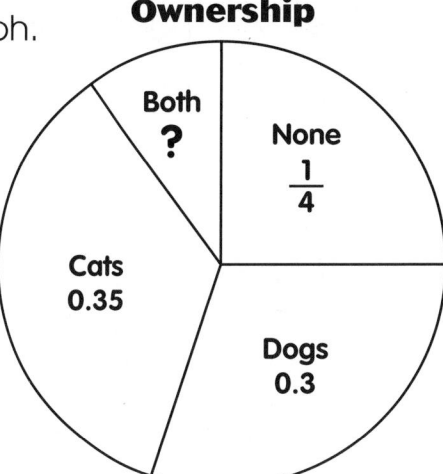

Dog and Cat Ownership

⑮ Refer to Question 14. Of all the cat owners surveyed, what is the probability that an owner also owns a dog?

Topics covered:

Question 14
- whole numbers
- decimals
- data management

Question 15
- fractions
- probability
- data management

ISBN: 978-1-77149-203-4

⑯ Two rectangular prisms have the same volume of 2475 cm³. Their heights are 9 cm and 5 cm. What is the difference between the area of their bases?

⑰ Roger will go swimming 3 times a week starting on Monday, June 17 until the end of the month. He swims on Mondays, Wednesdays, and Fridays. The swimming pool charges $2.75 on Mondays and Wednesdays, and $3.15 on Fridays. How much will Roger pay in total?

Hints

There are 30 days in June.

⑱ The faces that make a prism have a total of 14 right angles. Name the prism and the shape of its base. Explain your answer.

Topics covered:

Question 16	Question 17	Question 18
• whole numbers	• money	• shapes
• area	• time	• solids
• volume		

ISBN: 978-1-77149-203-4

Sandra bought 2 shirts (red and blue) for $25.40 each and 3 skirts (green, yellow, and black) for $27.55 each. What was the total cost? Draw a tree diagram to find the number of different shirt and skirt combinations she can wear.

⑳ Trixie did a science experiment. She grew Watermelons A and B in different soils. However, she lost some recordings by accident, but she knows that the watermelons grew steadily. Follow the patterns to fill in the missing data. What was the difference in mass of the watermelons by Week 8?

Masses of Watermelons

Week	Mass A	B
1		
2		
3		
4	900 g	900 g
5	1.05 kg	1.1 kg
6	1.2 kg	1.3 kg
7		
8		

Topics covered:

Question 19
• money
• probability

Question 20
• decimals
• mass
• patterning

ISBN: 978-1-77149-203-4

Students are required to solve multi-step questions which involve various topics in each.

Topics Covered

	Number Sense and Numeration	Measurement	Geometry and Spatial Sense	Patterning and Algebra	Data Management and Probability	My Record
1	fractions				probability	
2	decimals money	capacity				
3	decimals	time	solids			
4		area			probability	
5	decimals money					
6	whole numbers	time				
7		perimeter	solids			
8	whole numbers fractions				probability	
9		time temperature		patterning		
10	decimals		transformations			
11	fractions decimals				data management	
12	whole numbers	area	shapes			
13	whole numbers fractions					
14		volume	solids			
15	decimals	mass			data management	
16			transformations	patterning		
17	decimals money	area				
18			solids		probability	
19		area	shapes / Cartesian coordinate plane			
20			shapes transformations			

My Record: ✔ correct ✗ incorrect

ISBN: 978-1-77149-203-4

① Matthew has a box of marbles. $\frac{4}{25}$ of them are red, $\frac{6}{25}$ are blue, $\frac{7}{25}$ are green, and the rest are yellow. He randomly picked a marble and then replaced it. He picked a marble 100 times and picked his favourite colour 29 times. Which is Matthew's favourite colour?

② Shampoo is sold in 3 different sizes: 250 mL for $4.50, 500 mL for $8.90, and 1250 mL for $21.50. What is the cheapest way to buy 2.5 L of shampoo? How much will it cost?

③ It takes Hillary 0.5 s to draw a 2-cm line. How long will it take her to draw the net of a cube with a side length of 6 cm?

Topics covered:

Question 1	**Question 2**	**Question 3**
• fractions	• decimals	• decimals
• probability	• money	• time
	• capacity	• solids

ISBN: 978-1-77149-203-4

Jason creates a target using a series of squares as shown. Each section has a different colour. What is the probability of hitting each section?

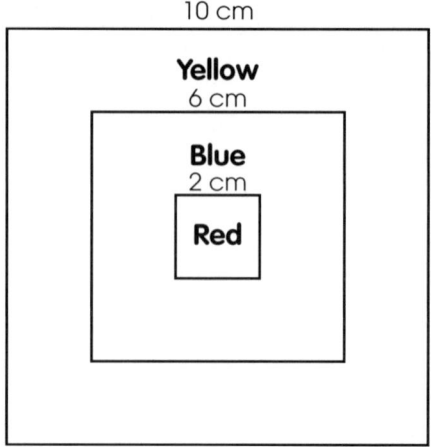

⑤ Jeanine played a game where she drops tokens on the board. Each section of the board is worth either 5¢, 10¢, or 25¢. Each token costs $0.10. Jeanine played 6 times and earned $0.15. How many tokens did she drop in each section if she dropped at least 1 token in each section?

Topics covered:

Question 4	Question 5
• area	• decimals
• probability	• money

ISBN: 978-1-77149-203-4

⑥ A flight of stairs has 12 steps. John walks up the stairs to get to his office. If he walked up a total of 108 steps from 7:52:18 to 7:54:33, how long did it take him to walk up 1 flight of stairs?

⑦ Virginia took apart the pyramid shown below and used as many sticks as possible to build a prism. What is the perimeter of the base of the prism?

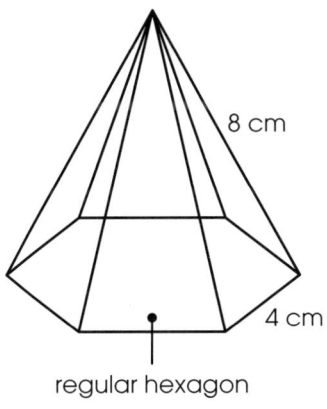

8 cm

4 cm

regular hexagon

Topics covered:

Question 6	**Question 7**
• whole numbers	• perimeter
• time	• solids

ISBN: 978-1-77149-203-4

⑧ The spinner was spun at a game booth. The pointer landed on the ball 624 times. About how many times was the spinner spun?

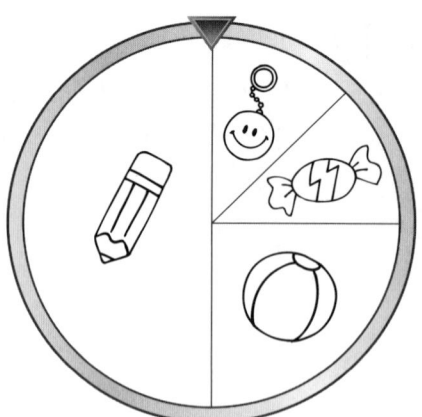

⑨ The temperature was 5°C below 0°C on Monday night. If the temperature rises 7°C in the morning and drops 4°C at night each day, what will the temperature be on Friday night?

⑩ Noah is biking on the routes as shown. He bikes 3.2 km to the right, 2.5 km down, 4.7 km to the left, and then 1.6 km down. If Noah wants to take the shortest route back, how should he bike and what is the distance?

Topics covered:

Question 8	**Question 9**	**Question 10**
• whole numbers	• time	• decimals
• fractions	• temperature	• transformations
• probability	• patterning	

ISBN: 978-1-77149-203-4

⑪ The mean amount of snowfall in 3 cities is 20.4 mm in a month. If City A has $24\frac{1}{2}$ mm and City B has 17.8 mm, what is the amount of snowfall in City C?

⑫ Farmer Dan has used 181 m of fencing to fence his patch of land. The land is made up of a triangle and a square as shown below. What is the area of the patch of land?

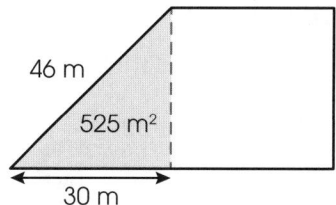

46 m

525 m²

30 m

⑬ Mrs. Anderson earns $3000 a month. Her rent is $1320 a month, her car loan is $4200 yearly, and she pays $\frac{1}{10}$ of what she earns for her insurance each month. How much money does Mrs. Anderson have left each month?

⑭ Jeremy has a rectangular prism that measures 16 cm by 24 cm by 20 cm. He wants to divide it into cubes. Should the cubes have side lengths of 4 cm or 6 cm? Explain. How many cubes will there be?

Topics covered:

Question 11	**Question 12**	**Question 13**	**Question 14**
• fractions	• whole numbers	• whole numbers	• volume
• decimals	• area	• fractions	• solids
• data management	• shapes		

ISBN: 978-1-77149-203-4

⑮ A bowling team has 4 members. They each have a bowling ball. Their bowling balls have a mean mass of 6.25 kg, a median mass of 6.15 kg, and a mode mass of 5.5 kg. What are the masses of the bowling balls?

⑯ Ronda created a pattern using the letter "R". The pattern rule is: "Make a $\frac{1}{2}$ rotation. Then reflect it horizontally".

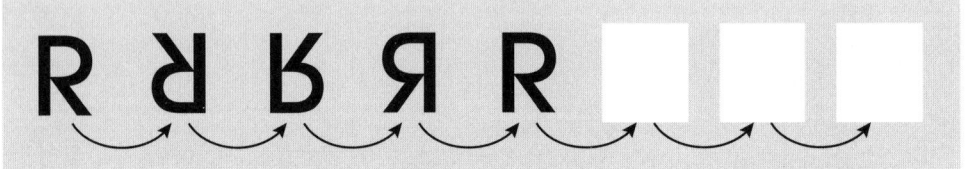

Draw the next 3 "R"s to continue the pattern. Identify the core. Then draw the 297th "R".

⑰ Lucas wants to replace the carpet in his bedroom. Every 1 m² of carpet costs $24. How much will it cost?

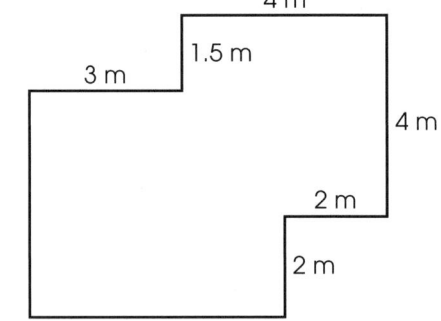

Topics covered:

Question 15	Question 16	Question 17
• decimals	• transformations	• decimals
• mass	• patterning	• money
• data management		• area

ISBN: 978-1-77149-203-4

⑱ Samantha rolled a 6-sided dice 30 times and got these results: 5 ♠ 16 ♥ 6 ♣ 3 ♦. How many of each symbol is on the dice?

⑲ Joey drew a shape that has (1,5), (5,7), and (1,9) as vertices. Name the shape in 2 ways. The area of the shape is 50.4 cm². What is the area of each square unit?

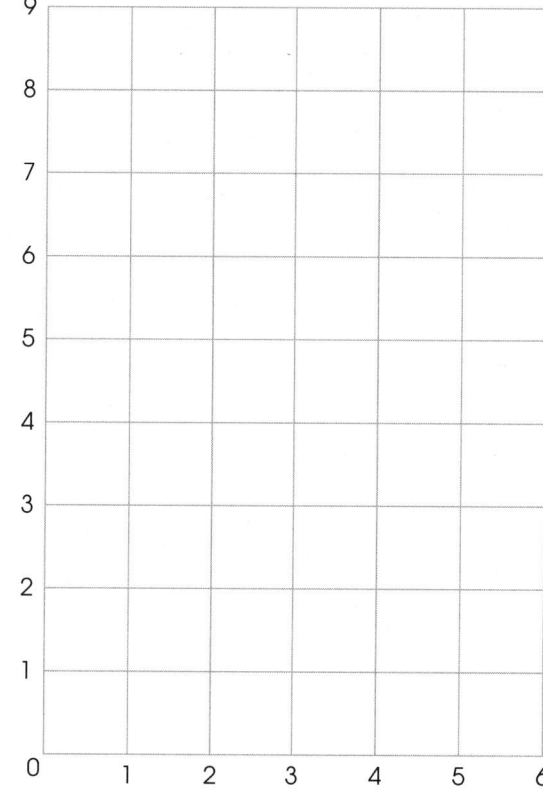

⑳ Refer to Question 19. Joey rotates the shape $\frac{1}{2}$ about (3,6). Draw the image. What is the combined shape? Write 3 of its properties.

Topics covered:

Question 18
• solids
• probability

Question 19
• area
• shapes
• Cartesian coordinate plane

Question 20
• shapes
• transformations

ISBN: 978-1-77149-203-4

Students are required to solve multi-step questions which involve various topics in each.

Topics Covered

	Number Sense and Numeration	Measurement	Geometry and Spatial Sense	Patterning and Algebra	Data Management and Probability	My Record ✔ correct ✘ incorrect
1	fractions money					
2		temperature			data management	
3	whole numbers	time				
4	whole numbers	volume capacity				
5			shapes solids		probability	
6	money			patterning		
7	whole numbers decimals					
8		perimeter volume	solids			
9	whole numbers				data management	
10		area volume			data management	
11		time area				
12	fractions	capacity			data management	
13	decimals	mass				
14			shapes transformations			
15	fractions			patterning		
16		time			probability	
17	money			patterning		
18			shapes / Cartesian coordinate plane			
19			shapes / Cartesian coordinate plane			
20		area	Cartesian coordinate plane			

ISBN: 978-1-77149-203-4

① Randy ate $\frac{3}{4}$ of a pizza. The pizza cost $12 and Randy paid exactly 5 coins for his portion. What coins did Randy pay with for the pizza?

② The mean temperature over 5 days was 21.6°C and the mode temperatures were 19.5°C and 23.6°C. What was the median temperature?

③ A laundry facility has 15 washing machines. It takes each machine 40 minutes to wash a load of laundry. From 8:30 a.m. to 3:50 p.m., how many loads of laundry can the facility wash?

Topics covered:

Question 1	**Question 2**	**Question 3**
• fractions	• temperature	• whole numbers
• money	• data management	• time

ISBN: 978-1-77149-203-4

④ Melissa bought a new fish tank. She added 42 L of water and some bags of gravel in it. Each bag of gravel has a volume of 240 cm³. If the water level is at 37 cm, how many bags of gravel did she add?

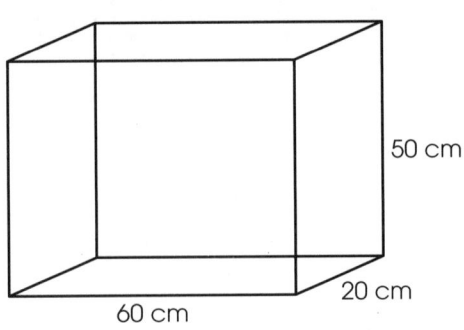

50 cm

20 cm

60 cm

⑤ Frank has 2 fair dice, one is a triangular prism and the other is a rectangular pyramid. If he throws both dice, what is the probability that both dice will land on a triangular face?

Topics covered:

Question 4	**Question 5**
• whole numbers	• shapes
• volume	• solids
• capacity	• probability

ISBN: 978-1-77149-203-4

⑥ Joan has 13 toonies and 7 loonies. She exchanges 2 toonies and a loonie each day for a $5 bill starting on Day 1. On which day will she have the same number of bills and coins?

⑦ 400 students are going on a field trip. Each student pays $12.35 and the remaining cost will be subsidized. It will cost $1750 for transportation and $5172 for museum tickets. How much will be subsidized for the field trip?

⑧ The 6 faces of a prism all have a perimeter of 24 cm. Name the prism and find its volume.

Topics covered:

Question 6	**Question 7**	**Question 8**
• money	• whole numbers	• perimeter
• patterning	• decimals	• volume
		• solids

ISBN: 978-1-77149-203-4

⑨ Howard graphed the heights of 6 prisms but he forgot to add the scale. He knows that the mean height is 25 cm. Add the scale and find the height of each prism.

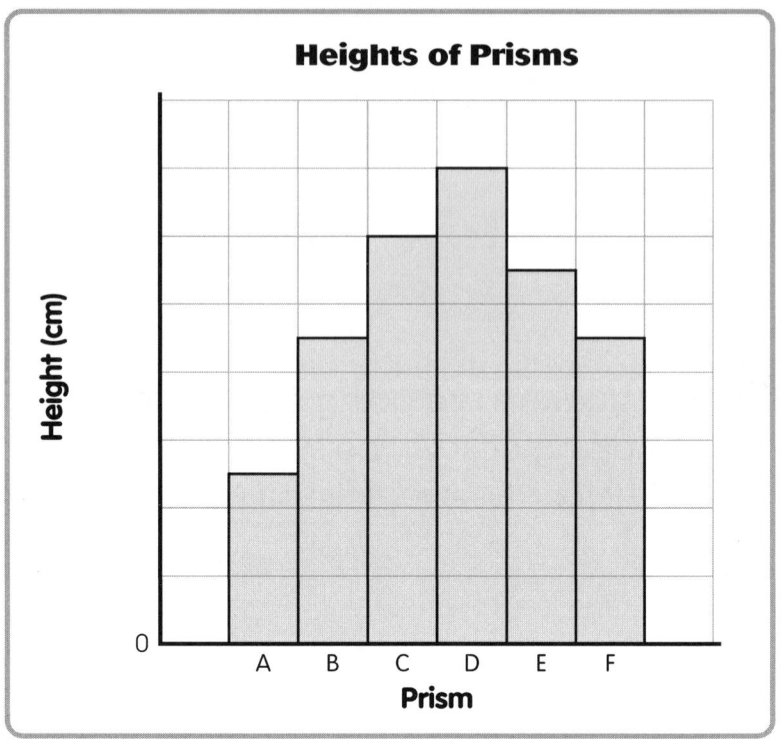

⑩ Refer to Question 9. The volumes of Prism C and Prism D are the same. The base of Prism D is a rectangle that measures 15 cm by 4 cm. What is the area of the base of Prism C?

Topics covered:

Question 9
- whole numbers
- data management

Question 10
- area
- volume
- data management

ISBN: 978-1-77149-203-4

⑪ Morgan started harvesting the crops on his farm at 10:40 a.m. and finished at exactly 2:00 p.m. If it took him 4 minutes to harvest 100 m² of crops, what is the area of his farm?

⑫ Out of 10 gift boxes, $\frac{1}{2}$ of them are Box A, $\frac{1}{5}$ are Box B, and the rest are Box C. What is the median capacity of the boxes in millilitres?

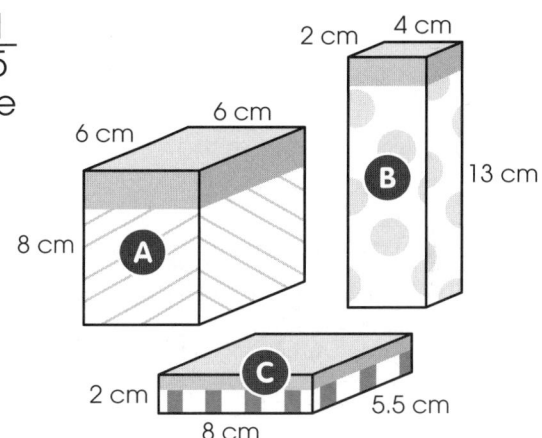

⑬ Tom and Leah put their money together to buy 1.6 kg of candies for $5. If Tom contributed $2, how many grams of candies should Tom and Leah each get?

Topics covered:

Question 11	**Question 12**	**Question 13**
• time	• fractions	• decimals
• area	• capacity	• mass
	• data management	

ISBN: 978-1-77149-203-4

⑭ A right isosceles triangle is combined with its reflection to make a bigger triangle. Name the bigger triangle in 2 ways.

⑮ In a class election, there were 4 candidates. Each candidate got twice the number of votes than the next best candidate. What fraction of the votes did the winner get if the smallest number of votes is 1?

⑯ The swimming pool is open from 9:00 a.m. to 3:00 p.m. for classes. Each class is 45 min long. If class times are assigned at random, what is the probability that a student's class time will start between 11:00 a.m. and 1:00 p.m.?

⑰ Patricia earns $2.25 on Day 1. On each following day, she is paid twice the amount from the previous day subtracted 1. On which day will she earn $11? If she is paid the same number of loonies and dimes, how many of each coin will she have?

Topics covered:

Question 14	Question 15	Question 16	Question 17
• shapes	• fractions	• time	• money
• transformations	• patterning	• probability	• patterning

ISBN: 978-1-77149-203-4

⑱ Jared wants to draw a shape with vertices at (2,4), (3,2), (4,5), (5,2), and (6,4) on the grid. Draw and name the shape. How many lines of symmetry does it have?

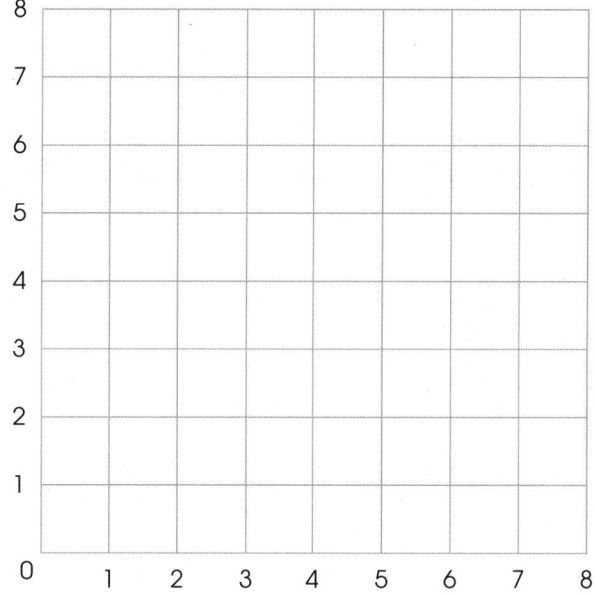

⑲ Refer to Question 18. Jared then wants to draw another shape with vertices at (1,4), (2,1), (4,6), (6,1), and (7,4). Draw the shape. Are the two shapes similar?

⑳ Refer to Questions 18 and 19. If the smaller shape has an area of 72 cm², what is the area of the bigger shape?

Topics covered:

Question 18	**Question 19**	**Question 20**
• shapes	• shapes	• area
• Cartesian coordinate plane	• Cartesian coordinate plane	• Cartesian coordinate plane

ISBN: 978-1-77149-203-4

Students are required to solve multi-step questions which involve various topics in each.

Topics Covered

	Number Sense and Numeration	Measurement	Geometry and Spatial Sense	Patterning and Algebra	Data Management and Probability	My Record ✔ correct ✘ incorrect
1	money	mass				
2	decimals	capacity				
3			solids	patterning	probability	
4		volume	solids transformations			
5		time	Cartesian coordinate plane			
6	fractions		solids			
7	decimals	temperature			data management	
8		time temperature		patterning		
9	whole numbers	mass				
10		volume		patterning		
11	fractions	time				
12	decimals	mass			data management	
13	money	volume		patterning		
14	money				data management	
15		area	shapes			
16	whole numbers				data management	
17	whole numbers				data management	
18		area	shapes transformations			
19	whole numbers fractions				probabillity	
20		perimeter area				

ISBN: 978-1-77149-203-4

① Every 500 g of flour is sold for $0.75 at a bulk food store. Sam paid 1 toonie, 1 loonie, and 3 quarters for flour. How many kilograms of flour did he buy?

② Mary has a cardboard that measures 15 cm by 12.5 cm. She cuts out four squares from each corner, each having a side length of 3 cm. She then folds the cardboard to make a box that has no top. What is the capacity of the box?

③ Calvin's top is shown. Each triangular face is labelled with a number starting at 1 and the number increases by 3 for each face. Calvin spins the top. What is the probability that it will land on a number that contains the digit "1"?

regular octagon

Topics covered:

Question 1	Question 2	Question 3
• money	• decimals	• solids
• mass	• capacity	• patterning
		• probability

ISBN: 978-1-77149-203-4

④ Paul has drawn half the net of a solid that will be completed by reflection in Line K. Complete the net and name the solid. Then find its volume by measuring its length, width, and height.

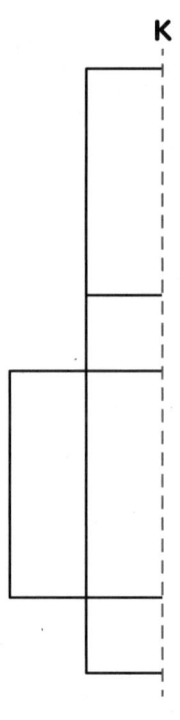

⑤ The park is at (3,7) and Joe's house is at (2,1). Joe started running on the path from the park to his house at 10:45:18 a.m. It took 20 min 24 s. He then biked back to the park on the same route. If he biked twice as fast as he ran, what time did he arrive at the park? How long did it take him to cover each unit by biking?

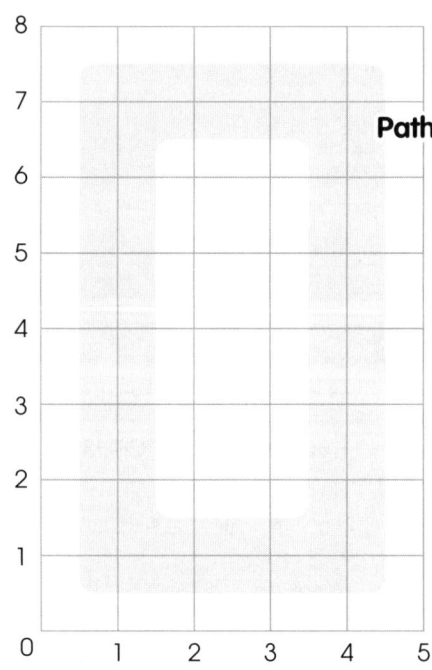

Topics covered:

Question 4
- volume
- solids
- transformations

Question 5
- time
- Cartesian coordinate plane

ISBN: 978-1-77149-203-4

⑥ Carmen took the gumdrops that were used to make the vertices of 3 pentagonal pyramids to build as many cubes as possible instead. What fraction of the gumdrops were used to make the cubes?

⑦ The mean temperature of the weekdays was 18.8°C and the mean of the weekend was 26.5°C. What was the mean temperature of the week?

⑧ It takes an air conditioner 34 min to cool down a house by 1.4°C. The air conditioner was turned on at 11:45 a.m. when the house was at 30°C. What time was it when the temperature dropped to 23°C?

⑨ A small block weighs 75 g and a large block weighs 94 g. A figure is made with 26 small and 18 large blocks. What is the total mass of the figure in kilograms?

Topics covered:

Question 6	**Question 7**	**Question 8**	**Question 9**
• fractions	• decimals	• time	• whole numbers
• solids	• temperature	• temperature	• mass
	• data management	• patterning	

ISBN: 978-1-77149-203-4

⑩ A staircase has 7 steps. All steps have a length and a height of 15 cm, whereas the width decreases by 30 cm as it goes up. The bottom step is 270 cm wide. What is the volume of the top step?

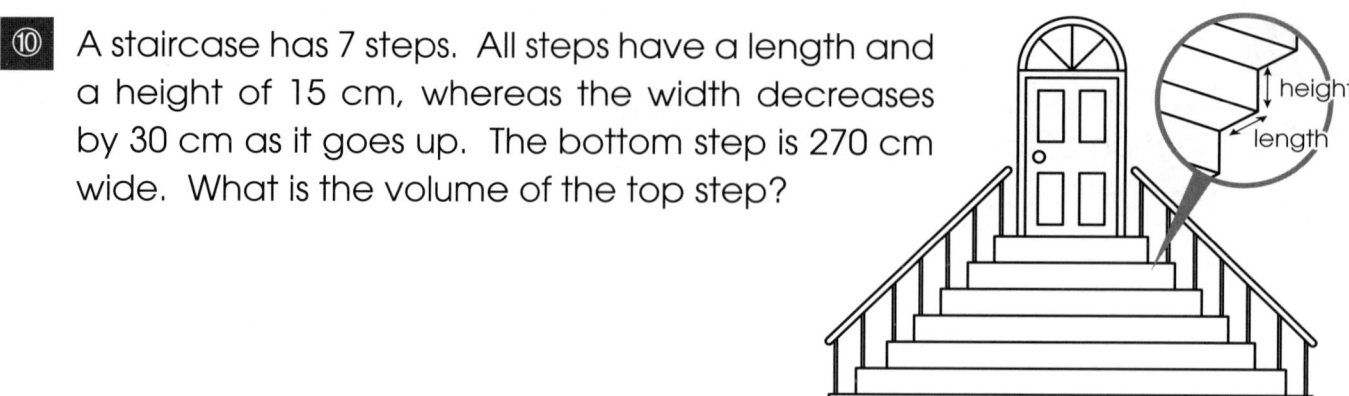

⑪ Alan makes $1\frac{1}{2}$ L of soup in $1\frac{3}{4}$ h. He finished making $4\frac{1}{2}$ L of soup at 6:38 p.m. What time did he start?

⑫ Robert has a box of 5 apples. The median mass is 210 g and the mean mass is 213.6 g. There are two modes and one of them is 197.5 g. What could the other mode be?

Topics covered:

Question 10
- volume
- patterning

Question 11
- fractions
- time

Question 12
- decimals
- mass
- data management

ISBN: 978-1-77149-203-4

⑬ A balloon that has a volume of 640 cm³ is leaking air. Its volume shrinks by half every 0.5 s. Its volume is 20 cm³ when deflated. How long will it take the balloon to deflate?

⑭ Jenny paid for 7 items with 4 $20 bills and received 1 loonie and 3 dimes in change. There was a sales tax of $9.05 on the items. What is the mean cost of the items before tax?

⑮ Timmy's rectangular garden has posts around it. The posts are 2 m apart and there are posts at all 4 corners. There are 14 posts in total. What is the greatest possible area of his garden?

Topics covered:

Question 13	**Question 14**	**Question 15**
• money	• money	• area
• volume	• data management	• shapes
• patterning		

⑯ A park charges an entrance fee. The revenue is shown in the line graph. What is the total revenue from the week?

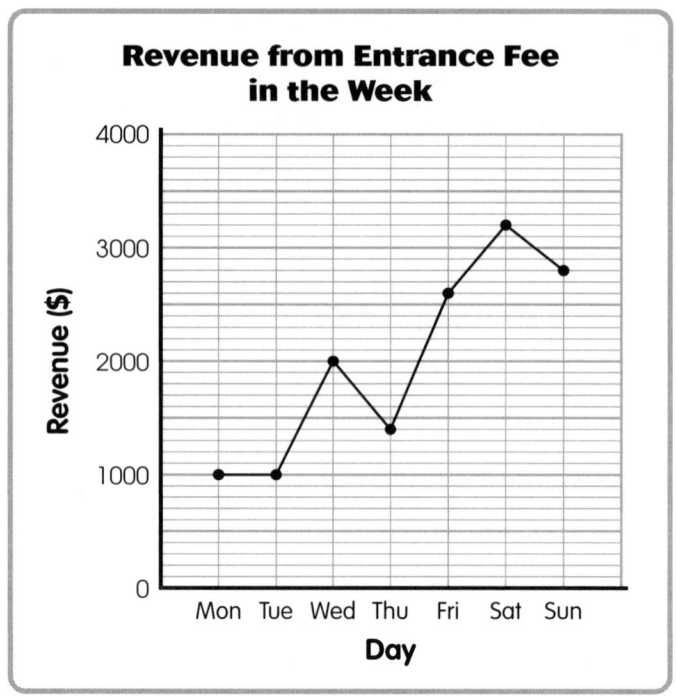

Revenue from Entrance Fee in the Week

⑰ Refer to Question 16. The entrance fee is $5 per visitor. What is the mean, median, and mode number of visitors each day?

Topics covered:

Question 16
- whole numbers
- data management

Question 17
- whole numbers
- data management

ISBN: 978-1-77149-203-4

⑱ The area of the shape is 16.5 cm². Erin performs 3 rotations to make a square. She makes a $\frac{1}{4}$ clockwise rotation, a $\frac{1}{2}$ rotation, and a $\frac{1}{4}$ counterclockwise rotation. About which point should she do the rotations? What will the area of the square be?

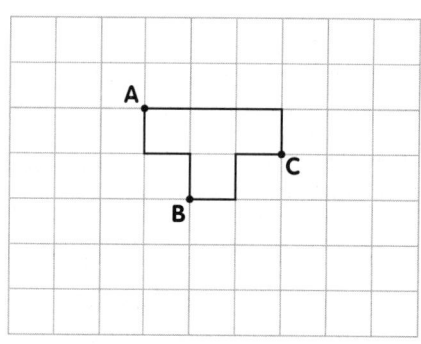

⑲ Rob had 6000 envelopes. $\frac{1}{4}$ of them were brown and the rest were white. If he used $\frac{4}{9}$ of the white envelopes, what is the probability of Rob picking a brown envelope at random from the remaining envelopes?

⑳ Tommy wants to separate a 12-m² field into an inner section and an outer section so that the two sections have the same area. If he wants to fence both sections, what length of fencing is needed in total?

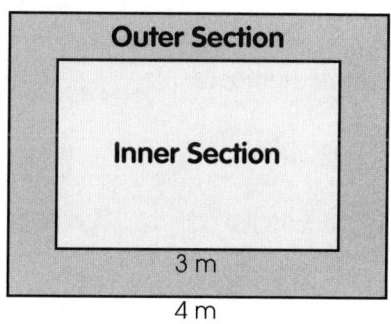

Topics covered:

Question 18	**Question 19**	**Question 20**
• area	• whole numbers	• perimeter
• shapes	• fractions	• area
• transformations	• probability	

ISBN: 978-1-77149-203-4

Students are required to solve multi-step questions which involve various topics in each.

Topics Covered

	Number Sense and Numeration	Measurement	Geometry and Spatial Sense	Patterning and Algebra	Data Management and Probability	My Record ✔ correct ✘ incorrect
1		time	transformations			
2		temperature			data management	
3	money				probability	
4	fractions decimals					
5	fractions				probability	
6	fractions				probability	
7	whole numbers	time				
8		area	shapes			
9	fractions decimals					
10		perimeter area		patterning		
11			shapes / Cartesian coordinate plane			
12		area	Cartesian coordinate plane			
13	whole numbers	volume capacity				
14	decimals	mass			data management	
15	decimals	perimeter	shapes			
16		area		patterning		
17		perimeter	shapes transformations			
18	fractions decimals		transformations			
19	fractions				data management	
20	fractions				data management	

ISBN: 978-1-77149-203-4

① On a clock, the hour hand has rotated $\frac{1}{6}$ clockwise. How many minutes have passed?

② The temperatures over 5 days were recorded. The mean was 15.6°C, the median was 16°C, and there was no mode. If the temperatures were all 2-digit whole numbers, what was the highest possible temperature?

③ Evan had $1.50 in 3 coins. The probability of picking a quarter from his coins was $\frac{2}{3}$. He received 3 more coins and has $2.05 in total now, but the probability of picking a quarter is the same as before. What coins did Evan receive?

④ Linda had $10. She spent $\frac{2}{5}$ of it on a drink and 0.25 of it on a Popsicle. How much does she have left?

Topics covered:

Question 1	Question 2	Question 3	Question 4
• time	• temperature	• money	• fractions
• transformations	• data management	• probability	• decimals

ISBN: 978-1-77149-203-4

⑤ Peter is playing a game where he spins two spinners to get a numerator and a denominator to make a fraction. If equivalent fractions are considered the same outcome, how many different outcomes are there?

Numerator

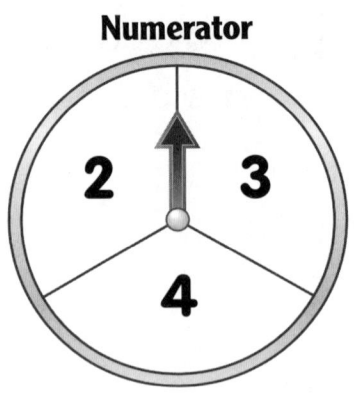

Denominator

⑥ Refer to Question 5. What is the probability of getting a fraction greater than $\frac{1}{2}$?

Topics covered:

Question 5
- fractions
- probability

Question 6
- fractions
- probability

ISBN: 978-1-77149-203-4

⑦ The blades on a wind turbine make 10 revolutions each minute. From 3:43:06 p.m. to 5:16:36 p.m., how many revolutions do the blades make?

⑧ A flooring design is in the shape of a square and part of it is covered by a rectangular carpet that has a width of 50 cm. The area overlapped by the design and the carpet is 4700 cm². What is the area of the design?

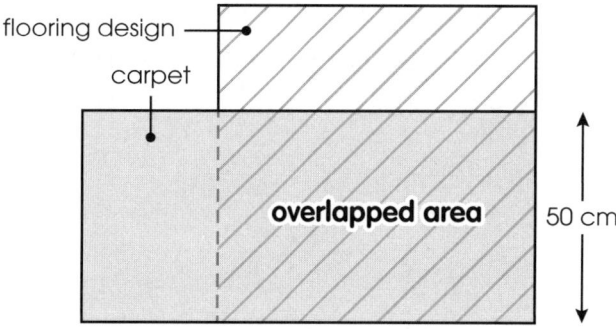

flooring design
carpet
overlapped area
50 cm

⑨ A taxi driver charges $0.90 for the first $1\frac{3}{4}$ km and $0.15 for each additional $\frac{1}{4}$ km. How much does it cost to travel 4 km?

Topics covered:

Question 7	**Question 8**	**Question 9**
• whole numbers	• area	• fractions
• time	• shapes	• decimals

ISBN: 978-1-77149-203-4

⑩ Cori has a piece of paper that measures 16 cm by 24 cm. Starting from the 16-cm side, she folds it in half, alternating between vertical and horizontal folds. What is the perimeter when the area of the folded paper is 24 cm²?

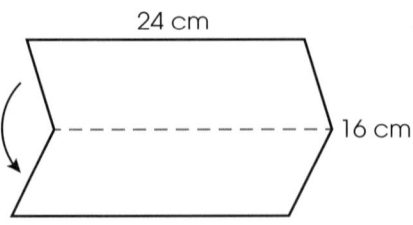

⑪ Rachel wants to draw an octagon with 4 lines of symmetry. Three of its vertices are at (1,5), (1,3), and (3,1). Draw the octagon. Write the coordinates of the remaining vertices.

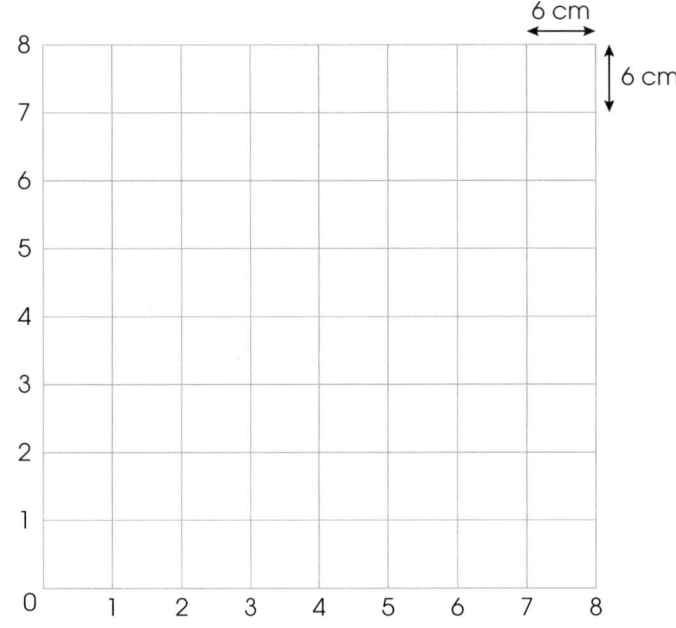

⑫ Refer to Question 11. What is the area of the octagon?

Topics covered:

Question 10	**Question 11**	**Question 12**
• perimeter	• shapes	• area
• area	• Cartesian coordinate plane	• Cartesian coordinate plane
• patterning		

ISBN: 978-1-77149-203-4

⑬ Part of the rectangular block is placed vertically into a glass tank. The tank will then be filled with water. Each cup holds 200 mL of water. Will 7 cups of water be enough to fill the tank?

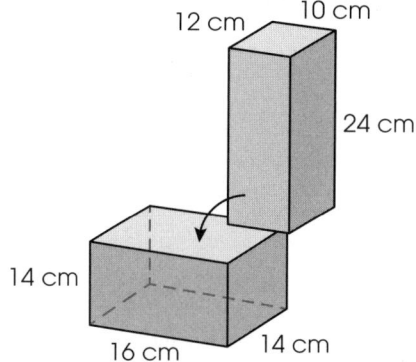

⑭ Mark recorded the masses of the crops that he harvested over 5 weeks. He harvested a mean of 9.48 kg each week. In Week 6, the mean increased by 920 g. What was the mass of the harvested crops in Week 6?

⑮ A snail moved along the edge of a regular pentagon. It travelled 3 times around the pentagon and covered a total distance of 51 cm. What was the side length of the pentagon?

Topics covered:

Question 13	**Question 14**	**Question 15**
• whole numbers	• decimals	• decimals
• volume	• mass	• perimeter
• capacity	• data management	• shapes

ISBN: 978-1-77149-203-4

⑯ The square tiles on a wall follow a pattern. Starting with a perimeter of 4 cm, the perimeter increases by 4 cm each time. What is the pattern rule for its area? What is the area of the 5th square?

⑰ Robin creates a design by rotating the rhombus about Point K $\frac{1}{8}$ clockwise 7 times. The perimeter of the rhombus is 5.36 cm. What will the perimeter of the design be?

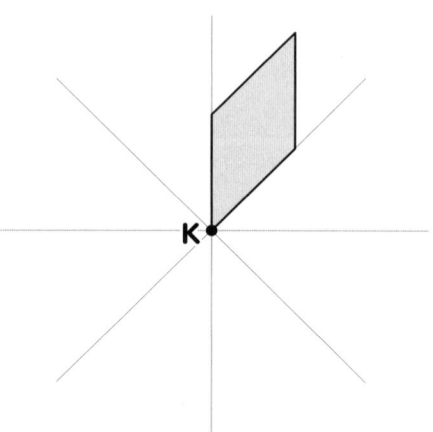

⑱ From her home, Serena walked 3 units to the right, $\frac{2}{3}$ of that distance up, and $1\frac{1}{3}$ of the original distance to the left. At this point, she has walked 5.4 km. How far will she have to walk down and to the right to get home?

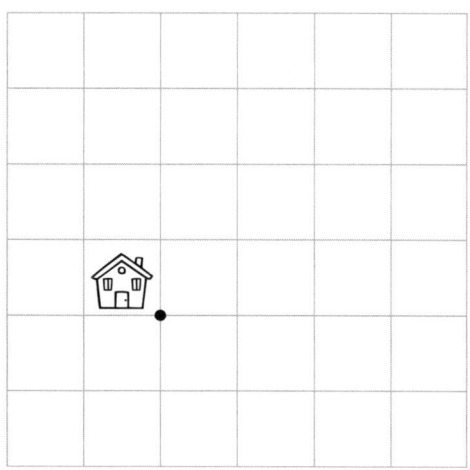

Topics covered:

Question 16	**Question 17**	**Question 18**
• area	• perimeter	• fractions
• patterning	• shapes	• decimals
	• transformations	• transformations

ISBN: 978-1-77149-203-4

⑲ Gilbert, Edmond, and Shane are having a picnic. The circle graph shows the number of grapes that Shane and Edmond have brought. If they share the grapes equally among themselves and Gilbert, what fraction of Edmond's and Shane's grapes will be given away?

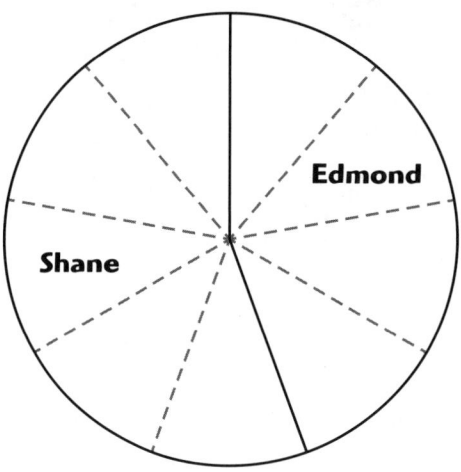

**Number of Grapes
Each Boy Has Brought**

⑳ Refer to Question 19. Each boy will have 54 grapes after sharing. How many grapes have Edmond and Shane each brought?

Topics covered:

Question 19
- fractions
- data management

Question 20
- fractions
- data management

ISBN: 978-1-77149-203-4

Students are required to solve multi-step questions which involve various topics in each.

Topics Covered

	Number Sense and Numeration	Measurement	Geometry and Spatial Sense	Patterning and Algebra	Data Management and Probability	My Record ✔ correct ✗ incorrect
1	fractions	volume capacity				
2	decimals	perimeter	shapes			
3		time			probability	
4	whole numbers	capacity				
5	decimals	time		patterning		
6	decimals	area				
7		volume	shapes solids			
8		time	Cartesian coordinate plane	patterning		
9		perimeter area				
10		mass			probability / data management	
11	fractions				probability	
12	money				probability	
13	whole numbers	area				
14	money	time		patterning		
15		temperature			data management	
16	fractions				data management	
17	fractions				data management	
18			shapes		probability	
19	decimals	time				
20			solids transformations			

ISBN: 978-1-77149-203-4

① Kelsey's fish tank measures 50 cm by 20 cm by 30 cm. If she fills the tank with 25 L of water, what fraction of the tank is not filled?

② Lisa has a square with a perimeter of 17 cm. She adds a parallelogram to it and the perimeter of the shape increases by 3.6 cm. What is the perimeter of the parallelogram?

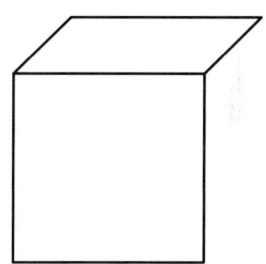

③ Randy's dentist appointment is at 2:05 p.m. Randy will arrive anytime from 1:50 p.m. to 2:25 p.m. What is the probability that Randy will not be late?

Topics covered:

Question 1	**Question 2**	**Question 3**
• fractions	• decimals	• time
• volume	• perimeter	• probability
• capacity	• shapes	

ISBN: 978-1-77149-203-4

④ Which is a better deal, a pack of twelve 355-mL cans of juice or two 2-L bottles of juice, if they both cost the same?

⑤ Annie had $0.75 in Jul. 2015, $1.39 in Aug. 2015, and $2.03 in Sep. 2015. How much did she have in Dec. 2015 if the pattern continued?

⑥ Melissa's table has a length of 2.2 m and a width of 1.2 m. She wants to customize it by extending either the length or the width by 80 cm. Which way will increase the area more and by how much?

⑦ Frank builds a rectangular prism using 8 cubes, each having a side length of 4 cm. What is the volume of the prism? What could the height of the prism be?

Topics covered:

Question 4	**Question 5**	**Question 6**	**Question 7**
• whole numbers	• decimals	• decimals	• volume
• capacity	• time	• area	• shapes
	• patterning		• solids

ISBN: 978-1-77149-203-4

⑧ At 10:19 a.m., Abby started walking 1 unit up and 1 unit to the left each time, and Ivy started walking 2 units up and 1 unit to the right each time. Both girls stopped at a park. Where was the park? Both girls covered a distance of 1 unit every minute. What time did they each stop at the park?

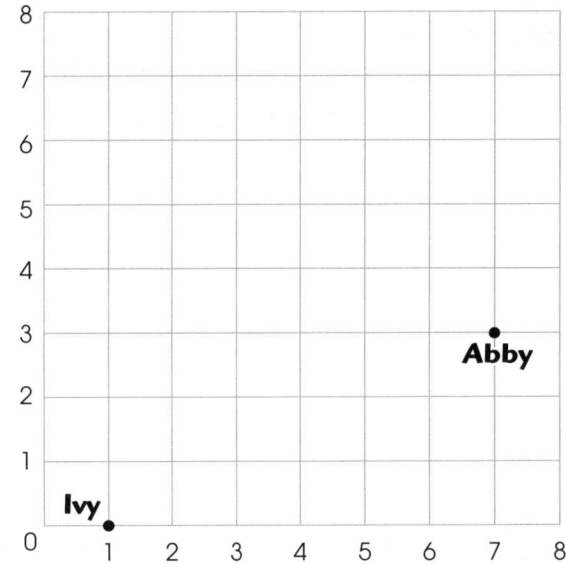

⑨ The diagram shows the dimensions of 3 brothers' rooms. Who has the biggest room? Whose room has the smallest perimeter?

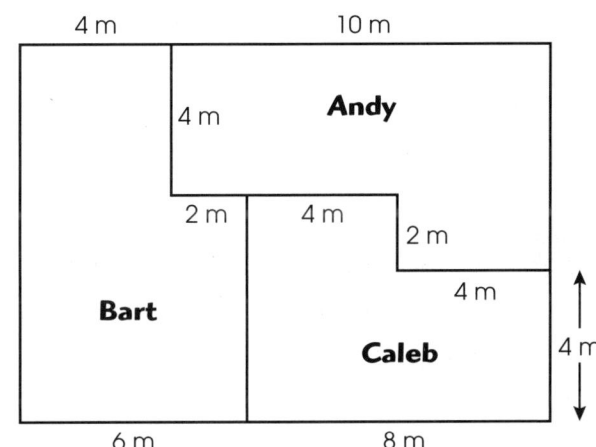

Topics covered:

Question 8	**Question 9**
• time	• perimeter
• Cartesian coordinate plane	• area
• patterning	

ISBN: 978-1-77149-203-4

⑩ Sandra weighs 5 strawberries. They have a median mass of 6.7 g and mode masses of 6.7 g and 9.3 g. If Sandra picks a strawberry at random, what is the probability that it weighs greater than 6.7 g?

⑪ Leo and his friends ordered 3 pizzas and they were cut into 8 equal slices. They ate $\frac{5}{8}$ of the pepperoni pizza, $\frac{3}{8}$ of the mushroom pizza, and $\frac{1}{2}$ of the cheese pizza. If Leo randomly took a leftover slice the next day, what was the probability that it was a slice of cheese pizza?

⑫ Alyssa has $2.10 in exactly 2 types of coins and there are 2 of each coin. If one of the coins is lost, what is the probability that the lost coin is a loonie?

Topics covered:

Question 10	**Question 11**	**Question 12**
• mass	• fractions	• money
• data management	• probability	• probability
• probability		

ISBN: 978-1-77149-203-4

⑬ Nadia plans to use tiles in the shape below to cover a wall that measures 2 m by 0.6 m. Measure the shape. How many tiles does Nadia need?

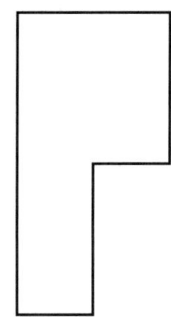

⑭ Natalie is saving for a present for her mom's birthday. Every 4 days, she saves 1 loonie and 1 nickel. If she has saved $17.80 on March 26, can she afford a $22 present by April 11?

⑮ Sheila recorded the temperatures over the last 5 days. What was the median temperature?

Temperatures Over the Last 5 Days

Day	Temperature
Mon	0°C
Tue	1°C below 0°C
Wed	3°C below 0°C
Thu	4°C
Fri	1°C

Topics covered:

Question 13
- whole numbers
- area

Question 14
- money
- time
- patterning

Question 15
- temperature
- data management

ISBN: 978-1-77149-203-4

16. For a science project, Eric showed the number of servings of each food group he had in a day in a bar graph. What fraction of Eric's food intake came from fruits and vegetables?

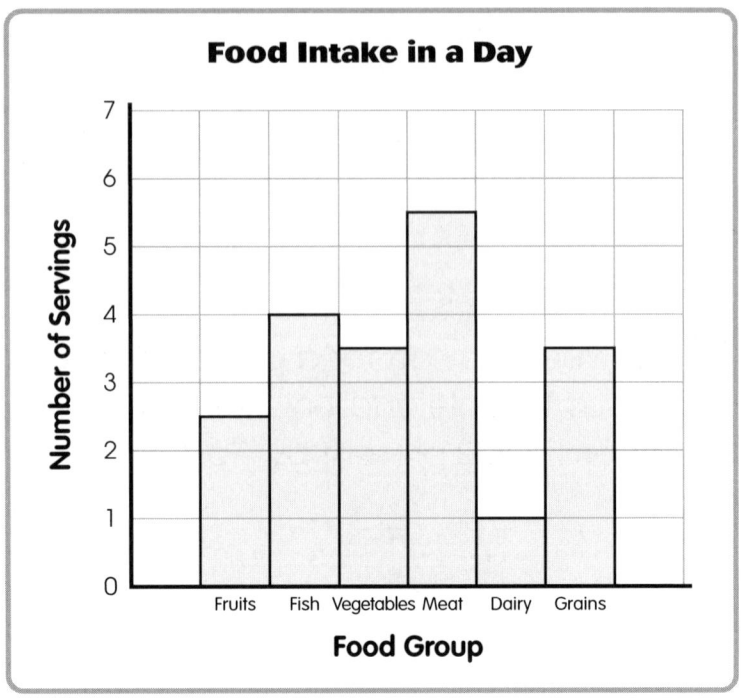

17. Refer to Question 16. Compare the recommended food intake shown in the circle graph with Eric's graph. How should Eric adjust his intake from fruits and vegetables?

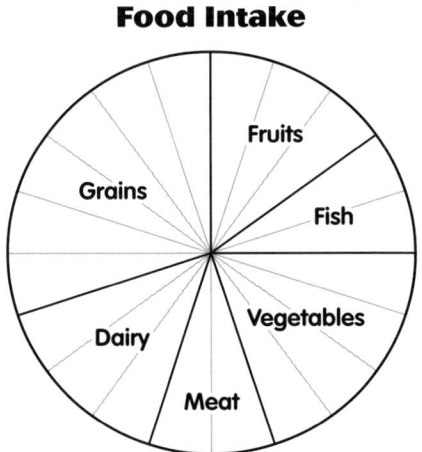

Recommended Daily Food Intake

Topics covered:

Question 16
- fractions
- data management

Question 17
- fractions
- data management

ISBN: 978-1-77149-203-4

⑱ David spins 2 spinners and draws a triangle according to the names spun, if possible. What is the probability that a triangle cannot be drawn with the outcomes?

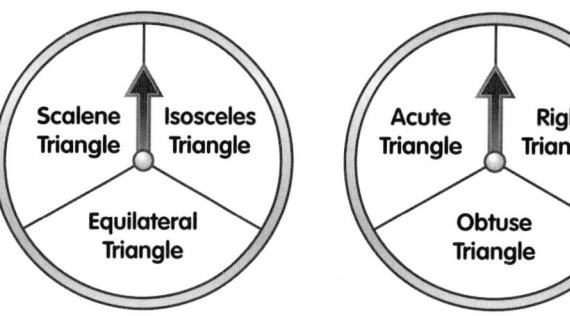

⑲ Dennis spends 1.5 hours every day on his computer. He promises his mom that for every 30 minutes on the computer, he will spend 12 minutes outdoors. How much time will he spend outdoors after a week?

⑳ Trisha drew the net of a solid by translating one shape on a grid 5 times. What is the shape? Name the solid the net makes.

Topics covered:

Question 18	**Question 19**	**Question 20**
• shapes	• decimals	• solids
• probability	• time	• transformations

ISBN: 978-1-77149-203-4

ISBN: 978-1-77149-203-4

■··Answers

1 Whole Numbers

Math Skills

1. 6344   a. 6108   b. 7750
c. 7076   d. 9457   e. 9805
2. 4914   a. 1754   b. 3099
c. 4465   d. 1369   e. 5846
3.
```
    26
  × 17
  ----
   182
   260
  ----
   442
```
a. 980   b. 817
c. 1752   d. 2886
e. 1400

4.
```
    156
  3)468
    3
    --
    16
    15
    --
    18
    18
```
a. 114   b. 140
c. 335R3   d. 859R1
e. 715R6

Problem Solving

1248 ; 1200 ; 1248 ; 1248

1. 46 × 28 = 1288
1288
```
    46
  × 28
  ----
   368
   920
  ----
  1288
```

2a. 23 × 36 = 828
828
```
    23
  × 36
  ----
   138
   690
  ----
   828
```

b. 45 × 16 = 720
```
    45
  × 16
  ----
   270
   450
  ----
   720
```
720 < 828
less

c. 15 × 15 = 225
```
    15
  × 15
  ----
    75
   150
  ----
   225
```
225

3. 344 ÷ 8 = 43
```
    43
  8)344
    32
    --
    24
    24
```
43

4. 455 ÷ 7 = 65
```
    65
  7)455
    42
    --
    35
    35
```
65

5. 1632 ÷ 8 = 204
204
```
     204
  8)1632
    16
    --
     32
     32
```

6a. 475 ÷ 9 = 52R7
```
    52R7
  9)475
    45
    --
    25
    18
    --
     7
```
7 beads will
be left over.

b. 475 ÷ 7 = 67R6
```
    67R6
  7)475
    42
    --
    55
    49
    --
     6
```
Yes, there will be
6 beads left over.

7a. 450 ÷ 8 = 56R2
The remaining 2 slices need
another pizza. The school
needs to order 57 pizzas.
```
    56R2
  8)450
    40
    --
    50
    48
    --
     2
```

b. 500 ÷ 9 = 55R5
The remaining $5 is not enough
for another pizza. 55 pizzas can
be ordered at most.
```
    55R5
  9)500
    45
    --
    50
    45
    --
     5
```

8. (1502 + 748) ÷ 9
= 2250 ÷ 9
= 250
There were 250 candies.
```
   1502       250
 +  748    9)2250
 ----      18
  2250     --
           45
           45
```

9. 12 × 25 – 126
= 300 – 126
= 174
174 cans of soup are left.
```
    12       300
  × 25     - 126
  ----     -----
    60       174
   240
  ----
   300
```

10. (5346 – 342) ÷ 4
= 5004 ÷ 4
= 1251
1251 toy cars can be
produced.
```
   5346      1251
 -  342    4)5004
 ----      4
  5004     --
           10
            8
           --
           20
           20
           --
            4
            4
```

11. (45 + 5) × 35
= 50 × 35
= 1750
Jimmy can type 1750 words.
```
    50
  × 35
  ----
   250
  1500
  ----
  1750
```

12a. 1248 + 368 × 6
= 1248 + 2208
= 3456
David has 3456 blocks.
```
   368      1248
 ×   6    + 2208
 ----     ------
  2208      3456
```

b. 3456 – 124 × 2
= 3456 – 248
= 3208
3208 blocks will remain.
```
   124      3456
 ×   2    -  248
 ----     ------
   248      3208
```

c. 3208 ÷ 4 = 802
Each child will get
802 blocks.
```
     802
  4)3208
    32
    --
     8
     8
```

13a. (2000 – 147) ÷ 8
= 1853 ÷ 8
= 231R5
There are 231 bundles
of newspapers.
```
   2000      231R5
 -  147    8)1853
 ----      16
  1853     --
           25
           24
           --
           13
            8
           --
            5
```

b. There are 5 newspapers
remaining.
8 – 5 = 3
3 more newspapers are needed.

ISBN: 978-1-77149-203-4

14a. $35 \times 24 \times 7$
$= 840 \times 7$
$= 5880$
Shuttle Bus A carries
5880 passengers.

$$\begin{array}{r} 35 \\ \times\ 24 \\ \hline 140 \\ 700 \\ \hline 840 \end{array} \qquad \begin{array}{r} 840 \\ \times\ 7 \\ \hline 5880 \end{array}$$

  b. Shuttle Bus B: $52 \times 18 \times 7 = 936 \times 7 = 6552$
Difference: $6552 - 5880 = 672$

$$\begin{array}{r} 52 \\ \times\ 18 \\ \hline 416 \\ 520 \\ \hline 936 \end{array} \qquad \begin{array}{r} 936 \\ \times\ 7 \\ \hline 6552 \end{array} \qquad \begin{array}{r} 6552 \\ -\ 5880 \\ \hline 672 \end{array}$$

Shuttle Bus B can carry 672 more passengers.

15. $2456 \div 50 = 49R6$
There are 49 plastic straws in a box.
$49 \times 27 = 1323$

$$\begin{array}{r} 49R6 \\ 50\overline{)2456} \\ 200 \\ \hline 456 \\ 450 \\ \hline 6 \end{array} \qquad \begin{array}{r} 49 \\ \times\ 27 \\ \hline 343 \\ 980 \\ \hline 1323 \end{array}$$

There are 1323 plastic straws.

16. $(2153 + 1207) \div 60 = 3360 \div 60 = 56$

$$\begin{array}{r} 2153 \\ +\ 1207 \\ \hline 3360 \end{array} \qquad \begin{array}{r} 56 \\ 60\overline{)3360} \\ 300 \\ \hline 360 \\ 360 \end{array}$$

It will take Mrs. Wynn 56 min.

17. $(490 \div 10) \times (6 \times 2)$
$= 49 \times 12$
$= 588$
Dan and his sister got 588 g
of coffee beans together.

$$\begin{array}{r} 49 \\ \times\ 12 \\ \hline 98 \\ 490 \\ \hline 588 \end{array}$$

2 Fractions

Math Skills

1a. $\dfrac{2}{5} < \dfrac{3}{5} < 1\dfrac{1}{5} < \dfrac{7}{5}$ b. $\dfrac{3}{7} < \dfrac{1}{2} < \dfrac{3}{4} < 1\dfrac{1}{2}$

  c. $\dfrac{4}{3} < 1\dfrac{3}{6} < 1\dfrac{2}{3} < \dfrac{11}{6}$

  d. $1\dfrac{5}{6} < \dfrac{10}{4} < \dfrac{16}{6} < \dfrac{11}{4}$

2a. 1 b. 1 c. $1\dfrac{1}{2}$ d. $1\dfrac{4}{5}$

  e. $1\dfrac{3}{7}$ f. 4 g. $3\dfrac{4}{5}$ h. $3\dfrac{2}{3}$

3a. $1\dfrac{1}{2}$ b. $\dfrac{1}{5}$ c. $\dfrac{3}{4}$ d. $1\dfrac{1}{6}$

  e. $\dfrac{2}{3}$ f. $1\dfrac{1}{2}$ g. 1 h. $1\dfrac{1}{2}$

Problem Solving

$$\dfrac{1}{3}\ ;\ \dfrac{7}{3}\ ;\ \dfrac{1}{3}\ ;\ \dfrac{1}{3}$$

1. $1\dfrac{1}{4} + \dfrac{7}{4} = 1\dfrac{1}{4} + 1\dfrac{3}{4} = 2\dfrac{4}{4} = 3\ ;\ 3$

2. Boys: $3\dfrac{3}{5} = \dfrac{18}{5}$ ← less than girls

$$\dfrac{20}{5} - \dfrac{18}{5} = \dfrac{2}{5}$$

girls ; $\dfrac{2}{5}$

3a. $\dfrac{16}{5} - 2\dfrac{4}{5} = \dfrac{16}{5} - \dfrac{14}{5} = \dfrac{2}{5}\ ;\ \dfrac{2}{5}$

  b. $2\dfrac{4}{5} + \dfrac{14}{5} = 2\dfrac{4}{5} + 2\dfrac{4}{5} = 4\dfrac{8}{5} = 5\dfrac{3}{5}\ ;\ 5\dfrac{3}{5}$

4. $2\dfrac{1}{4} + 1\dfrac{3}{4} = 3\dfrac{4}{4} = 4\ ;\ 4$

5a. $1\dfrac{3}{7} + \dfrac{9}{7} = 1\dfrac{3}{7} + 1\dfrac{2}{7} = 2\dfrac{5}{7}\ ;\ 2\dfrac{5}{7}$

  b. $2\dfrac{5}{7} + 1\dfrac{2}{7} = 3\dfrac{7}{7} = 4\ ;\ 4$

6. $3\dfrac{4}{5} + 2\dfrac{3}{5} = 5\dfrac{7}{5} = 6\dfrac{2}{5}$

Rosie drank $6\dfrac{2}{5}$ bottles of water.

7. $5 - 3\dfrac{1}{2} = 4\dfrac{2}{2} - 3\dfrac{1}{2} = 1\dfrac{1}{2}$

Aunt Vivian has $1\dfrac{1}{2}$ pies left.

8a. $6\dfrac{1}{12} - 4\dfrac{7}{12} = 5\dfrac{13}{12} - 4\dfrac{7}{12} = 1\dfrac{6}{12} = 1\dfrac{1}{2}$

The cat is $1\dfrac{1}{2}$ years older.

  b. $12 - 6\dfrac{1}{12} = 11\dfrac{12}{12} - 6\dfrac{1}{12} = 5\dfrac{11}{12}$

Amy is $5\dfrac{11}{12}$ years older.

9a. $\dfrac{1}{8} + \dfrac{5}{8} = \dfrac{6}{8} = \dfrac{3}{4}$

They weigh $\dfrac{3}{4}$ kg altogether.

  b. $9\dfrac{1}{8} + \dfrac{23}{8} = 9\dfrac{1}{8} + 2\dfrac{7}{8} = 11\dfrac{8}{8} = 12$

They weigh 12 kg altogether.

  c. $9\dfrac{1}{8} - \dfrac{5}{8} = 8\dfrac{9}{8} - \dfrac{5}{8} = 8\dfrac{4}{8} = 8\dfrac{1}{2}$

The watermelon is $8\dfrac{1}{2}$ kg heavier.

  d. $\dfrac{5}{8} - \dfrac{1}{8} = \dfrac{4}{8} = \dfrac{1}{2}$

The papaya is $\dfrac{1}{2}$ kg heavier.

  e. $\dfrac{23}{8} + \dfrac{1}{8} = \dfrac{24}{8} = 3$

The pineapple and the apple weigh exactly 3 kg altogether.

  f. $9\dfrac{1}{8} - 9 = \dfrac{1}{8}$

It is the apple.

ISBN: 978-1-77149-203-4

g. $\frac{23}{8} + 9\frac{1}{8} + \frac{1}{8} + \frac{5}{8} = 9\frac{30}{8} = 12\frac{6}{8} = 12\frac{3}{4}$

The total weight of all 4 fruits is $12\frac{3}{4}$ kg.

10. $10 - 4\frac{1}{6} - 3\frac{5}{6} = 9\frac{6}{6} - 4\frac{1}{6} - 3\frac{5}{6} = 2$

2 boxes are in storage.

11. $6\frac{4}{5} + 3\frac{3}{5} - 2\frac{2}{5} = 7\frac{5}{5} = 8$

8 cups of fried rice were served.

12a.

15 baseball cards are for sale.

b. $20 - 5 = 15$

$\frac{15}{20} = \frac{3}{4}$

$\frac{3}{4}$ of the collection remains.

13.

Scott has 18 crayons.

14a. $6\frac{7}{12} - 2\frac{5}{12} = 4\frac{2}{12} = 4\frac{1}{6}$

$4\frac{1}{6}$ cartons will be left.

b. $2\frac{5}{12} + 2\frac{5}{12} + 2\frac{5}{12} = 6\frac{15}{12} = 7\frac{1}{4}$

$7\frac{1}{4}$ cartons are needed.

c. $7\frac{1}{4} - 6\frac{7}{12} = 6\frac{15}{12} - 6\frac{7}{12} = \frac{8}{12} = \frac{2}{3}$

$\frac{2}{3}$ more of a carton is needed.

15a. $1\frac{2}{5} + \frac{9}{5} + \frac{8}{5} = 1\frac{2}{5} + 1\frac{4}{5} + 1\frac{3}{5} = 3\frac{9}{5} = 4\frac{4}{5}$

The total weight is $4\frac{4}{5}$ kg.

b. $10 - 4\frac{4}{5} = 9\frac{5}{5} - 4\frac{4}{5} = 5\frac{1}{5}$

The shelf can hold $5\frac{1}{5}$ more kilograms.

3 Decimals

Math Skills

1. 5.20 ; 9.86 a. 9.09   b. 17.86
   c. 9.19   d. 12.16   e. 23.16
2. 2.47 ; 5.27 a. 4.66   b. 3.23
   c. 7.45   d. 9.39   e. 11.71
3. 29.76 ; 23.67
   a. 65.6   b. 0.8   c. 25.36
   d. 141.2   e. 570

4.
$\begin{array}{r} 5.4 \\ 3\overline{)16.2} \\ 15 \\ \hline 12 \\ 12 \\ \hline \end{array}$ $\begin{array}{r} 0.55 \\ 4\overline{)2.2} \\ 20 \\ \hline 20 \\ 20 \\ \hline \end{array}$

a. 2.52   b. 0.9   c. 3.1
d. 2.5   e. 1.24

Problem Solving

10.54 ; 10 ; 54 ; 10.54

1. 3.79 − 1.28 = 2.51
   2.51

   $\begin{array}{r} 3.79 \\ -\ 1.28 \\ \hline 2.51 \end{array}$

2a. 2.14 + 1.96 = 4.1
    4.1

   $\begin{array}{r} 2.14 \\ +\ 1.96 \\ \hline 4.10 \end{array}$

b. 4.1 − 1.08 = 3.02
   3.02

   $\begin{array}{r} 4.10 \\ -\ 1.08 \\ \hline 3.02 \end{array}$

3. 2.49 + 3.16 = 5.65
   5.65

   $\begin{array}{r} 2.49 \\ +\ 3.16 \\ \hline 5.65 \end{array}$

4a. 0.78 + 1.05 + 1.2 = 3.03
    3.03

   $\begin{array}{r} 0.78 \\ 1.05 \\ +\ 1.20 \\ \hline 3.03 \end{array}$

b. 10 − 2.7 − 3.03 = 4.27
   4.27

   $\begin{array}{r} 10.00 \\ -\ 2.70 \\ \hline 7.30 \\ -\ 3.03 \\ \hline 4.27 \end{array}$

5. 1.33 − 0.24 − 0.24 − 0.24 = 0.61
   0.61

   $\begin{array}{r} 1.33 \\ -\ 0.24 \\ \hline 1.09 \\ -\ 0.24 \\ \hline 0.85 \\ -\ 0.24 \\ \hline 0.61 \end{array}$

6. 5.65 × 3 = 16.95
   Shawn has 16.95 m of
   ribbon in total.

   $\begin{array}{r} 5.65 \\ \times\ \ \ 3 \\ \hline 16.95 \end{array}$

7. 3.24 ÷ 9 = 0.36
   The average weight is 0.36 kg.

   $\begin{array}{r} 0.36 \\ 9\overline{)3.24} \\ 27 \\ \hline 54 \\ 54 \\ \hline \end{array}$

8. 7.36 ÷ 20 = 0.368
   Each customer was served
   0.368 L of soup.

   $\begin{array}{r} 0.368 \\ 20\overline{)7.360} \\ 60 \\ \hline 136 \\ 120 \\ \hline 160 \\ 160 \\ \hline \end{array}$

9. 1.78 × 5 = 8.9
   The total length of
   the tables is 8.9 m.

   $\begin{array}{r} 1.78 \\ \times\ \ \ 5 \\ \hline 8.90 \end{array}$

10a. 4 ÷ 8 = 0.5
     Each guest will get
     0.5 L of ice cream.

   $\begin{array}{r} 0.5 \\ 8\overline{)4.0} \\ 4.0 \\ \hline \end{array}$

b. 4 ÷ 10 = 0.4
   Each guest will get
   0.4 L of ice cream instead.

   $\begin{array}{r} 0.4 \\ 10\overline{)4.0} \\ 4.0 \\ \hline \end{array}$

ISBN: 978-1-77149-203-4

11. 3.08 × 6 = 18.48
The total weight of
6 robots is 18.48 kg.

$$\begin{array}{r} 3.08 \\ \times\ \ \ \ 6 \\ \hline 18.48 \end{array}$$

12. 0.8 × 7 = 5.6
Yes, Anita will reach
her goal.

$$\begin{array}{r} 0.8 \\ \times\ \ \ \ 7 \\ \hline 5.6 \end{array}$$

13. (60 − 24.16) × 9
= 35.84 × 9
= 322.56
Ms. Lee can drive 322.56 km farther.

$$\begin{array}{r} 60.00 \\ -\ 24.16 \\ \hline 35.84 \end{array} \quad \begin{array}{r} 35.84 \\ \times\ \ \ \ 9 \\ \hline 322.56 \end{array}$$

14. 362 ÷ 100 × 60 = 3.62 × 60 = 217.2
The weight is 217.2 g.

15. 0.453 ÷ 100 × 2000 = 0.00453 × 2000 = 9.06
Penelope needs 9.06 kg of tea leaves.

16a. 1.21 × 2 × 4
= 2.42 × 4
= 9.68
Gordon bikes 9.68 km in 4 days.

$$\begin{array}{r} 1.21 \\ \times\ \ \ \ 2 \\ \hline 2.42 \end{array} \quad \begin{array}{r} 2.42 \\ \times\ \ \ \ 4 \\ \hline 9.68 \end{array}$$

b. 9.68 + 1.21 + 2.45 = 13.34
Gordon biked 13.34 km
that week.

$$\begin{array}{r} 9.68 \\ 1.21 \\ +\ 2.45 \\ \hline 13.34 \end{array}$$

17a. Felix's total time: 15.24 × 5 = 76.2
Difference: 78.8 − 76.2 = 2.6

$$\begin{array}{r} 15.24 \\ \times\ \ \ \ 5 \\ \hline 76.20 \end{array} \quad \begin{array}{r} 78.8 \\ -\ 76.2 \\ \hline 2.6 \end{array}$$

The difference was 2.6 s.

b. 76.2 − (14.57 × 5) = 76.2 − 72.85 = 3.35

$$\begin{array}{r} 14.57 \\ \times\ \ \ \ 5 \\ \hline 72.85 \end{array} \quad \begin{array}{r} 76.20 \\ -\ 72.85 \\ \hline 3.35 \end{array}$$

Felix would have completed 3.35 s sooner.

c. Average time:
78.8 ÷ 5 = 15.76
Difference:
15.76 − 13.09 = 2.67
The difference was
2.67 s.

$$\begin{array}{r} 15.76 \\ 5\overline{)78.80} \\ \underline{5} \\ 28 \\ \underline{25} \\ 38 \\ \underline{35} \\ 30 \\ \underline{30} \end{array} \quad \begin{array}{r} 15.76 \\ -\ 13.09 \\ \hline 2.67 \end{array}$$

18a. 16.5 × 6 = 99
Shawn swam 99 laps.

$$\begin{array}{r} 16.5 \\ \times\ \ \ \ 6 \\ \hline 99.0 \end{array}$$

b. 7th day:
16.5 + 3.5 = 20
Average:
(99 + 20) ÷ 7
= 119 ÷ 7
= 17
The new average is 17 laps each day.

$$\begin{array}{r} 16.5 \\ +\ 3.5 \\ \hline 20.0 \end{array} \quad \begin{array}{r} 17 \\ 7\overline{)119} \\ \underline{7} \\ 49 \\ \underline{49} \end{array}$$

4   Money

Math Skills

1a. 196.20   b. 415.65   c. 401.45
d. 149.50   e. 370.95

2a. $2.45   b. $1

3a. $33.60

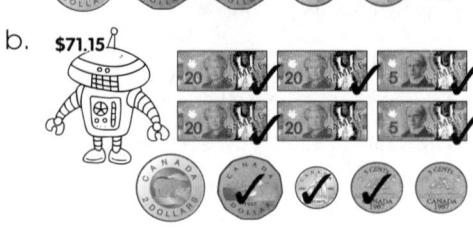

b. $71.15

Problem Solving

9.65 ; 9.65 ; 9.65

1. Money: $70
Amount needed:
$80.95 − $70 = $10.95
10.95

$$\begin{array}{r} 80.95 \\ -\ 70.00 \\ \hline 10.95 \end{array}$$

2a. Amount paid: $250
Change:
   $250 − $159.95 − $78.45
= $11.60
11.60

$$\begin{array}{r} 250.00 \\ -\ 159.95 \\ \hline 90.05 \\ -\ 78.45 \\ \hline 11.60 \end{array}$$

b. Total cost: $159.95 + $107.80 = $267.75
Amount needed: $267.75 − $250 = $17.75

$$\begin{array}{r} 159.95 \\ +\ 107.80 \\ \hline 267.75 \end{array} \quad \begin{array}{r} 267.75 \\ -\ 250.00 \\ \hline 17.75 \end{array}$$

17.75

c. 2 pairs of headphones:
$78.45 × 2 = $156.90
He will use 4 $50 bills for $200.
Change: $200 − $156.90 = $43.10

$$\begin{array}{r} 78.45 \\ \times\ \ \ \ 2 \\ \hline 156.90 \end{array} \quad \begin{array}{r} 200.00 \\ -\ 156.90 \\ \hline 43.10 \end{array}$$

4 ; 43.10

3. Amount paid: $319
Cost: $319 − $1.65 = $317.35

$$\begin{array}{r} 319.00 \\ -\ \ \ \ 1.65 \\ \hline 317.35 \end{array}$$

317.35

4a. $79.95 + $60.85 + $145.50 = $286.30
286.30

$$\begin{array}{r} 79.95 \\ 60.85 \\ +\ 145.50 \\ \hline 286.30 \end{array}$$

b. Amount paid: $300
Change: $300 − $286.30 = $13.70
13.70

$$\begin{array}{r} 300.00 \\ -\ 286.30 \\ \hline 13.70 \end{array}$$

ISBN: 978-1-77149-203-4

5a. Cost: $5.95 × 3 + $4.80 × 4
   = $17.85 + $19.20
   = $37.05
   Amount paid: $40
   Change: $40 – $37.05 = $2.95

5.95	4.80	17.85	40.00
× 3	× 4	+ 19.20	– 37.05
17.85	19.20	37.05	2.95

   Hugh's change is $2.95.

b. Cost: $5.95 × 2 + $4.80 × 3
   = $11.90 + $14.40
   = $26.30
   Amount paid: $25
   Amount needed: $26.30 – $25 = $1.30

5.95	4.80	11.90	26.30
× 2	× 3	+ 14.40	– 25.00
11.90	14.40	26.30	1.30

   No, 5 $5 bills will not be enough. He needs $1.30 more.

6a. Cost for 1 person:
   $202.60 ÷ 5 = $40.52
   Amount paid: $40

   ```
        40.52
   5)202.60
        20
        26
        25
        10
        10
   ```

   Amount needed: $40.52 – $40 = $0.52
   Conrad needs $0.52 more.

b. $50 – $40.52 = $9.48
   His change will be $9.48.

   ```
     50.00
   – 40.52
      9.48
   ```

7a. Cost of all 3 items:
   $4.95 + $7.50 + $2.75 – $2 = $13.20
   Amount paid: $15
   Change: $15 – $13.20 = $1.80

4.95	15.20	15.00
7.50	– 2.00	– 13.20
+ 2.75	13.20	1.80
15.20		

   Yes, 3 $5 bills would be enough. Her change would be $1.80.

b. Total cost: $7.50 + $2.75 = $10.25
   Change: $9.75
   Amount paid: $10.25 + $9.75 = $20

7.50	10.25
+ 2.75	+ 9.75
10.25	20.00

   Ellen paid $20.

8a. Cost for 1 person:
   $150.70 ÷ 2 = $75.35
   Amount saved: $55.25
   Amount needed:
   $75.35 – $55.25 = $20.10
   Leo needs to save $20.10 more.

   ```
        75.35       75.35
   2)150.70       – 55.25
        14           20.10
        10
        10
         7
         6
        10
        10
   ```

b. Amount saved: $78
   Amount left:
   $78 – $75.35 = $2.65
   Lenna will have $2.65 left.

   ```
     78.00
   – 75.35
      2.65
   ```

9a. Parking Lot A:
   $9.75 + $0.50 × 7 = $9.75 + $3.50 = $13.25
   Parking Lot B:
   $1.75 × 8 = $14
   Difference: $14 – $13.25 = $0.75

0.50	9.75	1.75	14.00
× 7	+ 3.50	× 8	– 13.25
3.50	13.25	14.00	0.75

   Parking Lot A has a better deal.
   The difference in cost is $0.75.

b. Amount paid: $14
   Change: $14 – $13.25 = $0.75
   Ms. Jones's change is $0.75.

   ```
     14.00
   – 13.25
      0.75
   ```

10a. The 6th shirt is free.
   Cost of 6 T-shirts:
   $23.40 × 5 = $117
   Cost of 1 T-shirt:
   $117 ÷ 6 = $19.50
   Each T-shirt will cost $19.50.

   ```
     23.40        19.5
   ×     5     6)117.0
   117.00         6
                 57
                 54
                 30
                 30
   ```

b. The 3rd T-shirt is free.
   Cost of 3 sweaters and 3 T-shirts:
   $36.10 × 3 + $23.40 × 2
   = $108.30 + $46.80
   = $155.10

36.10	23.40	108.30
× 3	× 2	+ 46.80
108.30	46.80	155.10

   Cost of each item:
   $155.10 ÷ 6 = $25.85
   Each item will cost $25.85 on average.

   ```
        25.85
   6)155.10
        12
        35
        30
        51
        48
        30
        30
   ```

c. Change: $44.90
   Amount paid:
   $44.90 + $155.10 = $200
   Sara paid $200.

   ```
      44.90
   + 155.10
     200.00
   ```

11a. Cost of 3 CDs and 2 DVDs:
   $19.99 × 3 + $25.99 × 2
   = $59.97 + $51.98
   = $111.95

19.99	25.99	59.97
× 3	× 2	+ 51.98
59.97	51.98	111.95

   Amount paid: $115
   Amount left:
   $115 – $111.95 = $3.05
   Jackson will have $3.05 left.

   ```
     115.00
   – 111.95
       3.05
   ```

b. Cost of 6 DVDs: $25.99 × 6 = $155.94
   Difference: $155.94 – $115 = $40.94

25.99	155.94
× 6	– 115.00
155.94	40.94

   Jackson needs $40.94 more for 6 DVDs.

ISBN: 978-1-77149-203-4

12a. $34.76 – $2 = $32.76
   A pair of shoes will be $32.76.
 b. There are 6 "25" in 168.26 and 7 "25" in 175.29.
   Boots: $168.26 – $2 × 6
      = $168.26 – $12
      = $156.26

$$\begin{array}{r} 168.26 \\ -\ \ 12.00 \\ \hline 156.26 \end{array}$$

   Heels: $175.29 – $2 × 7
      = $175.29 – $14
      = $161.29

$$\begin{array}{r} 175.29 \\ -\ \ 14.00 \\ \hline 161.29 \end{array}$$

   A pair of boots will be cheaper.
 c. Cost of 2 pairs of running shoes:
   $27.23 × 2 = $54.46
   There are 2 "25" in 54.46.
   Cost with discount: $54.46 – $2 × 2 = $50.46
   Money: $50
   Amount needed: $50.46 – $50 = $0.46

$$\begin{array}{r} 27.23 \\ \times\ \ \ \ \ 2 \\ \hline 54.46 \end{array} \qquad \begin{array}{r} 50.46 \\ -\ 50.00 \\ \hline 0.46 \end{array}$$

   No, 10 $5 will not be enough. $0.46 more
   is needed.

5 Time and Temperature

Math Skills

1a. 10:35:20 ; 11:40:50 ; 1 h 5 min 30 s
 b. 5:55:05 ; 7:10:45 ; 1 h 15 min 40 s
 c. 1 h 7 min 15 s   d. 1 h 43 min 35 s
 e. 3 h 22 min 55 s   f. 2 h 24 min 10 s
 g. 6 h 46 min 3 s
2a. 16 ; 13°C ; dropped ; 3
 b. 12°C ; 21°C ; rose by 9°C
 c. 36°C ; 29°C ; dropped by 7°C

Problem Solving

   2 h 55 min 30 s
1.
$$\begin{array}{r} {}^{14}\ \ {}^{70} \\ \cancel{15}{:}\cancel{10}{:}26 \\ -\ \ 7{:}45{:}15 \\ \hline 7{:}25{:}11 \end{array}$$
   7 h 25 min 11 s

2.
$$\begin{array}{r} 2{:}42{:}10 \\ +\ 4{:}37{:}00 \\ \hline \cancel{6}{:}\cancel{79}{:}10 \\ {}^{7}\ \ {}^{19} \end{array}$$
   7:19:10 p.m.

3.
$$\begin{array}{r} 8{:}56{:}31 \\ -\ 3{:}28{:}10 \\ \hline 5{:}28{:}21 \end{array}$$
   5:28:21 p.m.

4. From 1st coat to midnight:
$$\begin{array}{r} {}^{23}\ \ {}^{59}\ \ {}^{60} \\ \cancel{24}{:}\cancel{00}{:}\cancel{00} \\ -\ 14{:}48{:}51 \\ \hline 9{:}11{:}09 \end{array}$$

   From 1st coat to 2nd coat:
$$\begin{array}{r} 9{:}11{:}09 \\ +\ 10{:}31{:}05 \\ \hline 19{:}42{:}14 \end{array}$$

   19 h 42 min 14 s

5. Time needed:
   1 h 24 min 8 s + 1 h 24 min 8 s
   = 2 h 48 min 16 s
   10:28:04 a.m.
$$\begin{array}{r} {}^{12}\ \ {}^{76} \\ \cancel{13}{:}\cancel{16}{:}20 \\ -\ \ 2{:}48{:}16 \\ \hline 10{:}28{:}04 \end{array}$$

6a. Movie A: Movie B:
   9:21:59 p.m.   9:26:39 p.m.
$$\begin{array}{r} 7{:}46{:}12 \\ +\ \ 1{:}35{:}47 \\ \hline \cancel{8}{:}\cancel{81}{:}59 \\ {}^{9}\ \ {}^{21} \end{array} \qquad \begin{array}{r} 7{:}21{:}02 \\ +\ \ 2{:}05{:}37 \\ \hline 9{:}26{:}39 \end{array}$$
   A
 b.
$$\begin{array}{r} {}^{25}\ \ {}^{99} \\ 9{:}\cancel{26}{:}\cancel{39} \\ -\ 9{:}21{:}59 \\ \hline 0{:}04{:}40 \end{array}$$
   4 min 40 s
7a. Morning temperature: 9°C
   Current temperature: 9 + 7 = 16
   The current temperature is 16°C.
 b. Indoor temperature: 24°C
   Difference: 24 – 16 = 8
   It is 8°C warmer indoors than outdoors.
8a. From 12°C below 0°C to 0°C: 12°C
   Temperature above 0°C: 16 – 12 = 4
   The temperature of the turkey is 4°C.
 b.
$$\begin{array}{r} 74 \quad \leftarrow \text{from 74°C to 0°C} \\ +\ \ 12 \quad \leftarrow \text{from 0°C to 12°C below 0°C} \\ \hline 86 \end{array}$$
   The turkey is 86°C hotter.
9.
$$\begin{array}{r} 52 \quad \leftarrow \text{from 52°C to 0°C} \\ +\ \ \ 4 \quad \leftarrow \text{from 0°C to 4°C below 0°C} \\ \hline 56 \end{array}$$
   The microwave dinner was 56°C hotter
   after cooking.
10. Afternoon:
   2°C below 0°C increased to 0°C: 2°C
   Temperature above 0°C: 5 – 2 = 3
   Night:
   3°C dropped to 0°C: 3°C
   Temperature below 0°C: 10 – 3 = 7
   The temperature at night was 7°C below 0°C.
11a.
$$\begin{array}{r} 9{:}03{:}15 \\ +\ \ \ \ 4{:}32 \\ \hline 9{:}07{:}47 \end{array}$$
   It was 9:07:47 a.m.
 b.
$$\begin{array}{r} 13 \quad \leftarrow \text{from 13°C below 0°C to 0°C} \\ +\ \ \ 3 \quad \leftarrow \text{from 0°C to 3°C} \\ \hline 16 \end{array}$$
   The temperature had risen by 16°C.
12. Game time:
$$\begin{array}{r} {}^{104} \\ {}^{5}\ \ {}^{44}\ \ {}^{69} \\ \cancel{6}{:}\cancel{45}{:}\cancel{09} \\ -\ \ 4{:}57{:}22 \\ \hline 1{:}47{:}47 \end{array}$$
   Extra time:
$$\begin{array}{r} {}^{0}\ \ {}^{107} \\ \cancel{1}{:}\cancel{47}{:}47 \\ -\ \ \ 90{:}00 \\ \hline 17{:}47 \end{array} \qquad \begin{array}{r} 17{:}47 \\ -\ 15{:}00 \\ \hline 2{:}47 \end{array}$$
   The soccer game had 2 min 47 s of extra time.
13.
$$\begin{array}{r} {}^{44}\ \ {}^{81} \\ 15{:}\cancel{45}{:}\cancel{21} \\ -\ 11{:}34{:}24 \\ \hline 4{:}10{:}57 \end{array}$$
   It took 4 h 10 min 57 s
   to receive the reply.
14.
$$\begin{array}{r} {}^{16}\ \ {}^{63} \\ \text{Sep. 29} \quad \cancel{17}{:}\cancel{03}{:}17 \\ -\ \text{Sep. 24} \quad 11{:}47{:}03 \\ \hline \text{5 days} \quad 5{:}16{:}14 \end{array}$$
   The voyage was
   5 days 5 h 16 min
   14 s long.
15a.
$$\begin{array}{r} 23{:}45 \\ -\ 10{:}00 \\ \hline 13{:}45 \end{array}$$
   The pool is open for 13 h 45 min
   on Fridays.

ISBN: 978-1-77149-203-4

b. Saturdays: 13 h 45 min

Tuesdays: $\begin{array}{r} 21{:}30 \\ -\ 8{:}00 \\ \hline 13{:}30 \end{array}$ Difference: $\begin{array}{r} 13{:}45 \\ -\ 13{:}30 \\ \hline 0{:}15 \end{array}$

The pool is open for 15 min longer.

16a. $\begin{array}{r} \text{Jun. 15} \quad 22{:}36 \\ +\ \qquad\quad 5{:}19 \\ \hline \text{Jun. \cancel{15}}\ \ \cancel{27}{:}55 \\ {}_{16}\qquad {}_{3} \end{array}$ The flight will arrive on June 16 at 3:55 a.m.

b. $\begin{array}{r} 3{:}55 \\ -\ 3{:}00 \\ \hline 0{:}55 \end{array}$ The flight will arrive at 12:55 a.m.

c. $\begin{array}{r} 0{:}\ 55 \\ +\ 1{:}\ 57 \\ \hline \cancel{1}{:}\cancel{112} \\ {}_{2}\qquad {}_{52} \end{array}$ The flight will arrive at 2:52 a.m.

17a. Temperature change: 30 – 22 = 8
No. of 16-min periods: 8 ÷ 2 = 4
Elapsed time: 16 × 4 = 64
64 min = 1 h 4 min
A room will cool to
22°C at 6:57 p.m.

$\begin{array}{r} 5{:}53 \\ +\ 1{:}04 \\ \hline 6{:}57 \end{array}$

b. $\begin{array}{r} {}_{10}\ {}_{79} \\ \cancel{11}{:}\cancel{19} \\ -\ 9{:}43 \\ \hline 1{:}36 \end{array}$

1 h 36 min = 96 min
No. of 16-min periods: 96 ÷ 16 = 6
Temperature change: 2 × 6 = 12
The room will be 12°C cooler.

6 Perimeter and Area

Math Skills

1. A: 17 ; 9   B: 18 cm ; 13 cm²
   C: 17 cm ; 11 cm²   D: 15 cm ; 9.5 cm²
   E: 15 m ; 8 cm²
2. 5 × 4 ; 20 ; 5 × 5 ; 25
3. (3 + 5) × 2 ; 16 (m) ; 3 × 5 ; 15 (m²)
4. 8 × 4 ; 32 (mm) ; 8 × 8 ; 64 (mm²)

Problem Solving

60 ; 60
1. (80 + 60) × 2 = 140 × 2 = 280 ; 280
2. (0.8 + 1.2) × 2 = 2 × 2 = 4 ; 4
3a. 23 × 4 = 92 ; 92
 b. Side length: 23 + 1.5 = 24.5
   Perimeter: 24.5 × 4 = 98
   98
4a. Shape A: 5.5 + 10.5 + 6 + 6 + 4.2 = 32.2
   Shape B: 5 + 5 + 5.5 + 11.4 = 26.9
   B
 b. 32.2 + 26.9 = 59.1 ; 59.1
5. Shape A: 1 + 3 + 5 + 5 = 14
   Shape B: 5 + 3 + 3 = 11
   Shape C: 3 + 1.4 + 2.8 + 5 = 12.2
   Shape D: 3 + 3 + 3 + 1.4 = 10.4
   Shape E: 3 + 2 + 5 + 2.8 = 12.8
   A

6. 72 × 72 = 5184
   The area of the table is 5184 cm².
7. 200 ÷ 16 = 12.5
   The width of the board is 12.5 cm.
8a. 15 × 8 = 120
   The area of the tile is 120 cm².
 b. Area of panel: 290 × 85 = 24 650
   Area of 200 tiles: 120 × 200 = 24 000
   No, 200 tiles will not be enough.
9a. Length of photo: 24 – 2 – 2 = 20
   Width of photo: 16 – 2 – 2 = 12
   Area of photo: 20 × 12 = 240
   The area of the photo is 240 cm².
 b. Area of frame and photo: 24 × 16 = 384
   Area of frame: 384 – 240 = 144
   The area of the frame alone is 144 cm².
10a. 3 × 2.6 = 7.8
   The area of the parking space is 7.8 m².
 b. 7.8 m² = 78 000 cm²
   The area of the parking space is 78 000 cm².
11a. 0.24 km = 240 m
   4000 cm = 40 m
   240 × 40 = 9600
   The area is 9600 m².
 b. 4000 cm = 40 m = 0.04 km
   (0.24 + 0.04) × 2 = 0.28 × 2 = 0.56
   The perimeter is 0.56 km.
12a. Perimeter: (32 + 16) × 2 = 48 × 2 = 96
   Area: 32 × 16 = 512
   The piece of string is 96 cm long. The area of the rectangle is 512 cm².
 b. Side length: 96 ÷ 4 = 24
   Area: 24 × 24 = 576
   The area of the square will be 576 cm².
13. Length: 16 + 8 = 24
   Perimeter: (24 + 16) × 2 = 40 × 2 = 80
   Area: 24 × 16 = 384
   The perimeter is 80 cm and the area is 384 cm².
14. Area of door: 200 × 50 = 10 000
   Area of window: 30 × 30 = 900
   Area of door with window:
   10 000 – 900 = 9100
   The area of the door is 9100 cm² after the cut-out.
15a. James's bedroom: 7 × 8.5 = 59.5
   Janet's bedroom: 8 × 8 = 64
   Jinny's bedroom: 7.6 × 8 = 60.8
   The area of the biggest room is 64 m².
 b. 64 + 60.8 = 124.8
   The total area is 124.8 m².

ISBN: 978-1-77149-203-4

16a. Area of Painting A: $16 \times 15 = 240$
Width of Painting B: $15 - 3 = 12$
Length of Painting B: $240 \div 12 = 20$
The length of Painting B is 20 cm.

b. Perimeter of Painting A:
$(16 + 15) \times 2 = 31 \times 2 = 62$
Perimeter of Painting B:
$(20 + 12) \times 2 = 32 \times 2 = 64$
Painting B has a greater perimeter.

7 Volume, Capacity, and Mass

Math Skills

1. A: $18 \times 7 \times 25$; 3150
   B: $15 \times 15 \times 40$; 9000 (cm³)
   C: $10 \times 10 \times 10$; 1000 (mm³)
   D: $2 \times 1.5 \times 0.3$; 0.9 (m³)
   E: $56 \times 50 \times 50$; 140 000
   F: $19 \times 14 \times 28$; 7448 (mL)
   G: $60 \times 30 \times 40$; 72 000 (mL)
   H: $12 \times 12 \times 60$; 8640 (mL)
   I: 4.905 ; 4 905 000
   J: 3650 ; 3 650 000
   K: 2.37 ; 2 370 000
   L: 0.375 ; 375 000

Problem Solving

384 ; 384
1. $5 \times 3 \times 12 = 180$; 180
2. 0.54 m = 54 cm   0.42 m = 42 cm
   $54 \times 30 \times 42 = 68\ 040$; 68 040
3. $12 \times 12 \times 7.5 = 1080$; 1080
4. Height: $10 \times 2 = 20$
   Length: $2000 \div 10 \div 20 = 10$
   10
5. $35 \times 28 \times 45 = 44\ 100$
   44 100 cm³ = 44 100 mL
   44 100
6. $13 \times 13 \times 20 = 3380$
   3380 cm³ = 3380 mL
   3380
7. $600 \times 240 \times 280 = 40\ 320\ 000$
   40 320 000 cm³ = 40 320 L
   40 320
8. $9 \times 9 \times 9 = 729$
   729 cm³ = 0.729 L
   No, the glass cube cannot hold 1 L of water.
9. $152 \times 75 \times 18 = 205\ 200$
   205 200 cm³ = 205.2 L
   The capacity of the sandbox is 205.2 L.
10a. 78 L = 78 000 cm³
   Height: $78\ 000 \div 65 \div 48 = 25$
   The height of the cooler is 25 cm.

b. $65 \times 48 \times 16 = 49\ 920$
   49 920 cm³ = 49.92 L
   There is 49.92 L of water in the cooler.
11a. 62 000 g = 62 kg   0.006 t = 6 kg
   6 kg < 56 kg < 62 kg
   The mailman should put Parcel A at the bottom, Parcel B in the middle, and Parcel C at the top.

b. $62 + 56 + 6 = 124$
   Yes, the trolley can be used.
12a. Length: $25 \div 4 = 6.25$
   Width: $12 \div 2 = 6$
   Height: 8 cm
   The dimensions of each piece are 6.25 cm by 6 cm by 8 cm.

b. $1.648 \div 8 = 0.206$
   The mass of each piece is 0.206 kg.
13a. $3.5 \times 2 \times 0.9 = 6.3$
   The capacity is 6.3 m³.

b. $3.5 \times 2 \times 0.6 = 4.2$
   4.2 m³ = 4 200 000 cm³ = 4 200 000 mL
   There is 4 200 000 mL of water.

c. 20 cm = 0.2 m
   $3.5 \times 2 \times 0.2 = 1.4$
   The volume of Alex is 1.4 m³.
14a. Volume of a box: $12 \times 12 \times 12 = 1728$
   Volume of the bin: $1728 \times 6 = 10\ 368$
   The volume of the bin is 10 368 cm³.

b. $5.65 \times 6 = 33.9$
   The mass of the bin is 33.9 kg.
15a. 7.2 L = 7200 cm³
   Length: $7200 \div 16 \div 15 = 30$
   The length of the aquarium is 30 cm.

b. New volume: $30 \times 15 \times 18 = 8100$
   Volume of 5 decorations: $8100 - 7200 = 900$
   Volume of 1 decoration: $900 \div 5 = 180$
   The volume of one decoration is 180 cm³.

c. Volume of aquarium: 9 L = 9000 cm³
   Remaining volume: $9000 - 8100 = 900$
   No. of decorations: $900 \div 180 = 5$
   The aquarium can hold 5 more decorations.
16a. 72 000 L = 72 m³
   Height: $72 \div 12 = 6$
   The tank is 6 m tall.

b. Decrease in water level: $72 \div 6 \div 6 = 2$
   The water level will decrease by 2 m.

8 Shapes and Solids

Math Skills

1. A: parallelogram   B: pentagon
   C: triangle   D: trapezoid
   E: hexagon

ISBN: 978-1-77149-203-4

2. A: equilateral triangle ; acute triangle
   B: isosceles triangle ; right triangle
   C: scalene triangle ; obtuse triangle
3.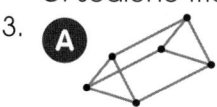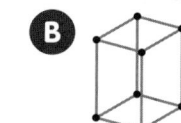

   A: triangular prism ; 5 ; 6 ; 9
   B: rectangular prism ; 6 ; 8 ; 12
   C: rectangular pyramid ; 5 ; 5 ; 8
   D: hexagonal pyramid ; 7 ; 7 ; 12

Problem Solving

   2 ; 2
1-14. (Suggested drawings)
   1.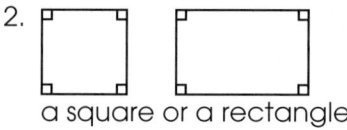
      obtuse angle — obtuse angle
      acute angle — acute angle
      2 acute angles and 2 obtuse angles
   2.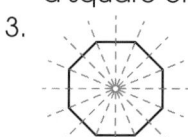
      a square or a rectangle
   3.
      octagon
   4.
      isosceles triangle ; right triangle
   5.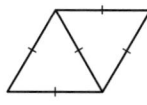
      isosceles triangles ; acute triangles
   6a. 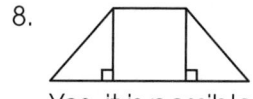   b.
      rhombus   hexagon
   7.
      There will be 16 pieces.
      Each piece is a right triangle
      and a scalene triangle.
   8.   9.
      Yes, it is possible.   Yes, Jake is correct.

10. 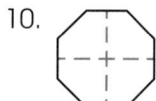 The shape is an octagon.

11a. 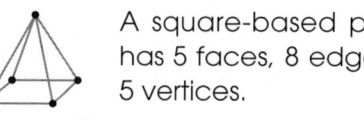 A square-based pyramid
      has 5 faces, 8 edges, and
      5 vertices.
   b. 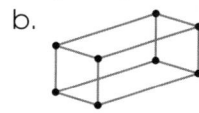 A rectangular prism has
      6 faces, 12 edges, and
      8 vertices.

12a.    b.
      triangular   pentagonal
      pyramid   pyramid
   c. 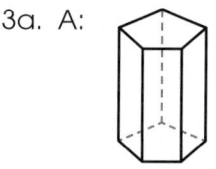   d.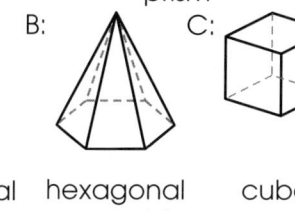
      sphere   hexagonal
                      prism

13a. A: B: C:

      pentagonal   hexagonal   cube
      prism   pyramid
   b. Net C ; Net A ; Net B
14a. Heptagonal pyramid: 8 vertices, 14 edges
      No, Lucy does not have enough materials.
      She needs more sticks.
   b.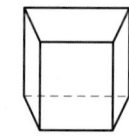
      The triangles are isosceles
      triangles and acute triangles.

15. The solid is a hexagonal pyramid. The solid
    has 6 triangular faces.
16. Yes, the base is a regular hexagon.
17. (Suggested drawing)

      It has 4 rectangular faces.

9 Cartesian Coordinate Plane
Math Skills

1a. (3,5)   b. (7,3)   c. (7,10) d. (1,1)
   e. (6,6)   f. (2,7)   g. (1,9)   h. (5,8)
2a. pineapple   b. kiwi
   c. mango   d. watermelon
3a. move 4 units to the right and 5 units up
   b. move 2 units to the left and 4 units down

ISBN: 978-1-77149-203-4

Problem Solving

2 unit(s) to the right ; 1 unit(s) down ; 2 unit(s) down; 3 unit(s) to the left

1. Route 1: Emma ➔ pencil ➔ book: 8 units
   Route 2: Emma ➔ book ➔ pencil: 9 units
   3 units up, 3 units to the left, and 2 units down

2.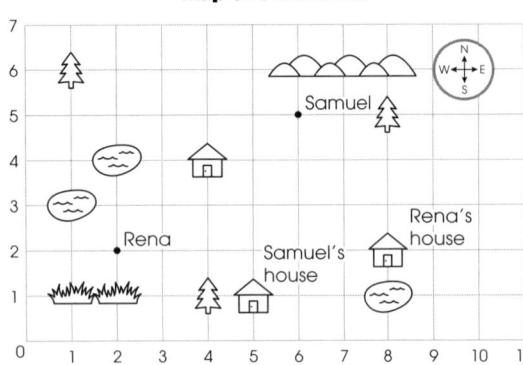

Map of Greensvilla

a. Forests: (1,6), (4,1), (8,5)
   Houses: (4,4), (5,1), (8,2)
   Mountains: (6,6), (7,6), (8,6)
   Ponds: (1,3), (2,4), (8,1)

c. Closest forest: 2 units to the right and 1 unit down
   Farthest forest: 6 units to the right and 3 units up

d. Closest pond: 4 units to the left and 1 unit down
   Farthest pond: 5 units to the left and 2 units down

e. 10   h. 8   i. 6
j. (7,1) ; (6,2)

3a.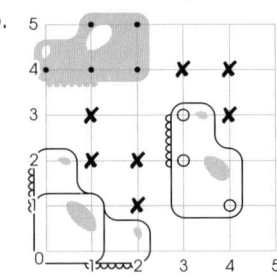

b. She travels 18 units on the bus.
c. She travels 20 units on the train.
d. 100 × 20 = 2000
   Jeannie will travel 2000 m.

4.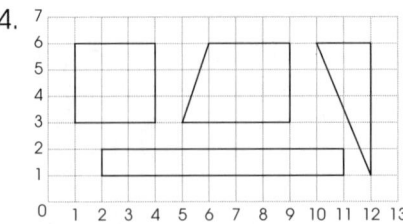

a. The coordinates of the square's vertices are (1,3), (1,6), (4,3), and (4,6).
   The coordinates of the rectangle's vertices are (2,1), (2,2), (11,1), and (11,2).

b. It is a trapezoid.

c. The coordinates of its vertices are (10,6), (12,6), and (12,1).

5a.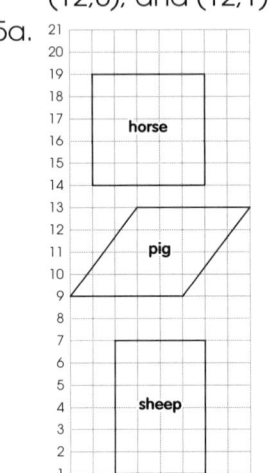

b. Horse: (6,14)
   Pig: (5,9)
   Sheep: (2,1)

c. Horse:
   25 square units
   Pig:
   20 square units
   Sheep:
   24 square units
   The horse pen has the greatest area.

d. A rhombus has 4 equal sides.
   5 × 4 = 20
   The perimeter of the pig pen is 20 units.

e. Horse: 20 units   Pig: 20 units
   Sheep: 20 units
   Perimeter in units: 20 + 20 + 20 = 60
   Perimeter in m: 10 × 60 = 600
   The total length of fencing is 600 m.

6.

c. Yes, Jack can uncover the remaining parts. The coordinates are (3,1) and (4,2).

d. The possible coordinates are (0,2), (0,1), (0,0), (1,1), (1,0), and (2,0).

e. The coordinates (0,1), (0,0), (1,1), and (1,0) must contain part of a fossil.

ISBN: 978-1-77149-203-4

10 Transformations

Math Skills

1a. Translate it 5 units to the right and 1 unit up.
 b. Reflect it in Line R.
 c. Make a $\frac{1}{2}$ rotation about Point O.
 d. Reflect it in Line S.
 e. Rotate it $\frac{1}{4}$ clockwise about Point P.
 f. Translate it 2 units to the left and 2 units up.
 g. Yes, because an image that is created by translations is always congruent to its original figure.

Problem Solving

3 ; Line R ; 3 ; Line R

1. (3,4), (5,4), (5,2), (4,1), and (3,2)

2.
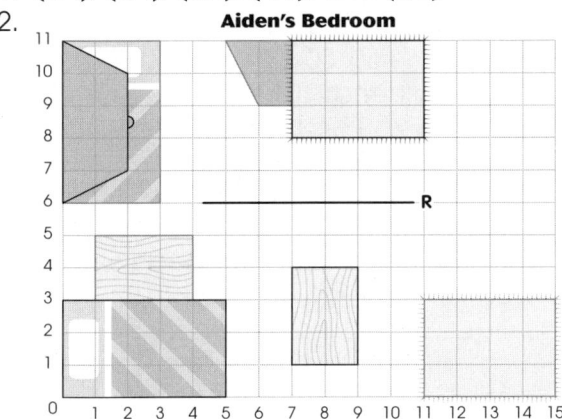

 c. (Suggested answer)
   The desk was rotated $\frac{1}{4}$ counterclockwise about (4,5). Then it was translated 3 units to the right and 1 unit down.
 e. (Suggested answer)
   The dresser was rotated $\frac{1}{4}$ counterclockwise about (10,11). Then it was translated 10 units to the left.
 f. No, Aiden is not correct because even though the location of the bed will be the same, the orientation will be different.
 g. (Suggested answers)
   Bed: Rotate the bed $\frac{1}{4}$ counterclockwise about (3,11). Then translate it 8 units down and 3 units to the left.
   Rug: Translate the rug 1 unit up and reflect it in Line R. Then translate it 4 units to the left.
   Desk: Rotate the desk $\frac{1}{4}$ counterclockwise about (4,3). Then translate it 5 units to the right and 1 unit up.

3a. No, he is not correct. He can also use reflection and rotation.
 b. Translate it 4 units down.
   Reflect it in Line M.
   Make a $\frac{1}{2}$ rotation about (3,4).
4a. Yes, Nancy is correct.
 b. Reflect it in Line N.
5a. Translations:
   Translate the square 3 times: 3 units to the right, 3 units up, and 3 units to the right and 3 units up.
   Rotations:
   Rotate the square about (3,3) 3 times: $\frac{1}{4}$ clockwise, $\frac{1}{2}$, and $\frac{3}{4}$ clockwise.
 b. No, she cannot use another point as the centre.
 c. (Individual labelling)
   Square 1: (1,1), (1,2), (2,1) ,(2,2)
   Square 2: (1,4), (1,5), (2,4), (2,5)
   Square 3: (4,1), (4,2), (5,1), (5,2)
   Square 4: (4,4), (4,5), (5,4), (5,5)
6a. All images are congruent to Figure A.
 b. Translations, reflections, and rotations will create congruent images.
 c. Yes, it is.
 d. The similar pairs are A and D, and B and E. The remaining triangle is C.
 e.
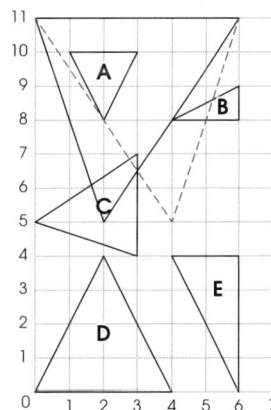

The possible coordinates of the vertex are (2,5) and (4,5).

7. (Suggested drawing)

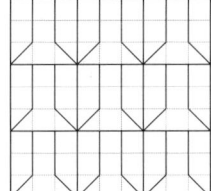

ISBN: 978-1-77149-203-4

8a. Make a $\frac{1}{2}$ rotation about (1,2).

b. Translate it 2 units to the right.

c. Make a $\frac{1}{2}$ rotation about (2,2).

d.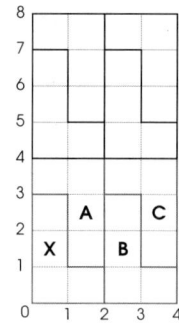

11 Patterning

Math Skills

1a. 19 ; 22 ; 25 ; Add 3 each time.

b. 30 ; 23 ; 16 ; Subtract 7 each time.

c. 160 ; 320 ; 640 ; Multiply by 2 each time.

d. 22 ; 28 ; 35 ; Add 1. Then increase the number to be added by 1 each time.

2. Jane's savings:
20 ; 24 ; The amount of savings is 4 times the number of days.
Chloe's savings:
30 ; 36 ; The amount of savings is 3 times the number of days.

Problem Solving

9 ; 2 ; 18 ; 36 ; 72 ; 72

1.
Day	Mon	Tue	Wed	Thu	Fri	Sat
Push-ups	5	8	11	14	17	20

+ 3

20

2.
Hour	0	1	2	3	4	5	6	7
Height	28	27	25	22	18	13	7	0

– 1 – 2 – 3 – 4 – 5 – 6 – 7

7

3.
Minute	0	1	2	3	4	5	6
Kernels unpopped	512	256	128	64	32	16	8

÷ 2

a. 32   b. 6

4.
Day	No. of Cranes
5	9
6	11
7	13
8	15
9	17
10	19

+ 2

Billy folds 2 more cranes each day.

a. 15   b. Day 10

5.
Week	Amount of Water (mL)
4	48
5	30
6	21

÷ 2 + 6

Each week, the amount of water was divided by 2 and then added 6.

21

6. 70 ; 83

a. None ; Plant A ; Plant B

b. Plant B was taller after 5 months.

c. Plant A: 70 + 15 + 15 = 100
Plant B: 83 + 12 + 12 = 107
Plant A was 100 cm tall and Plant B was 107 cm tall. Plant B was taller.

d. Month 8: 100 + 15 = 115
Month 9: 115 + 15 = 130
It took Plant A 9 months to reach 130 cm.

7a.

b. 7 ; 9 ; 11

c. Starting with 3 sticks. Each frame uses 2 more sticks.

d. The number of sticks is twice the frame number and add 1.

e. Frame 7: 7 × 2 + 1 = 15
Julia needs 15 sticks.
Frame 10: 10 × 2 + 1 = 21
Julia needs 21 sticks.
Frame 50: 50 × 2 + 1 = 101
Julia needs 101 sticks.

8a.
No. of Bounces	0	1	2	3	4	5	6
Height (cm)	108	96	84	72	60	48	36

– 12

The ball's height will be 36 cm.

b.
No. of Bounces	6	7	8	9
Height (cm)	36	24	12	0

– 12

It will take the ball 9 bounces to stop bouncing.

9. Prize B:
Week	1	2	3
Prize ($)	10	20	40

× 2   ← Total prize is $70.

Prize B is better.

10a.
No. of Years	0	5	10	15	20	25	30
Money ($)	200	400	800	1600	3200	6400	12 800

× 2

Sheila will have $12 800 after 30 years.

b.
No. of Years	0	5	10	15	20	25	30
Money ($)	200	300	500	900	1700	3300	6500

× 2 – 100

Sheila will have $6500 instead.

11.
No. of Minutes	1	2	3	4
Turtle (cm)	10	20	30	40
Grasshopper (cm)	5	10	20	40

+10 (Turtle)
× 2 (Grasshopper)

It will take the grasshopper 4 minutes.

ISBN: 978-1-77149-203-4

12.

Quiz	1	2	3	4	5	6
Score	30	46	54	58	60	61

+(16 ÷ 2) +(8 ÷ 2) +(4 ÷ 2) +(2 ÷ 2)

Michael's score on Quiz 6 will be 61.

13.

Fill-up	0	1	2	3	4	5	6
Gas (L)	80	48	32	24	20	18	17

÷ 2 + 8

Marcus will have 17 L of gas after filling his tank 6 times.

14.

Hour	0–2	3	4	5	6	7
Bill ($)	7	10	13	16	19	22

+ 3

a. Julie spent 5 hours at the Internet cafe.
b. There are 4 stamps.
Amount spent: $5 × 4 = $20
Spending 7 hours at the cafe costs $22.
Julie needs at least 7 hours to complete the stamp card.

12 Data Management

Math Skills

1. A: 5 ; 4 ; 3   B: 5 ; 4 ; 4, 8
   C: 15 ; 15.5 ; None   D: 14.9 ; 13 ; 12
   E: 5.3 ; 5.8 ; 3.2   F: 6.32 ; 6.75 ; 2.3, 8.9
2. Ice cream: 3.50 ; $3.60 ; $3.90
   Plant: 12.6 ; 13.15 cm ; None
   Pumpkin: 4.6 ; 4.6 kg ; 4.3 kg, 5 kg

Problem Solving

   6.22 ; 6.22 ; 6.30 ; 7.15
1. (6.3 + 3.8 + 7.15 + 4.7 + 7.15) ÷ 5 = 5.82
   3.8   4.7   (6.3)   (7.15   7.15)
                   ↑   ↑
                 median   mode
   The mean is now $5.82. The median and mode stay the same.
2. (2.3 + 1.6 + 3.7 + 2.2 + 3.2) ÷ 5 = 2.6 ; 2.6
3. (0.8 + 0.8 + 1.3 + 1.3 + 1.3) ÷ 5 = 1.1 ; 1.1
4. Total height: 1.2 × 5 = 6
   Eddie's height: 6 – 1.3 – 1.1 – 1.5 – 0.8 = 1.3
   1.3
5. (11.2 + 9.6 + 10.4) ÷ 3 = 10.4
   Books A, B, and C
6a. Total score: 82 × 6 = 492
   Quiz 6: 492 – 82 – 79 – 81 – 79 – 90 = 81 ; 81
b. (79   79)   (81   81)   82   90
           ↑   ↑
         mode   median
   81 ; 79 and 81
7a. French ; English   b. English ; Math
c. Jane ; 20   d. Ashley ; 20
e. 96 ; 86

8.

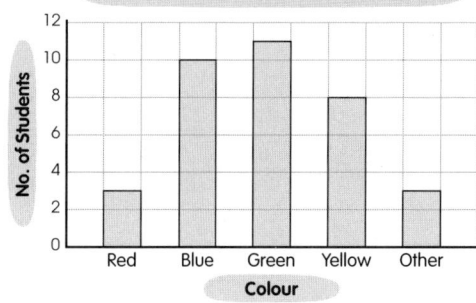

Grade 5 Students' Favourite Colours

a. 7 ; 3
b. (3 + 10 + 11 + 8 + 3) ÷ 5 = 7 ; 7
9a. • Lowest temperature:
      It was recorded on Wednesday.
    • Highest temperature:
      It was recorded on Thursday.
b. The highest temperature was 17°C.
c. (8 + 6 + 11 + 2 + 17 + 12 + 7) ÷ 7 = 9
   The mean temperature was 9°C.
d. It occurred between Wednesday and Thursday.
e. (8 + 6 + 11 + 2 + 17 + 12 + 7 + 5 + 6 + 7) ÷ 10
   = 8.1
   ┌ mode   ┌ median
   2   5   (6   6) (7   7)   8   11   12   17
   The mean was 8.1°C, the median was 7°C, and the modes were 6°C and 7°C.

10. Soccer: $\frac{1}{8}$ Baseball: $\frac{2}{8}$

    Basketball: $\frac{2}{8}$ Hockey: $\frac{3}{8}$

a. It is hockey.
b. $\frac{1}{8}$ of his friends picked it. It is soccer.
c. "Baseball" is 2 times the size of "soccer".
   13 × 2 = 26
   26 people picked basketball.
d. "Soccer" is 1 of the 8 sections in the graph.
   13 × 8 = 104
   104 people were surveyed in total.
e. Baseball: 13 × 2 = 26
   Basketball: 13 × 2 = 26
   Difference: (26 + 26) – 13 = 39
   39 more people picked baseball or basketball than soccer.

13 Probability

Math Skills

1a. 1, 2, 3, 4, 5, 6   b. 1, 2, A, E, U
   $\frac{1}{6}$; $\frac{1}{2}$; $\frac{1}{3}$ $\frac{1}{2}$; $\frac{1}{2}$; 0
c. ♡, ☆, ⌣   d. 1, 2, 3, 4, 5, 6, 7, 8
   $\frac{1}{4}$; 1 ; 0 $\frac{1}{8}$; $\frac{1}{4}$; $\frac{1}{2}$

ISBN: 978-1-77149-203-4

■ ·· Answers

Problem Solving

$\frac{1}{3}$; $\frac{1}{3}$

1. Possible outcomes: 1 2 3 4 5 6 | 7 8
   <u>smaller than 7</u>

   $\frac{6}{8} = \frac{3}{4}$; $\frac{3}{4}$

2a. [hearts 2, star 6, star 8, heart 7 cards]

   $\frac{4}{9}$

b. [heart 2, heart 8, heart 7 cards]   c. [star A, heart 2, star A cards]

   $\frac{3}{9} = \frac{1}{3}$; $\frac{1}{3}$ $\frac{3}{9} = \frac{1}{3}$; $\frac{1}{3}$

d. There is 1 "Win!" card. So there are 8 cards that are not "Win!" cards.

   $\frac{8}{9}$

e. There are no number cards with ☽.

   0

3a. • Red: • Blue:
   Total: 7 + 11 = 18   Total: 6 + 14 = 20
   Probability: $\frac{11}{18}$ Probability: $\frac{14}{20} = \frac{7}{10}$

   • Green:
   Total: 12 + 10 = 22
   Probability: $\frac{10}{22} = \frac{5}{11}$

   $\frac{11}{18}$; $\frac{7}{10}$; $\frac{5}{11}$

b. Total: 7 + 6 + 12 = 25
   Red or blue: 7 + 6 = 13
   Probability: $\frac{13}{25}$
   $\frac{13}{25}$

c. Total: 7 + 11 + 6 + 14 + 12 + 10 = 60
   Probability: $\frac{6}{60} = \frac{1}{10}$
   $\frac{1}{10}$

4a. A ; C ; B

b. Spinner A: $\frac{1}{2}$ Spinner B: $\frac{1}{8}$

   Spinner C: $\frac{1}{3}$

   Liz should choose Spinner A.

c. Spinner A: $\frac{3}{4}$ Spinner B: $\frac{5}{8}$

   Spinner C: $\frac{2}{3}$

   Liz should choose Spinner A.

d. Spinner A: $\frac{1}{2}$ Spinner B: $\frac{3}{4}$

   Spinner C: $\frac{1}{2}$

   Liz should choose Spinner B.

5a.

Sums of 2 Dice

+	1	2	3	4	5	6
1	2	3	4	5	6	7
2	3	4	5	6	7	8
3	4	5	6	7	8	9
4	5	6	7	8	9	10
5	6	7	8	9	10	11
6	7	8	9	10	11	12

b. • Sum of 3: $\frac{2}{36} = \frac{1}{18}$

   The probability is $\frac{1}{18}$.

   • Sum greater than 9: $\frac{6}{36} = \frac{1}{6}$

   The probability is $\frac{1}{6}$.

   • A 3 on one of the dice: $\frac{11}{36}$

   The probability is $\frac{11}{36}$.

   • Sum less than 12: $\frac{35}{36}$

   The probability is $\frac{35}{36}$.

   • A 7 on one of the dice:
   A 7 cannot be rolled on either dice. The probability is 0.

c. There are 5 ways to get a sum of 6. 2 of the ways are with a 2 and a 4 on the dice.

   The probability is $\frac{2}{5}$.

6.

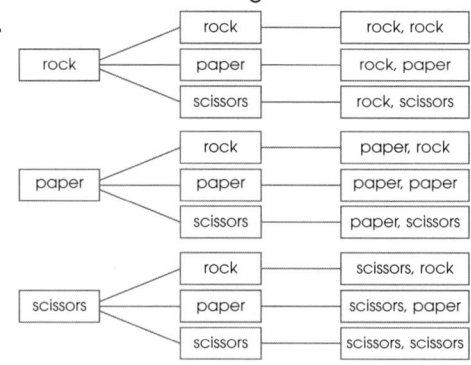

a. • Tied game: $\frac{3}{9} = \frac{1}{3}$

   The probability is $\frac{1}{3}$.

   • Scissors and loses: $\frac{2}{9}$

   The probability is $\frac{2}{9}$.

ISBN: 978-1-77149-203-4

b. $\frac{1}{3}$ of 100 is about 33.

There will be about 33 tied games.

7a. Claire's box: $\frac{2}{5}$

Eva's box: $\frac{4}{5}$

The probability is $\frac{2}{5}$ from Claire's box and $\frac{4}{5}$ from Eva's box.

b. Both boxes now have 1 red, 3 green, and 1 blue balls.

The probability is $\frac{3}{5}$ for both boxes.

c. Probability: $\frac{1}{5}$

$\frac{1}{5}$ of 50 is 10.

A blue ball will be picked about 10 times.

d. Claire's box: 3 red, 3 green, 1 blue balls

The probability of picking a red ball is $\frac{3}{7}$.

e. $\frac{3}{7}$ of 70 is 30.

A red ball will be picked about 30 times.

Critical-thinking Questions

Unit 1

1. $1.536 \div 3 = 0.512$; $100 - $26.20 = $73.80 ;
$73.80 \div 3 = $24.60 ; 0.512 kg ; $24.60

2. From 7:26 a.m. to 8:39 a.m.:
1 h 13 min = 73 min
Distance run: $0.22 \times 73 = 16.06$ km
Corey ran 16.06 km.

3.
Week	Temperature
1	9°C below 0°C
2	7°C below 0°C
3	5°C below 0°C
4	3°C below 0°C
5	1°C below 0°C
6	1°C
7	3°C

(+2°C)

The temperature will be 3°C in Week 7.

4. $8.25 - $3.25 = $5
The amount of allowance Ann saves alternates between $8.25 and $5.

Week	Money Saved ($)
1	10
2	18.25
3	23.25
4	31.50
5	36.50
6	44.75
7	49.75
8	58

+ 8.25
+ 5
+ 8.25
+ 5
+ 8.25
+ 5
+ 8.25

It will take Ann 8 weeks to save $58.

5.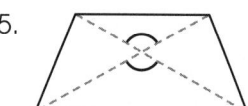

The highlighted angles are obtuse angles.

So, there are two obtuse triangles.

The probability is $\frac{1}{2}$.

6. Capacity of tank: $30 \times 40 \times 60 = 72\,000$ (mL)
4.8 L = 4800 mL

Fraction filled: $\frac{4800}{72000} = \frac{1}{15}$

$\frac{1}{15}$ of the tank is filled.

7. Winter: $1 - 0.4 - 0.25 - 0.15 = 0.2$
0.2 is half of 0.4. So, half of the number of people who voted for summer voted for winter.

No. of people voted for winter: $16 \div 2 = 8$
8 people voted for winter.

8. Area of 1 unit square: $3 \times 3 = 9$
No. of unit squares in rectangle: $135 \div 9 = 15$
Possible dimensions:
1 unit by 15 units ← too big for grid
3 units by 5 units

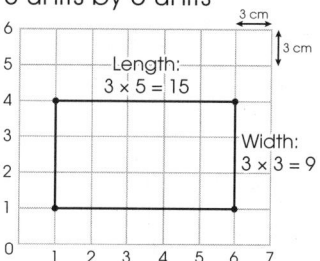

The coordinates of the remaining vertices are (1,1), (6,4), and (6,1). The length and width of the rectangle are 15 cm and 9 cm respectively.

9. Total distance:
$2456 + 2624 + 1946 + 1203 + 981 = 9210$
Mean: $9210 \div 5 = 1842$
The mean distance is 1842 m.

10. Claire's rotation:

$\frac{1}{4}$ clockwise and $2\frac{1}{2}$ clockwise

↓

$\frac{1}{4}$ clockwise and $\frac{1}{2}$ clockwise

↓

$\frac{3}{4}$ clockwise

↓

$\frac{1}{4}$ counterclockwise ← same as Clement's

Yes, they will be in the same orientation.

11. Side length of hexagon: $15.3 \div 6 = 2.55$
Area of rectangle: $2.55 \times 8 = 20.4$
The area of each rectangle is 20.4 cm².

12. From 3:47:17 p.m. to 4:16:02 p.m.:
28 min 45 s = 28.75 min
Memory used: $28.75 \times 14 = 402.5$
Arnold's video will use 402.5 MB of memory.

ISBN: 978-1-77149-203-4

13. Mean: $(\frac{7}{6} + \frac{5}{6} + \frac{4}{6} + 1\frac{3}{6} + \frac{5}{6}) \div 5 = 1$

Median: $\frac{4}{6}$ $\frac{5}{6}$ $(\frac{5}{6})$ $\frac{7}{6}$ $1\frac{3}{6}$

Mode: $\frac{5}{6}$

The mean elapsed time is 1 hour, the median is $\frac{5}{6}$ hour, and the mode is $\frac{5}{6}$ hour.

14. Elapsed days: 31 days in May, 30 days in June, 31 days in July, 8 days in August

31 + 30 + 31 + 8 = 100

Plant growth: 0.02 × 100 = 2

Height: 2.7 + 2 = 4.7

Its height was 4.7 cm on August 8.

15. Volume of a brick: 10 × 5 × 20 = 1000 (cm³)

0.5 m³ = 500 000 cm³

No. of bricks: 500 000 ÷ 1000 = 500

Weight of bricks: 2.26 × 500 = 1130

The bricks will weigh 1130 kg.

16.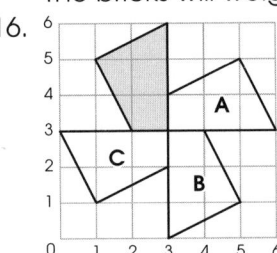

The transformations are rotations of the shape $\frac{1}{4}$ clockwise (or $\frac{3}{4}$ counterclockwise) about (3,3) each time.

The shape covers 4 squares.

Area of each square: 368 ÷ 4 = 92

Each square on the grid is 92 cm².

17.

Predictions on the Revenue from the Sales of Heaters

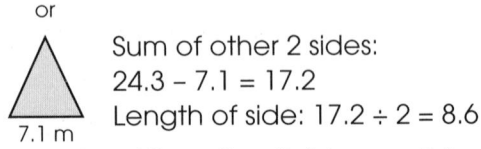

The revenue decreases by $1200 and then by $200 less each month.

Total revenue:

$5200 + $4000 + $3000 + $2200 + $1600 + $1200 + $1000 = $18 200

The revenue could be $18 200.

18. Capacities:

10 × 10 × 5 = 500 ← 2 containers

11 × 10 × 4 = 440 ← 4 containers

12 × 8 × 6 = 576 ← 4 containers (10 – 2 – 4 = 4)

Mean:

(500 × 2 + 440 × 4 + 576 × 4) ÷ 10 = 506.4

Median:

440 440 440 440 (500)(500) 576 576 576 576

Mode: 440 and 576

The mean is 506.4 mL, the median is 500 mL, and the modes are 440 mL and 576 mL.

19.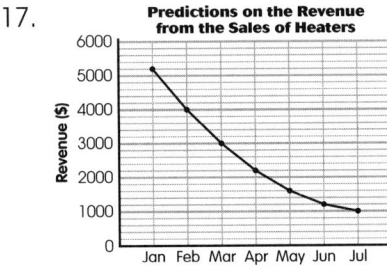

7.1 m

Second side: 7.1

Third side: 24.3 – 7.1 – 7.1 = 10.1

or

7.1 m

Sum of other 2 sides:

24.3 – 7.1 = 17.2

Length of side: 17.2 ÷ 2 = 8.6

The lengths of the other 2 sides are 7.1 m and 10.1 m, or 8.6 m and 8.6 m.

20.

Day	No. of Pages
1	39 ⎞ – 1
2	38 ⎟ – 2
3	36 ⎟ – 3
4	33 ⎟ – 4
5	29 ⎟ – 5
6	24 ⎟ – 6
7	18 ⎠

Each day, Dave reads 1 more page fewer than the previous day.

Mean:

(39 + 38 + 36 + 33 + 29 + 24 + 18) ÷ 7 = 31

Dave reads a mean of 31 pages each day.

Unit 2

1. 12 × 25 = 300; 540 × 300 = 162 000; 162 000 cm²

2. Hummingbird in 1 min: 54 × 60 = 3240

Difference in 1 min: 3240 – 1080 = 2160

Difference in 5 min: 2160 × 5 = 10 800

The hummingbird flaps its wings 10 800 times more than the butterfly in 5 minutes.

3. Volume of a box: 15 × 13 × 2 = 390

No. of boxes: 1800 ÷ 20 = 90

Volume of carton: 390 × 90 = 35 100

Its volume is 35 100 cm³.

4.

Day	Money Earned ($)
Fri	8816 ⎞ ÷ 2
Thu	4408 ⎠
Wed	2204
Tue	1102
Mon	551

$551 was earned last Monday.

5. No. of 2-room apartments: $\frac{3}{5} = \frac{30}{50}$

There are 30 2-room apartments.

No. of 3-room apartments: 50 – 30 = 20

Rooms in 2-room apartments: 30 × 2 = 60

Rooms in 3-room apartments: 20 × 3 = 60

Total no. of rooms: 60 + 60 = 120

Probability: $\frac{60}{120} = \frac{1}{2}$

The probability of getting a room in a 2-room apartment is $\frac{1}{2}$.

ISBN: 978-1-77149-203-4

6. Water needed: 78 × 77 = 6006
Volume of tank: 2 × 2 × 0.75 = 3
Capacity of tank: 3 m³ = 3000 L
No. of refills: 6006 ÷ 3000 = 2R6
A refill is needed for the remaining 6 L.
Amy needs to refill it at least 3 times.

7.
180 cm
2 m
(200 cm)

Total length:
(200 + 180) × 2 = 760
Cost of wire: $0.05 × 760 ÷ 8 = $4.75
Change: $6 – $4.75 = $1.25
Ruben's change will be $1.25.

8.

Week	Chocolate Milk Powder (g)	
1	60	
2	55	– 5
3	48	– 7
4	39	– 9
5	28	– 11
6	15	– 13

Each week, Carl reduces his chocolate milk powder by 2 g more than the previous week.

Carl will use only 15 g in Week 6.

9. Additional distance: $4\frac{1}{2} - 2 = 2\frac{1}{2}$

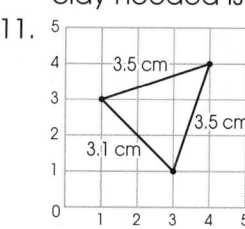 There are 5 "$\frac{1}{2}$" in "$2\frac{1}{2}$".

Total: $3.90 + $1.25 × 5 = $10.15
The taxi fare will cost $10.15.

10. Triangular prism: 6 vertices
Square-based pyramid: 5 vertices
Heptagonal pyramid: 8 vertices
Mean: (6 + 6 + 6 + 6 + 6 + 5 + 5 + 8) ÷ 8 = 6
The mean number of balls of modelling clay needed is 6.

11.
The triangle is an isosceles triangle and an acute triangle.

Perimeter: 3.1 + 3.5 + 3.5 = 10.1
The perimeter of the triangle is 10.1 cm.

12. From 1:30 p.m. to 5:30 p.m.: 4 hours
From 2:15 p.m. to 3:00 p.m.: 45 minutes
4 hours = 240 minutes
Probability: $\frac{45}{240} = \frac{3}{16}$

The probability is $\frac{3}{16}$.

13.

No. of Sweaters	Cost ($)
1	17.50
2	35 ← $5 + $5 + $5 + $20
3	52.50
4	70 ← $20 + $20 + $20 + $10
5	87.50 ← too expensive (4 $20 is $80)

Anita could have bought 2 or 4 sweaters.

14.

Design	No. of Squares
1	1
2	5
3	9
4	13
5	17
6	21

+ 4

Each design has 4 more squares.

Area of 1 square: 3 × 3 = 9
The 6th design has 21 squares.
Area of 6th design: 9 × 21 = 189
The area of the 6th design is 189 cm².

15. Image C will complete the net.
(Suggested answer)
The transformations involved are a rotation of $\frac{1}{2}$ about (3,3) and then a translation of 1 unit to the right.

16. Female musicians: 0.37 + 0.18 = 0.55
Male musicians: $\frac{6}{20} + \frac{3}{20} = \frac{9}{20} = \frac{45}{100} = 0.45$
There were more people who picked female musicians.

17. From 3:00 p.m. to 7:00 p.m. = 4 hours
Total change in temperature:
8°C to 4°C below 0°C = 12°C
Decrease in temperature each hour:
12°C ÷ 4 = 3°C

Time	Temperature
3:00 p.m.	8°C
4:00 p.m.	5°C
5:00 p.m.	2°C
6:00 p.m.	1°C below 0°C
7:00 p.m.	4°C below 0°C

– 3°C
fall below 0°C

The temperature fell below 0°C between 5:00 p.m. and 6:00 p.m.

18. The triangle covers 2 squares.
The parallelogram covers 6 squares.
The area of the parallelogram is 3 times the triangle's.
Area of parallelogram: 2.75 × 3 = 8.25
The area of the parallelogram is 8.25 cm².

19.

Layer	No. of Blocks
1	4
2	9
3	16
4	25
5	36

+ 5
+ 7
+ 9
+ 11

The second layer increases by 5 blocks. Then each layer increases by 2 more blocks.

Total no. of blocks: 4 + 9 + 16 + 25 + 36 = 90
Weight of structure: 15 × 90 = 1350
The weight of the structure is 1350 g.

ISBN: 978-1-77149-203-4

20.

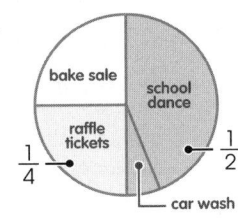

School dance and car wash ($\frac{1}{2}$ of the circle graph):
$4382 + $642 = $5024
Raffle tickets:
$\frac{1}{4}$ is half of $\frac{1}{2}$.
$5024 ÷ 2 = $2512
$2512 was raised from selling raffle tickets.

Unit 3

1. $16 \times 500 = 8000$; $8000 \div 1600 = 5$;
$75.20 \times 5 = $376 ; $376

2. Area of a square: $2 \times 2 = 4$
Triangular prism:

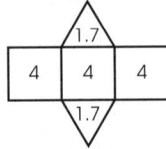

Area:
$4 + 4 + 4 + 1.7 + 1.7 = 15.4$

Square-based pyramid:

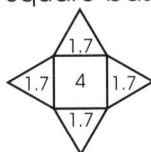

Area:
$4 + 1.7 + 1.7 + 1.7 + 1.7 = 10.8$
Difference: $15.4 - 10.8 = 4.6$
The net for the triangular prism has a bigger area by 4.6 cm².

3.

Year	Value ($)
0	6504 ⎤ ÷ 2
1	3252
2	1626
3	813
4	406.50

It will be worth $406.50 after 4 years.

4. $2\frac{1}{6}$ h = 2 h 10 min $3\frac{1}{4}$ h = 3 h 15 min
Start time:
2 h 10 min before 1:46 p.m. = 11:36 a.m.
Current time:
3 h 15 min after 11:36 a.m. = 2:51 p.m.
The current time is 2:51 p.m.

5. Total value of coins: $0.10 \times 6 = $0.60
Possible combinations:
6 dimes ✗ ← need at least 1 nickel and quarter
1 quarter, 2 dimes, 3 nickels ✔
Fred has 1 quarter, 2 dimes, and 3 nickels.

6.

Perimeter: $1.9 \times 4 + 1.6 \times 4 + 1.5 \times 4 = 20$
The perimeter of the design is 20 cm.

7. 0.23 L = 230 mL
$\frac{7}{20}$ L = $\frac{350}{1000}$ L = 0.35 L = 350 mL
Capacities:

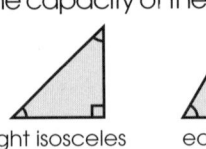

Each size is 120 mL bigger.
The capacity of the biggest cup size is 590 mL.

8.

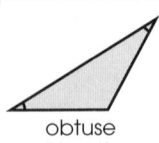

| right isosceles triangle | equilateral triangle | obtuse triangle |
| 2 acute angles | 3 acute angles | 2 acute angles |

There are 9 angles in total and 7 of them are acute angles.
$\frac{7}{9}$ of the angles are acute.

9. Rotations:
$2\frac{1}{4}$ clockwise → $\frac{1}{4}$ clockwise
$1\frac{3}{4}$ counterclockwise → $\frac{3}{4}$ counterclockwise
$\frac{5}{4}$ clockwise → $\frac{1}{4}$ clockwise

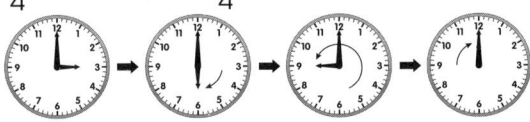

The clock shows 12:00 now.

10.

Parallelograms have 2 pairs of equal sides.
Sum of remaining 2 sides: $14.7 - 5.9 - 5.9 = 2.9$
Length of side: $2.9 \div 2 = 1.45$
The lengths of the other sides are 5.9 cm, 1.45 cm, and 1.45 cm.

11.

Prism	Length (cm)	Width (cm)	Height (cm)	Volume (cm³)
1	10 ⎤−1	1 ⎤×2	16 ⎤−3	10×1×16 = 160
2	9	2	13	9×2×13 = 234
3	8	4	10	8×4×10 = 320
4	7	8	7	7×8×7 = 392
5	6	16	4	6×16×4 = 384
6	5	32	1	5×32×1 = 160

Mean volume:
$(160 + 234 + 320 + 392 + 384 + 160) \div 6 = 275$
The mean volume of the prisms is 275 cm³.

12.

The pool takes up 8 squares.
Area of 1 square:
$1152 \div 8 = 144$
$144 = 12 \times 12$
The side length of a square is 12 m.
Length of pool: $12 \times 4 = 48$
Width of pool: $12 \times 2 = 24$
The dimensions are 48 m by 24 m.

ISBN: 978-1-77149-203-4

13. No. of minutes to Stop A: 420 ÷ 60 = 7
No. of minutes to Stop B: 540 ÷ 60 = 9
Time to Stop A: 2:15 p.m. + 7 min = 2:22 p.m.
Time to Stop B: 2:15 p.m. + 9 min = 2:24 p.m.
Mac will miss the bus at Stop A but he can catch it at Stop B. So, Mac should go to Stop B.

14.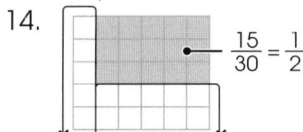

$\frac{15}{30} = \frac{1}{2}$

Volume of whole cake: 36 × 25 × 8 = 7200
Volume of remaining cake: $\frac{1}{2}$ of 7200 is 3600.
Remaining mass: $\frac{1}{2}$ of 6 is 3.
The volume is 3600 cm³ and the mass is 3 kg.

15. Possible outcomes:

Coins Lost				Amount Lost
$2	$1	$1	$0.25	
•	•			$3
•		•		$3
•			•	$2.25
	•	•		$2
	•		•	$1.25
		•	•	$1.25

There are 6 possible outcomes. 3 of them are more than $2.
Probability: $\frac{3}{6} = \frac{1}{2}$

The probability is $\frac{1}{2}$.

16.

Box	Cost ($)
1	29.75
2	28.40
3	27.05
4	25.70
5	24.35

$\Big\}$ – $1.35

Mean cost: ($29.75 + $28.40 + $27.05 + $25.70 + $24.35) ÷ 5 = $27.05
The mean cost is $27.05.

17. Cost of 1 pepperoni pizza: $1.50 × 6 = $9
Cost of 1 vegetarian pizza: $3.25 × 2 = $6.50
Total cost: $9 + $6.50 + $6.50 = $22
Change: $40 – $22 = $18
Jim's change will be 1 $10 bill, 1 $5 bill, 1 toonie, and 1 loonie.

18.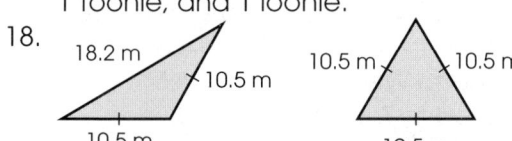

Isosceles triangle: 18.2 + 10.5 + 10.5 = 39.2
Equilateral triangle: 10.5 × 3 = 31.5
Difference: 39.2 – 31.5 = 7.7
Perimeter of field: 18.2 + 10.5 + 10.5 + 10.5 = 49.7
The perimeter of the isosceles triangle is 7.7 m longer. The perimeter of his field is 49.7 m.

19. Abby: 500 × 3 = 1500
Danny: 850 × 2 = 1700
Difference: 1700 – 1500 = 200
Danny filled 200 mL more water.

20. Water in tank: 12.5 × 20 × 7.4 = 1850
Abby: 500 mL   Betty: 1100 mL
Cathy: 750 mL   Danny: 850 mL
1850 = 1100 (Betty) + 750 (Cathy)
Betty and Cathy are the two children.

Unit 4

1. (3.53 + 5.38 + 1.52 + 1.83 + 2.04) ÷ 5 ;
14.3 ÷ 5 ; 2.86 ; 3

2. Capacity of juice box: 4.2 × 5 × 9 = 189
Total drunk: $\frac{2}{3} \overset{\times 63}{=} \frac{126}{189}$ $\frac{2}{3}$ of 189 is 126.

126 mL = 0.126 L
Juliet drank 0.126 L of juice.

3. Harry and Sally in 1 min: 55 + 45 = 100
Time needed: 2500 ÷ 100 = 25
Time: 3:15 p.m. + 25 min = 3:40 p.m.
They will meet each other at 3:40 p.m.

4. Carly: $\frac{3}{4} = \frac{45}{60}$ $\frac{3}{4}$ of 60 is 45.
Jessie: 45 × 0.8 = 36   Rae: 36 + 12 = 48
Mean points: (45 + 36 + 48) ÷ 3 = 43
Rae got the most points and the mean was 43 points.

5. $1\frac{3}{4}$ counterclockwise $1\frac{1}{2}$ clockwise
↓ $\frac{3}{4}$ counterclockwise   ↓ $\frac{1}{2}$ clockwise

same orientation as original

| original | 1st | 2nd | 3rd | 4th | 5th |

2 of the rectangles would be in the same orientation as the original.

6. Pentagonal pyramid: 10 edges, 6 vertices
Sticks: 16¢ × 10 = 160¢ = $1.60
Balls: 75¢ × 6 = 450¢ = $4.50
Total cost: $1.60 + $4.50 = $6.10
3 toonies and 1 quarter: $6.25
Change: $6.25 – $6.10 = $0.15
Nicole will have $0.15 left.

7. From 7:15 a.m. to 8:45 a.m.:
1 h 30 min = 90 min
Times with the number 6: 7:16, 7:26, 7:36, 7:46, 7:56, 8:06, 8:16, 8:26, 8:36
There are 9 "times" that contain "6".
$\frac{9}{90} = \frac{1}{10}$
The probability is $\frac{1}{10}$.

ISBN: 978-1-77149-203-4

8.

Mileage (km)	Value ($)
65 000	12 000
75 000	11 000
85 000	10 000
95 000	9000
105 000	8000

+1000 on mileage, –1000 on value

The value decreases by $1000 for every 10 000 km of mileage.
The value is $8000.

9. 2.6 kg = 2600 g
No. of 100 g in 2600 g: 2600 ÷ 100 = 26
Cost: 55¢ × 26 = 1430¢ = $14.30
Change: $20 – $14.30 = $5.70
Jackson will get $5.70.

10. Side length: 104 ÷ 4 = 26
Total area: 26 × 26 = 676
Area of grass: 676 – 45.8 = 630.2
630.2 m² of the diamond is covered with grass.

11. From 11:30 a.m. to 5:30 p.m.: 6 h
He needs to pay for 6 hours.
Cost of 5 additional hours: $0.60 × 5 = $3
Total cost for 6 hours: $0.75 + $3 = $3.75
The flat rate is cheaper. So, Michael will pay $3.

12.

Bounce	Height (cm)
4	8
3	16
2	32
1	64
0	128

× 2

The ball was initially dropped at 128 cm.

13. Total no. of students: 25 × 3 = 75

$$\underset{\substack{\text{smallest class:} \\ 75 - 24 - 30 = 21}}{\underline{21}} \qquad \underset{\text{median}}{\underline{24}} \qquad \underset{\substack{\text{largest class:} \\ 75 \times 0.4 = 30}}{\underline{30}}$$

There are 21, 24, and 30 students in the classes.

14. 900 m = $\frac{3}{4}$ of the path

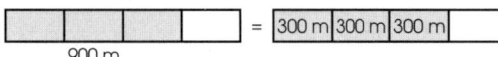

= 300 m 300 m 300 m

900 m

Length of path: 300 × 4 = 1200

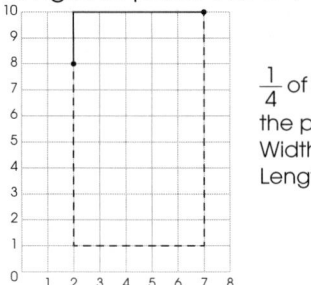

$\frac{1}{4}$ of the path is 7 units. So, the path is 28 units long.
Width: 5
Length: (28 – 5 – 5) ÷ 2 = 9

The path is 1200 m long. The coordinates are (7, 10), (2, 10), (2, 1), and (7, 1).

15. Area of room: 6 × 5 = 30
Area of closet: 3 × 1.5 = 4.5
Tiling area: 30 – 4.5 = 25.5
Cost of tiling: $65 × 25.5 ÷ 3 = $552.50
No, $500 is not enough to cover her room.

16.

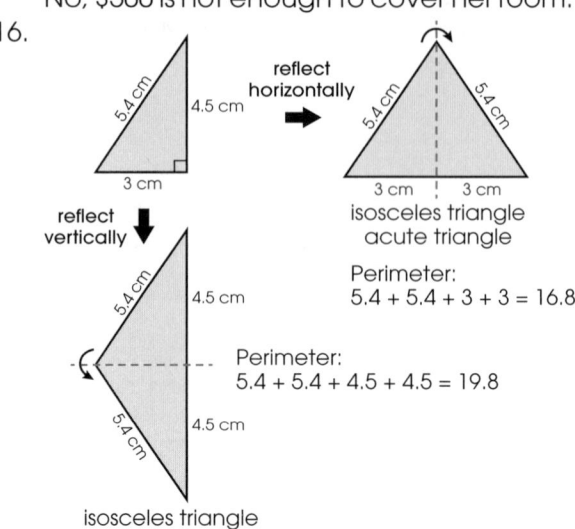

reflect horizontally

isosceles triangle
acute triangle

Perimeter:
5.4 + 5.4 + 3 + 3 = 16.8

reflect vertically

isosceles triangle
obtuse triangle

Perimeter:
5.4 + 5.4 + 4.5 + 4.5 = 19.8

(Suggested answer)
The big triangle is an isosceles triangle and an acute triangle. Its perimeter is 16.8 cm.

17.

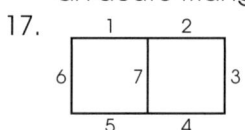

The fencing is divided into 7 sides.
Side length of square: 10.5 ÷ 7 = 1.5
Perimeter of square: 1.5 × 4 = 6
The perimeter of each pen is 6 m.

18. No. of drops each day: 2 × 2 × 3 = 12
No. of drops in July: 12 × 31 = 372
Amount needed: 372 × 0.8 = 297.6
Bottles needed: 297.6 ÷ 80 = 3.72
Katie needs 4 bottles of eye drops.

19. Mon: 23°C   Tue: 17.5°C   Wed: 11°C
Thu: 19.5°C   Fri: 8°C   Sat: 3.5°C
Mean: (23 + 17.5 + 11 + 19.5 + 8 + 3.5) ÷ 6
= 13.75
Median: 3.5 8 11 17.5 19.5 23
(11 + 17.5) ÷ 2 = 14.25
The mean is 13.75°C, the median is 14.25°C, and there are no modes.

20. Mon to Tue: 23 – 17.5 = 5.5
Tue to Wed: 17.5 – 11 = 6.5
Wed to Thu: 19.5 – 11 = 8.5
Thu to Fri: 19.5 – 8 = 11.5 ← biggest change
Fri to Sat: 8 – 3.5 = 4.5
Sat to Sun: 3.5°C to 4°C below 0°C = 7.5
The biggest change in temperature occurred between Thursday and Friday.

ISBN: 978-1-77149-203-4

Unit 5

1. $32 \times 14 = 448$; $28 \times 19 = 532$; $532 - 448 = 84$;
   84 points

2. From 5:41 p.m. to 9:26 p.m. = 3 h 45 min
   $1\frac{1}{2}$ h = 1 h 30 min $\frac{3}{4}$ h = 45 min
   Time spent on reading:
   3 h 45 min – 1 h 30 min – 45 min = 1 h 30 min
   Anna read for 1 h 30 min.

3.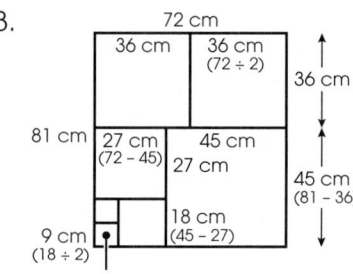
   Area: $9 \times 9 = 81$
   The area of the smallest tile is 81 cm².

4. Capacity of fish tank: $20 \times 20 \times 20 = 8000$
   Amount filled: $\frac{3}{4} = \frac{6000}{8000}$
   Amount needed: $\frac{7}{8} = \frac{7000}{8000}$
   Amount to be filled: $7000 - 6000 = 1000$
   1000 mL of water is needed.

5.
Total: 1250 m	
$210 \div 3 = 70$ (s)	$1040 \div 2 = 520$ (s) $\uparrow$ $1250 - 210$

   Total time: 70 s + 520 s = 590 s = 9 min 50 s
   Finish time:
   11:06:48 a.m. + 9 min 50 s = 11:16:38 a.m.
   Dory finished swimming at 11:16:38 a.m.

6. Side length of pentagonal base: $10 \div 5 = 2$
   2-cm sticks were used for the bases.

   2-cm sticks: 10
   5-cm sticks: 5
   Total: 15
   Probability: $\frac{5}{15} = \frac{1}{3}$
   The probability is $\frac{1}{3}$.

7. Cary: 600 g = $\frac{600}{1000}$ kg = $\frac{3}{5}$ kg
   Ashley: $\frac{3}{5} + 1\frac{3}{5} = 2\frac{1}{5}$
   Brock: $2\frac{1}{5} - \frac{7}{5} = \frac{4}{5}$
   Total: $\frac{3}{5} + 2\frac{1}{5} + \frac{4}{5} = 3\frac{3}{5}$
   The total mass of the candies is $3\frac{3}{5}$ kg.

8.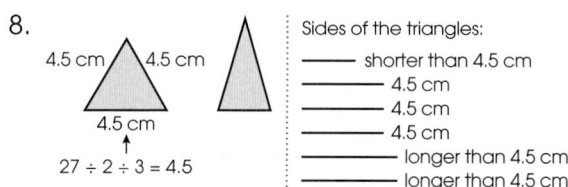
   $27 \div 2 \div 3 = 4.5$
   Mean: $27 \div 6 = 4.5$
   Median:
   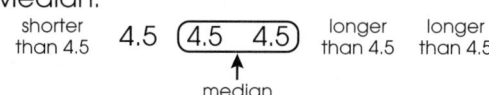
   Mode: 4.5
   Yes, Emily is correct.

9. Capacity of tank: $17.5 \times 10 \times 12 = 2100$
   Amount of water:
   2100 – 630 = 1470 (cm³) = 1470 (mL)
   The tank can hold 1470 mL of water.

10.
Year	Amount ($)
1	13.75
2	27.5
3	55
4	110
5	220

    $\times 2$
    It will take 5 years.

11.
No. of Dimes	No. of Nickels	Total (¢)	
4	4	60	✗
5	5	75	✗
6	6	90	✔

    Height of dimes: $1.22 \times 6 = 7.32$
    Height of nickels: $1.76 \times 6 = 10.56$
    Total height: 7.32 + 10.56 = 17.88
    The stack will be 17.88 mm tall.

12.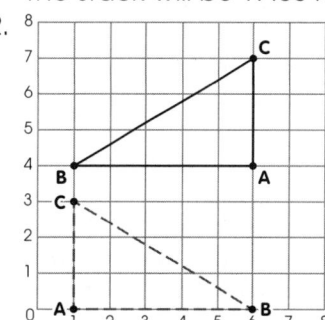
    It is a scalene triangle and a right triangle.

13. The coordinates of Point C is (1,3).
    Point C is translated 5 units to the left and 4 units down.

14. The people who own at least one dog are the people who chose "Dogs" and "Both".
    Dogs: $1200 \times 0.3 = 360$
    Both: $1 - 0.25 - 0.35 - 0.3 = 0.1$
    $\quad \frac{1}{4} = \frac{25}{100} = 0.25$
    $1200 \times 0.1 = 120$
    Total: 360 + 120 = 480
    480 people own at least one dog.

ISBN: 978-1-77149-203-4

15. Owners with cats: 0.35 + 0.1 = 0.45
No. of owners with cats: 1200 × 0.45 = 540
No. of owners with both: 1200 × 0.1 = 120
Probability: $\frac{120}{540} = \frac{2}{9}$

The probability is $\frac{2}{9}$.

16. Base area of 9-cm tall prism: 2475 ÷ 9 = 275
Base area of 5-cm tall prism: 2475 ÷ 5 = 495
Difference: 495 − 275 = 220
The difference in area is 220 cm².

17.

S	M	T	W	Th	F	S
	⃝17	18	⃝19	20	⃝21	22
23	⃝24	25	⃝26	27	⃝28	29
30						

• 4 Mondays and Wednesdays
• 2 Fridays
Amount for Mon and Wed: $2.75 × 4 = $11
Amount for Fri: $3.15 × 2 = $6.30
Total: $11 + $6.30 = $17.30
Roger will pay $17.30 in total.

18. Any prism must have at least 3 rectangular faces.
No. of right angles in 3 rectangular faces:
4 × 3 = 12
The remaining 2 angles must be for the bases. So both bases are triangles and each base has 1 right angle. Therefore, the base is a right triangle.

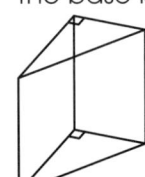

This prism is a triangular prism.

19. Cost of 2 shirts: $25.40 × 2 = $50.80
Cost of 3 skirts: $27.55 × 3 = $82.65
Total cost: $50.80 + $82.65 = $133.45

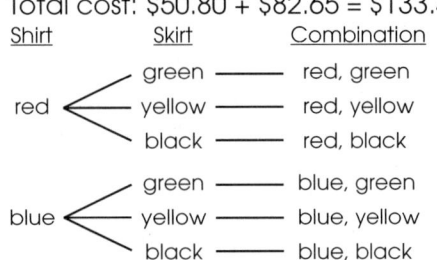

Shirt	Skirt	Combination
red	green	red, green
	yellow	red, yellow
	black	red, black
blue	green	blue, green
	yellow	blue, yellow
	black	blue, black

The total cost was $133.45. Sandra has 6 different shirt and skirt combinations she can wear.

20.

Masses of Watermelons

Week	Mass A	Mass B
1	450 g	300 g
2	600 g	500 g
3	750 g	700 g
4	900 g	900 g
5	1.05 kg	1.1 kg
6	1.2 kg	1.3 kg
7	1.35 kg	1.5 kg
8	1.5 kg	1.7 kg

(A: − 150 g } + 0.15 kg) (B: − 200 g } + 0.2 kg)

Each week, the mass of Watermelon A increased by 0.15 kg and Watermelon B's mass increased by 0.2 kg.
Difference: 1.7 − 1.5 = 0.2
The difference in mass was 0.2 kg.

Unit 6

1. Red: $\frac{4}{25} = \frac{16}{100}$ Blue: $\frac{6}{25} = \frac{24}{100}$
Green: $\frac{7}{25} = \frac{28}{100}$ ← closest to 29
Yellow: 100 − 16 − 24 − 28 = 32
Matthew's favourite colour is green.

2.

Shampoo Size and Cost	Cost of 2.5 L
250 mL for $4.50	$4.50 × 10 = $45 ↑ 10 250-mL in 2.5 L
500 mL for $8.90	$8.90 × 5 = $44.50 ↑ 5 500-mL in 2.5 L
1250 mL for $21.50	$21.50 × 2 = $43 ↑ 2 1250-mL in 2.5 L

Buying two 1250-mL shampoo is the cheapest. It will cost $43.

3.

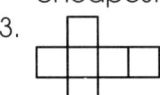

There are 19 6-cm lines.
Total length: 6 × 19 = 114
No. of 2-cm lines: 114 ÷ 2 = 57
Time needed: 0.5 × 57 = 28.5
It will take Hillary 28.5 seconds.

4. Total area: 10 × 10 = 100
Area of yellow section: 10 × 10 − 6 × 6 = 64
Probability of yellow section: $\frac{64}{100} = \frac{16}{25}$
Area of blue section: 6 × 6 − 2 × 2 = 32
Probability of blue section: $\frac{32}{100} = \frac{8}{25}$
Area of red section: 2 × 2 = 4
Probability of red section: $\frac{4}{100} = \frac{1}{25}$
The probability of hitting the yellow section is $\frac{16}{25}$, blue is $\frac{8}{25}$, and red is $\frac{1}{25}$.

ISBN: 978-1-77149-203-4

5. Total cost to play: $0.10 × 6 = $0.60
   Total won: $0.60 + $0.15 = $0.75 = 75¢
   To get 75¢, she must have got three 5¢, one 10¢, and two 25¢.

6. From 7:52:18 to 7:54:33: 2 min 15 s = 135 s
   No. of flights walked: 108 ÷ 12 = 9
   Time spent on 1 flight: 135 ÷ 9 = 15
   It took John 15 seconds to walk up 1 flight of stairs.

7. There are 6 4-cm sticks and 6 8-cm sticks.
   Possible prisms:

    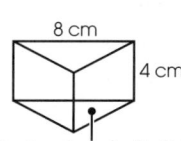

   Perimeter: 4×3=12   Perimeter: 8×3=24
   The perimeter of the base is 12 cm or 24 cm.

8. Fraction of ball: $\frac{1}{4}$
   $\frac{1}{4}$ of the total is 624.
   Total: 624 × 4 = 2496
   The spinner was spun about 2496 times.

9. Change in temperature: 7 – 4 = 3
   Each day, the temperature rises 3°C from the previous night.

Night	Temperature
Mon	5°C below 0°C
Tue	2°C below 0°C
Wed	1°C
Thu	4°C
Fri	7°C

   + 3°C

   It will be 7°C on Friday night.

10.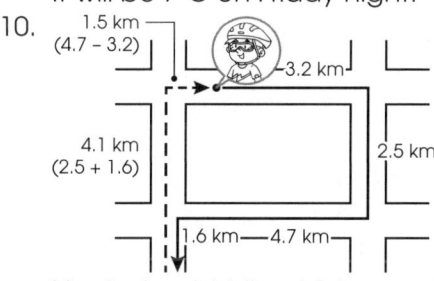

    1.5 km (4.7 – 3.2)
    3.2 km
    4.1 km (2.5 + 1.6)
    2.5 km
    1.6 km — 4.7 km

    Noah should bike 4.1 km up and 1.5 km to the right.

11. Total snowfall: 20.4 × 3 = 61.2
    $24\frac{1}{2} = 24.5$
    Snowfall in City C: 61.2 – 24.5 – 17.8 = 18.9
    The amount of snowfall in City C is 18.9 mm.

12. Total side length of 3 sides of square:
    181 – 46 – 30 = 105
    Side length of square: 105 ÷ 3 = 35
    Area of square: 35 × 35 = 1225
    Total area: 525 + 1225 = 1750
    The area of the patch is 1750 m².

13. Monthly car loan: $4200 ÷ 12 = $350
    Monthly insurance:
    $\frac{1}{10} = \frac{300}{3000}$ $\frac{1}{10}$ of $3000 is $300.
    Amount left:
    $3000 – $1320 – $350 – $300 = $1030
    Mrs. Anderson has $1030 left each month.

14.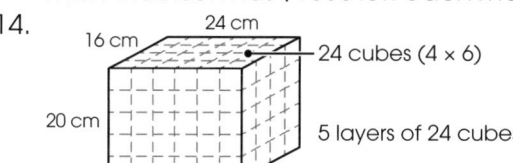

    24 cm
    16 cm
    20 cm
    24 cubes (4 × 6)
    5 layers of 24 cubes

    The cubes should have side lengths of 4 cm because 24, 16, and 20 can all be divided by 4 without remainders.
    No. of cubes: 24 × 5 = 120
    There will be 120 cubes.

15. Total mass: 6.25 × 4 = 25
    Masses of balls:
    5.5   5.5   6.8   7.2
    mode   6.15 × 2 – 5.5   25 – 5.5 – 5.5 – 6.8
    The masses of the balls are 5.5 kg, 5.5 kg, 6.8 kg, and 7.2 kg.

16. core

    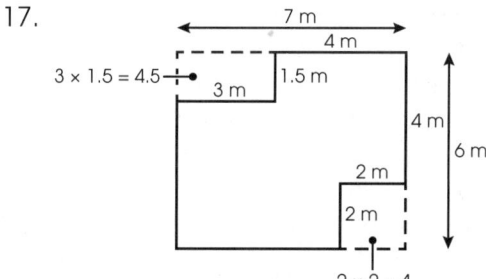

    Ronda's pattern repeats the 4 "R"s in the core.
    297 ÷ 4 = 74R1 ← The 297th "R" is the first "R" in the core.

    The 297th "R" is **R** .

17. 7 m
    4 m
    3 × 1.5 = 4.5
    3 m   1.5 m
    4 m   6 m
    2 m
    2 m
    2 × 2 = 4

    Area of carpet: 7 × 6 – 4.5 – 4 = 33.5
    Total cost: $24 × 33.5 = $804
    It will cost $804.

18. No. of times a side should land: 30 ÷ 6 = 5
    5 ♠: 5 ← 1 side has ♠.
    16 ♥: about 15 ← 3 sides have ♥.
    6 ♣: about 5 ← 1 side has ♣.
    3 ♦: fewer than 5 ← 1 side has ♦.
    There are 1 ♠, 3 ♥, 1 ♣, and 1 ♦ on the dice.

ISBN: 978-1-77149-203-4

19.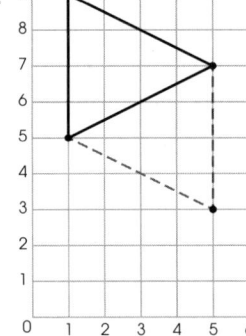

It is an isosceles triangle and an acute triangle.

The shape covers 8 squares.
Area of each square: 50.4 ÷ 8 = 6.3
Each square unit is 6.3 cm².

20. The shape is a parallelogram.
(Suggested properties)
It has 2 pairs of parallel sides, 2 pairs of equal angles, and no right angles.

Unit 7

1.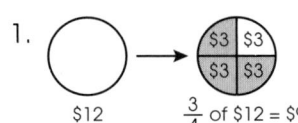

$\frac{3}{4}$ of $12 = $9

Randy paid $9 with 4 toonies and 1 loonie.

2. Total temperature: 21.6 × 5 = 108
Remaining temperature:
108 – 19.5 – 19.5 – 23.6 – 23.6 = 21.8
Temperatures from least to greatest:
19.5   19.5   (21.8)   23.6   23.6
                median
The median temperature was 21.8°C.

3. From 8:30 a.m. to 3:50 p.m.:
7 h 20 min = 440 min
Loads on each machine: 440 ÷ 40 = 11
Total loads: 11 × 15 = 165
The facility can wash 165 loads.

4. Total volume: 60 × 20 × 37 = 44 400
Volume of gravel: 44 400 – 42 000 = 2400
                            └ 42 L = 42 000 cm³
No. of bags: 2400 ÷ 240 = 10
Melissa added 10 bags of gravel.

5.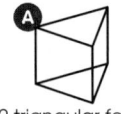

2 triangular faces   4 triangular faces
3 rectangular faces   1 rectangular face

B＼A	△	△	□	□	□
△	✔	✔			
△	✔	✔			
△	✔	✔			
△	✔	✔			
□					

Total no. of outcomes: 25
No. of outcomes with 2 △ : 8
The probability is $\frac{8}{25}$.

6.

Day	No. of Toonies	No. of Loonies	No. of $5 Bills
0	13 ⎫ ₋₂	7 ⎫ ₋₁	0 ⎫ ₊₁
1	11 ⎭	6 ⎭	1 ⎭
2	9	5	2
3	7	4	3
4	5	3	4
5	3	2	5 ← 5 coins, 5 bills

Joan will have the same number of bills and coins on Day 5.

7. Total cost: $1750 + $5172 = $6922
Amount students paid: $12.35 × 400 = $4940
Difference: $6922 – $4940 = $1982
$1982 will be subsidized for the field trip.

8. A prism that has the same perimeter on all its 6 faces must be a cube.
Side length of face: 24 ÷ 4 = 6
Volume of cube: 6 × 6 × 6 = 216
It is a cube with a volume of 216 cm³.

9. Total squares in the bars: 30
Mean no. of squares: 30 ÷ 6 = 5
Mean height of the bars: 5 squares
Height each square represents: 25 ÷ 5 = 5

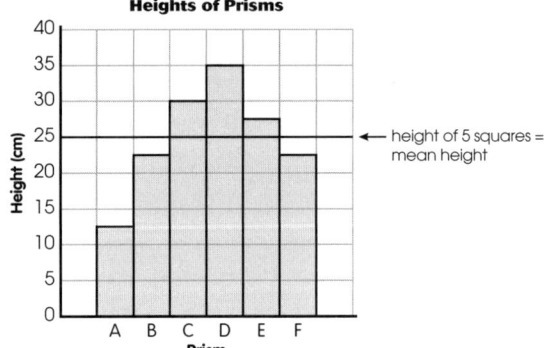

The heights of Prisms A, B, C, D, E, and F are 12.5 cm, 22.5 cm, 30 cm, 35 cm, 27.5 cm, and 22.5 cm respectively.

10. Volume of Prism D: 15 × 4 × 35 = 2100
Area of Prism C's base: 2100 ÷ 30 = 70
The area of the base of Prism C is 70 cm².

11. From 10:40 a.m. to 2:00 p.m.:
3 h 20 min = 200 min
No. of "4 min": 200 ÷ 4 = 50
Area of farm: 100 × 50 = 5000
The area of Morgan's farm is 5000 m².

12. Capacity of Box A: 6 × 6 × 8 = 288
Capacity of Box B: 4 × 2 × 13 = 104
Capacity of Box C: 8 × 5.5 × 2 = 88
There are 5 Box A, 2 Box B, and 3 Box C.
Capacities ordered from least to greatest:
88 88 88 104 (104 288) 288 288 288 288
Median: (104 + 288) ÷ 2 = 196
The median capacity is 196 mL.

ISBN: 978-1-77149-203-4

13. Tom: $2   Leah: $5 – $2 = $3
    Divide the candies into 5 equal parts:
    2 for Tom and 3 for Leah.
    1 part of candies: 1.6 ÷ 5 = 0.32
    Tom's candies: 0.32 kg × 2 = 0.64 kg = 640 g
    Leah's candies: 0.32 kg × 3 = 0.96 kg = 960 g
    So, Tom should get 640 g and Leah should
    get 960 g of candies.

14.
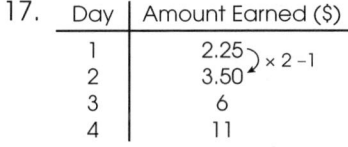
    • has 2 equal sides
    • has 1 right angle

    The bigger triangle is an isosceles triangle
    and a right triangle.

15. No. of votes: $1 \xrightarrow{\times 2} 2 \xrightarrow{\times 2} 4 \xrightarrow{\times 2} 8$
    Total: 1 + 2 + 4 + 8 = 15
    The winner got $\frac{8}{15}$ of the votes.

16. Class times:
    9:00 a.m – 9:45 a.m.   9:45 a.m. – 10:30 a.m.
    10:30 a.m. – 11:15 a.m.   11:15 a.m. – 12:00 p.m.
    12:00 p.m. – 12:45 p.m.   12:45 p.m. – 1:30 p.m.
    1:30 p.m. – 2:15 p.m.   2:15 p.m. – 3:00 p.m.
    Probability: $\frac{3}{8}$ ← 3 classes start between 11:00 a.m. and 1:00 p.m.
    ← 8 classes in total

    The probability is $\frac{3}{8}$.

17.
Day	Amount Earned ($)
1	2.25
2	3.50
3	6
4	11

    × 2 – 1

    10 loonies and 10 dimes: $10 + $1 = $11
    Patricia will earn $11 on Day 4. She will
    have 10 loonies and 10 dimes.

18.
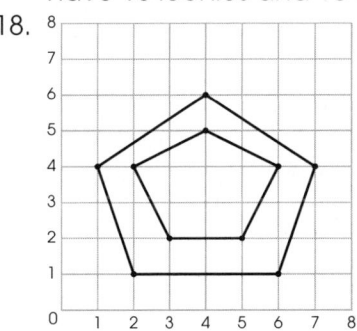
    It is a pentagon with 1 line of symmetry.

19. No, the shapes are not similar.

20. No. of squares in the smaller shape: 8
    Area of each square: 72 ÷ 8 = 9
    No. of squares in the bigger shape: 21
    Area of bigger shape: 9 × 21 = 189
    The area of the bigger shape is 189 cm².

Unit 8

1. 1 toonie, 1 loonie, and 3 quarters: $3.75
   There are 5 $0.75 in $3.75.
   Amount of flour: 500 g × 5 = 2500 g = 2.5 kg
   Sam bought 2.5 kg of flour.

2. Dimensions of cardboard after cut-out:
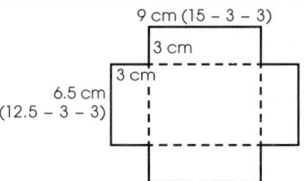

   Length: 9 cm
   Width: 6.5 cm
   Height: 3 cm
   Capacity: 9 × 6.5 × 3 = 175.5
   175.5 cm³ = 175.5 mL
   The capacity of the box is 175.5 mL.

3. Numbers: ① 4   7 ⑩ ⑬ ⑯ ⑲ 22
   There are 8 numbers in total. 5 numbers
   have the digit "1".

   The probability is $\frac{5}{8}$.

4.
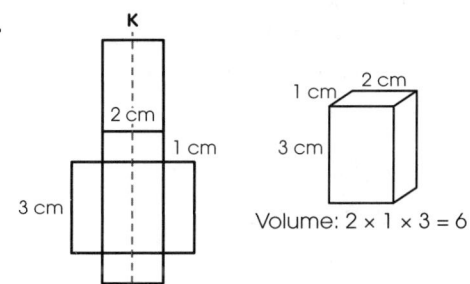

   Volume: 2 × 1 × 3 = 6

   The solid is a rectangular prism. Its volume
   is 6 cm³.

5.
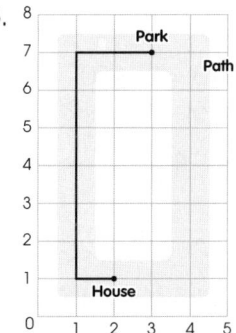

   Time needed to bike:
   20 min 24 s ÷ 2 = 10 min 12 s
   Elapsed time:
   20 min 24 s + 10 min 12 s = 30 min 36 s
   Time:
   10:45:18 a.m. + 30 min 36 s = 11:15:54 a.m.
   Time needed to cover each square:
   10 min 12 s ÷ 9 = 612 s ÷ 9 = 68 s
   Joe arrived at the park at 11:15:54 a.m. It
   took him 68 seconds to cover each unit
   by biking.

ISBN: 978-1-77149-203-4

6.

6 vertices   8 vertices

Gumdrops for 3 pentagonal pyramids:

$6 \times 3 = 18$

Gumdrops used for cubes:

$16 \leftarrow$ for 2 cubes

Fractions: $\dfrac{16}{18} = \dfrac{8}{9}$

$\dfrac{8}{9}$ of the gumdrops were used to make cubes.

7. Total on weekdays: $18.8 \times 5 = 94$
Total on weekend: $26.5 \times 2 = 53$
Mean: $(94 + 53) \div 7 = 21$
The mean temperature was 21°C.

8.

Time	Temperature (°C)
11:45 a.m.	30
12:19 p.m.	28.6
12:53 p.m.	27.2
1:27 p.m.	25.8
2:01 p.m.	24.4
2:35 p.m.	23

34 min (between 11:45 a.m. and 12:19 p.m.) −1.4

It was 2:35 p.m.

9. Mass of small blocks: $75 \times 26 = 1950$
Mass of large blocks: $94 \times 18 = 1692$
Total mass:
$1950\,g + 1692\,g = 3642\,g = 3.642\,kg$
The total mass is 3.642 kg.

10.

Step	Width (cm)
1	270
2	240
3	210
4	180
5	150
6	120
7	90

−30

Volume: $15 \times 90 \times 15 = 20\,250$
The volume of the top step is 20 250 cm³.

11. There are 3 "$1\dfrac{1}{2}$" in "$4\dfrac{1}{2}$".
Time needed:
$1\dfrac{3}{4}\,h + 1\dfrac{3}{4}\,h + 1\dfrac{3}{4}\,h = 5\dfrac{1}{4}\,h = 5\,h\ 15\,min$
5 h 15 min before 6:38 p.m.: 1:23 p.m.
Alan started at 1:23 p.m.

12. Total mass: $213.6 \times 5 = 1068$
Sum of the remaining mass:
$1068 - 210 - 197.5 \times 2 = 463$
Possible masses:

197.5   197.5   210   231.5   231.5
     mode   mode: $463 \div 2$

197.5   197.5   210   210   253
     mode   mode   ($463 - 210$)

The other mode could be 231.5 g or 210 g.

13.

Volume (cm³)	Time (s)
640	0
320	0.5
160	1
80	1.5
40	2
20	2.5

÷2 (640, 320)   (0, 0.5) +0.5

It will take 2.5 seconds.

14. 4 $20 bills: $80
1 loonie, 3 dimes: $1.30
Amount paid: $80 – $1.30 = $78.70
Cost before tax: $78.70 – $9.05 = $69.65
Mean: $69.65 ÷ 7 = $9.95
The mean cost is $9.95.

15. Possible dimensions:

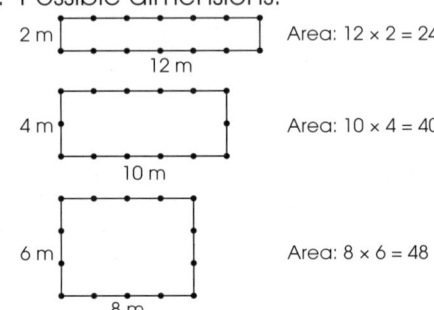

2 m   Area: $12 \times 2 = 24$
      12 m

4 m   Area: $10 \times 4 = 40$
      10 m

6 m   Area: $8 \times 6 = 48$
      8 m

The greatest possible area is 48 m².

16. $1000 + 1000 + 2000 + 1400 + 2600 + 3200 + 2800 = 14\,000$
The total revenue from the week is $14 000.

17.

Day	Revenue ($)	No. of Visitors
Mon	1000	200
Tue	1000	200
Wed	2000	400
Thu	1400	280
Fri	2600	520
Sat	3200	640
Sun	2800	560
Total:		2800

÷5

Mean: $2800 \div 7 = 400$
Median: 200 200 280 (400) 520 560 640
                            median
Mode: 200
The mean, median, and mode are 400, 400, and 200 respectively.

18.

Erin should do the rotations about Point B.
Area: $16.5 \times 4 = 66$
The area will be 66 cm².

ISBN: 978-1-77149-203-4

19. Brown envelopes:

$\dfrac{1}{4} = \dfrac{1500}{6000}$ 1500 brown envelopes

White envelopes: 6000 – 1500 = 4500
White envelopes used:

$\dfrac{4}{9} = \dfrac{2000}{4500}$ 2000 white envelopes were used.

Remaining envelopes: 6000 – 2000 = 4000

Probability: $\dfrac{1500}{4000} = \dfrac{3}{8}$

The probability is $\dfrac{3}{8}$.

20. Area of inner section: 12 ÷ 2 = 6

	Outer Fencing	Inner Fencing
Length (m)	4	3
Width (m)	12 ÷ 4 = 3	6 ÷ 3 = 2
Perimeter (m)	(4 + 3) × 2 = 14	(3 + 2) × 2 = 10

Total fencing: 14 + 10 = 24
24 m of fencing is needed in total.

Unit 9

1. A clock face shows 12 hours.

$\dfrac{1}{6} = \dfrac{2}{12}$ $\dfrac{1}{6}$ of 12 h is 2 h.

2 hours = 120 minutes
120 minutes have passed.

2. Sum of temperatures: 15.6 × 5 = 78
Having no mode means all temperatures are different. To find the highest possible temperature, the other temperatures must be as low as possible.

10   11   16   17   24
          ↑ median   ↑ 78 – 10 – 11 – 16 – 17

The highest possible temperature was 24°C.

3. Evan had 2 quarters and 1 loonie.
Money received: $2.05 – $1.50 = $0.55

Probability: $\dfrac{2}{3} = \dfrac{4}{6}$ ← 4 quarters
                              ← 6 coins in total

Evan received 2 quarters and 1 nickel.

4. Drink: $\dfrac{2}{5} = \dfrac{4}{10}$ $\dfrac{2}{5}$ of $10 is $4.

Popsicle: $10 × 0.25 = $2.50
$10 – $4 – $2.50 = $3.50
Linda has $3.50 left.

5. Possible outcomes:

Numerator → Denominator ↓	2	3	4
5	$\boxed{\dfrac{2}{5}}$	$\dfrac{3}{5}$	$\dfrac{4}{5}$
6	$\dfrac{2}{6}$	$\bigcirc\dfrac{3}{6}$	$\dfrac{4}{6}$
8	$\dfrac{2}{8}$	$\dfrac{3}{8}$	$\boxed{\dfrac{4}{8}}$
10	$\dfrac{2}{10}$	$\dfrac{3}{10}$	$\boxed{\dfrac{4}{10}}$

◯, ☐: the same
There are 10 different outcomes.

6. Fractions greater than $\dfrac{1}{2}$:

$\dfrac{3}{5}, \dfrac{4}{5}, \dfrac{4}{6}$ ← 3 fractions

Probability: $\dfrac{3}{12} = \dfrac{1}{4}$

The probability is $\dfrac{1}{4}$.

7. From 3:43:06 p.m. to 5:16:36 p.m:
1 h 33 min 30 s = 93.5 min
No. of revolutions: 10 × 93.5 = 935
The blades make 935 revolutions.

8.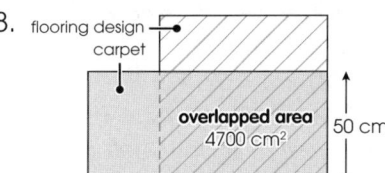

Side length of square: 4700 ÷ 50 = 94
Area of square: 94 × 94 = 8836
The area of the design is 8836 cm².

9. Additional distance: $4 - 1\dfrac{3}{4} = 2\dfrac{1}{4}$

There are 9 "$\dfrac{1}{4}$" in "$2\dfrac{1}{4}$".

Additional cost: $0.15 × 9 = $1.35
Total cost: $0.90 + $1.35 = $2.25
It costs $2.25 to travel 4 km.

10.

Fold	Length (cm)	Width (cm)	Area (cm²)
0	24	16 ⎫÷2	384
1	÷2 ⎛ 24	8 ⎭	192
2	⎝ 12	8 ⎫÷2	96
3	÷2 ⎛ 12	4 ⎭	48
4	⎝ 6	4	24

Perimeter: (6 + 4) × 2 = 20
The perimeter is 20 cm.

ISBN: 978-1-77149-203-4

11.
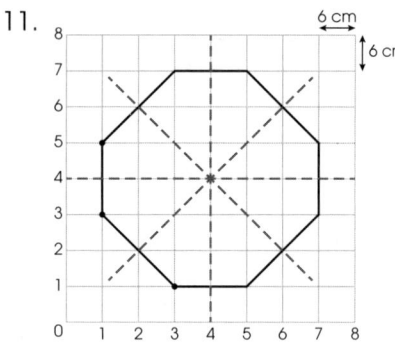

The coordinates of the remaining vertices are (5,1), (7,3), (7,5), (5,7), and (3,7).

12. No. of squares: 28
Area: 6 × 6 × 28 = 1008
The area of the octagon is 1008 cm².

13. Capacity of tank: 16 × 14 × 14 = 3136
Volume of block in the tank:
12 × 10 × 14 = 1680
Amount of water needed:
3136 – 1680 = 1456
7 cups of water: 200 × 7 = 1400
No, 7 cups of water will not be enough.

14. Total mass in 5 weeks: 9.48 × 5 = 47.4
Total mass in 6 weeks:
(9.48 + 0.92) × 6 = 62.4
Mass in Week 6: 62.4 – 47.4 = 15
The mass was 15 kg in Week 6.

15. Perimeter of pentagon: 51 ÷ 3 = 17
Side length of pentagon: 17 ÷ 5 = 3.4
The side length of the pentagon was 3.4 cm.

16.

Perimeter (cm)	Side Length (cm)	Area (cm²)
4	1	1
8	2	4
12	3	9
16	4	16
20	5	25

+4 ↓   ÷4 →   +3, +5, +7, +9

Pattern rule for area:
Start with 1, add 3. Then increase the number to be added by 2 each time.
The area of the 5th square is 25 cm².

17.
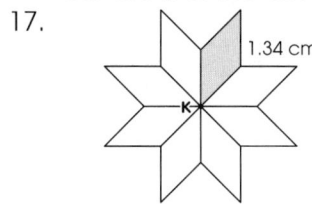
1.34 cm

Side length of rhombus: 5.36 ÷ 4 = 1.34
Perimeter of design: 1.34 × 16 = 21.44
The perimeter will be 21.44 cm.

18. Serena walked 9 squares.

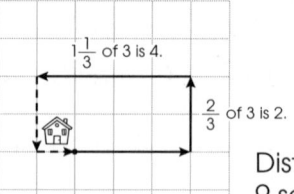
$1\frac{1}{3}$ of 3 is 4.
$\frac{2}{3}$ of 3 is 2.
Distance travelled: 9 squares

Length of each square: 5.4 ÷ 9 = 0.6
Distance down: 0.6 × 2 = 1.2
Distance to the right: 0.6
Serena will have to walk 1.2 km down and 0.6 km to the right.

19. The graph shows 9 portions.
Portions for each boy: 9 ÷ 3 = 3

Number of Grapes Each Boy Has Brought
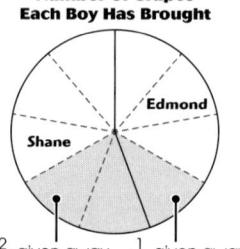
$\frac{2}{5}$ given away $\frac{1}{4}$ given away

$\frac{1}{4}$ of Edmond's grapes and $\frac{2}{5}$ of Shane's grapes will be given away.

20. Total no. of grapes: 54 × 3 = 162
Edmond: $\frac{4}{9} = \frac{72}{162}$ $\frac{4}{9}$ of 162 is 72.
Shane: $\frac{5}{9} = \frac{90}{162}$ $\frac{5}{9}$ of 162 is 90.
Edmond has brought 72 grapes and Shane has brought 90 grapes.

Unit 10

1. Capacity of tank: 50 × 20 × 30 = 30 000
30 000 cm³ = 30 000 mL = 30 L
Tank not filled: 30 – 25 = 5
Fraction: $\frac{5}{30} = \frac{1}{6}$
$\frac{1}{6}$ of the tank is not filled.

2.
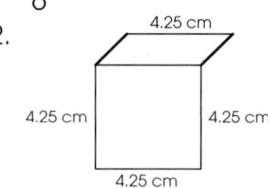
4.25 cm
4.25 cm   4.25 cm
4.25 cm

Side length of square: 17 ÷ 4 = 4.25
The increase in perimeter is from the sides in bold. So, the sides in bold have the total length of 3.6 cm.
Perimeter: 3.6 + 4.25 + 4.25 = 12.1
The perimeter of the parallelogram is 12.1 cm.

ISBN: 978-1-77149-203-4

3. From 1:50 p.m. to 2:05 p.m.: 15 min
   From 1:50 p.m. to 2:25 p.m.: 35 min
   Probability: $\frac{15}{35} = \frac{3}{7}$

   The probability is $\frac{3}{7}$.

4. Twelve 355-mL cans: 355 mL × 12 = 4260 mL
   Two 2-L bottles: 2 L × 2 = 4 L = 4000 mL
   A pack of twelve 355-mL cans is a better deal.

5.
Month	Amount ($)
Jul. 2015	0.75
Aug. 2015	1.39
Sep. 2015	2.03
Oct. 2015	2.67
Nov. 2015	3.31
Dec. 2015	3.95

   +0.64

   Annie gains $0.64 each month.

   Annie had $3.95 in Dec. 2015.

6.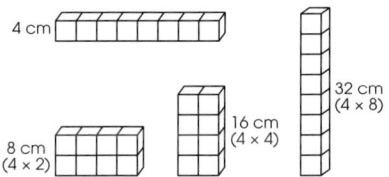
   3 m (2.2+0.8)   1.2 m
   Area: 3 × 1.2 = 3.6
   2.2 m
   2 m (1.2+0.8)
   Area: 2.2 × 2 = 4.4
   Difference: 4.4 – 3.6 = 0.8
   Extending the width will increase the area by 0.8 m² more.

7. Volume of prism: 4 × 4 × 4 × 8 = 512
   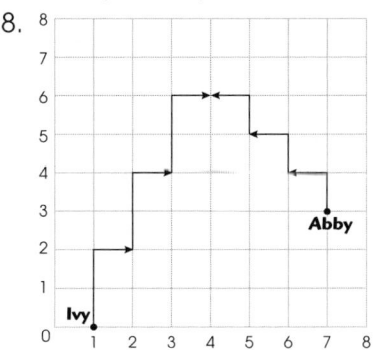
   4 cm
   8 cm (4 × 2)
   16 cm (4 × 4)
   32 cm (4 × 8)

   The volume of the prism is 512 cm³. The height of the prism could be 4 cm, 8 cm, 16 cm, or 32 cm.

8.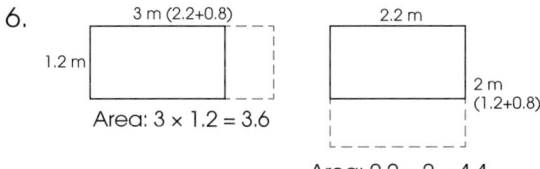

   Abby

   Ivy

   The park was at (4,6).
   No. of min Abby took: 6
   6 min after 10:19 a.m. is 10:25 a.m.
   No. of min Ivy took: 9
   9 min after 10:19 a.m. is 10:28 a.m.
   Abby and Ivy stopped at the park at 10:25 a.m. and 10:28 a.m. respectively.

9.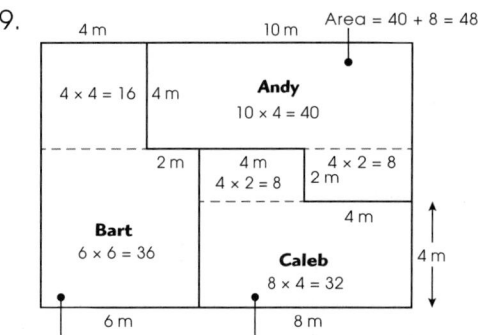
   4 m   10 m   Area = 40 + 8 = 48
   4 × 4 = 16   4 m
   Andy   10 × 4 = 40
   2 m   4 m   4 × 2 = 8   2 m
   4 × 2 = 8
   4 m
   Bart   6 × 6 = 36
   Caleb   8 × 4 = 32
   4 m
   6 m   8 m
   Area = 36 + 16 = 52   Area = 32 + 8 = 40

   Perimeter:
   Andy: 10 + 6 + 4 + 2 + 6 + 4 = 32
   Caleb: 4 + 2 + 4 + 4 + 8 + 6 = 28
   Bart: 4 + 4 + 2 + 6 + 6 + 10 = 32
   Bart has the biggest room. Caleb's room has the smallest perimeter.

10. Masses of strawberries:
    ?   6.7   6.7   9.3   9.3
    greater than 6.7
    The probability is $\frac{2}{5}$.

11.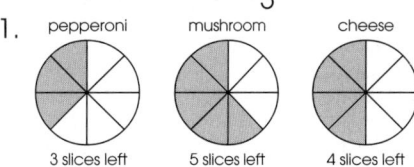
    pepperoni   mushroom   cheese
    3 slices left   5 slices left   4 slices left
    Total slices left: 3 + 5 + 4 = 12
    Probability: $\frac{4}{12} = \frac{1}{3}$

    The probability was $\frac{1}{3}$.

12. 2 loonies and 2 nickels: $2.10
    Probability: $\frac{2}{4}$ ← no. of loonies / ← total no. of coins

    The probability is $\frac{1}{2}$.

13.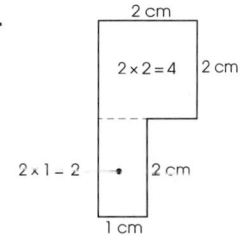
    2 cm
    2 × 2 = 4   2 cm
    2 × 1 = 2   2 cm
    1 cm

    Area of tile: 4 + 2 = 6
    Area of wall:
    2 m × 0.6 m
    = 200 cm × 60 cm
    = 12 000 cm²
    No. of tiles: 12 000 ÷ 6 = 2000
    Nadia needs 2000 tiles.

ISBN: 978-1-77149-203-4

14. 1 loonie and 1 nickel: $1.05

Date	Amount Saved ($)
Mar. 26	17.80
Mar. 30	18.85
Apr. 3	19.90
Apr. 7	20.95
Apr. 11	22

+4 (Mar. 26 / Mar. 30)   (17.80 / 18.85) +1.05

Yes, Natalie can afford it.

15. From least to greatest:
   3°C below 0°C
   1°C below 0°C
   0°C ← median
   1°C
   4°C
   The median temperature was 0°C.

16. Total no. of servings:
   $2.5 + 4 + 3.5 + 5.5 + 1 + 3.5 = 20$
   Fruits and vegetables servings:
   $2.5 + 3.5 = 6$
   Fraction: $\frac{6}{20} = \frac{3}{10}$
   $\frac{3}{10}$ of Eric's food intake came from fruits and vegetables.

17.
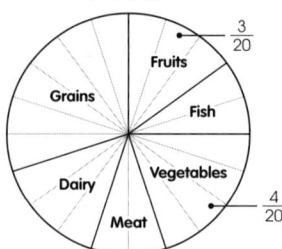

Recommended Daily Food Intake

Eric should increase fruit intake by 0.5 serving and vegetable intake by 0.5 serving.

18. Possible outcomes:
   scalene triangle, acute triangle ✔
   scalene triangle, right triangle ✔
   scalene triangle, obtuse triangle ✔
   isosceles triangle, acute triangle ✔
   isosceles triangle, right triangle ✔
   isosceles triangle, obtuse triangle ✔
   equilateral triangle, acute triangle ✔
   equilateral triangle, right triangle ✘
   equilateral triangle, obtuse triangle ✘
   2 out of 9 outcomes cannot be drawn.

   The probability is $\frac{2}{9}$.

19. There are 3 "30 min" in 1.5 h.
   Time spent outdoors in 1 day:
   12 min × 3 = 36 min
   Time spent outdoors in 1 week:
   36 min × 7 = 252 min = 4 h 12 min
   Dennis will spend 4 h 12 min outdoors.

20. Since the shape is only translated, it must be a square. The net makes a cube.

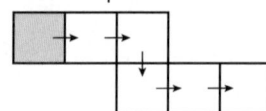

ISBN: 978-1-77149-203-4